Z (pronounced *zed*) is a formal notation for specifying and de and software. Formal methods are useful when problems are no must meet requirements for safety, security, accuracy or other critical properties. This book is a self-contained tutorial on Z and formal methods for experienced professionals and serious students in programming, software engineering and computer science.

By using realistic case studies emphasizing safety-critical systems and other examples drawn from embedded controls, real-time and concurrent programming, computer graphics, games, text processing, databases, artificial intelligence, and object-oriented programming, the author motivates the use of formal methods and discusses practical issues concerning how to apply them in real projects. He also teaches how to apply formal program derivation and formal verification to implement Z specifications in real programming languages through examples in C.

The book includes exercises with solutions, reference materials, and a guide to further reading directing readers to more case studies, experience reports, recent research, and other formal notations and methods.

If you want to try out formal methods, or just want to find out more about them, this book is for you.

The Way of Z

THE WAY OF Z
Practical Programming with Formal Methods

Jonathan Jacky
Department of Radiation Oncology
University of Washington

CAMBRIDGE
UNIVERSITY PRESS

CAMBRIDGE UNIVERSITY PRESS
Cambridge, New York, Melbourne, Madrid, Cape Town, Singapore, São Paulo, Delhi

Cambridge University Press
32 Avenue of the Americas, New York, NY 10013-2473, USA

www.cambridge.org
Information on this title: www.cambridge.org/9780521559768

First published 1997
7th printing 2008

Printed in the United States of America

A catalog record for this publication is available from the British Library.

Library of Congress Cataloging in Publication Data

Jacky, Jonathan.
The way of Z : Practical programming with formal methods / Jonathan Jacky.
    p. cm.
ISBN 0-521-55041-6 (hbk.) – ISBN 0-521-55976-6 (pbk.)
1. Z (Computer program language) I. Title.
QA76.73.Z2J33   1996
005.1'2 – dc20   96-13537
                                                              CIP

ISBN 978-0-521-55976-8 paperback

To my parents Norman and Elinor,
and my wife Noreen

Contents

Preface

I learned Z (pronounced *zed*) when I got tired of programming by trial and error.

I write large programs for a serious purpose. I work in a clinical department in a research hospital. My first project here was a program that assists in planning radiation therapy treatments for cancer, by performing physics simulations – radiation dose calculations – with 3-D interactive graphics. Our planning system took more than two years to develop and comprised 40,000 lines of code. We spent plenty of time on design, coded carefully, and ran lots of tests.

Like most software, our system *usually* worked. It did most of what the users asked for – and some things that they didn't. It handled most cases correctly – then every so often it did the wrong thing, locked up, or crashed. We, the developers, were as surprised by the bizarre behavior as anyone else. Fortunately, the computations were done before patients' treatments began and every result was reviewed thoroughly. We could detect and work around the problems. We could live with it – though it wasn't always convenient.

We had to do better. Our next project was the computer control system for a unique radiation therapy machine at our clinic. Typical software quality wasn't good enough. We had recently learned of another therapy control system that had *killed* people!

I surveyed every development method I could find, including many packaged as software products with nice facilities for drawing diagrams and producing documents. I was disappointed. Most of them emphasize how a system is structured but are weak on describing behavior. Above all, we needed a complete and unambiguous description of what our system would do. A few methods and products did attempt to do this, but they weren't very expressive and didn't provide a clear way to represent the important features of our system.

To my surprise, I found that the only methods that really hit the nail on the head were the *formal methods*. Formal methods apply logic and simple mathematics to programming. They enabled us to create complete, yet concise, descriptions of what we were trying to do and helped us write the programs so we knew they would work.

I chose Z for this book because it is the formal notation which is the most accessible and best explained. It already has a rich literature of case studies that provide examples and inspiration. Z is among the first of the formal description languages to break out of the research world and be used on large projects in industry: Industry leaders with IBM, Inmos and others say it has saved them millions. Z has been applied to embedded controls, commercial transaction processing, floating point microcode, and other applications. It is also beginning to be taught at colleges and universities. Z works with any programming language and supports different programming styles, including object-oriented programming, functional programming, and others. You can get started easily: You don't need to buy any expensive tools, and it can work on a small scale – even for a single programmer.

Formal programming methods have a frustrated history. They have a reputation for being esoteric and impractical. This reputation derives from how they are customarily presented, not from their actual content or difficulty. Most of the literature has been written by researchers for other researchers. They have honed the methods to a very sharp point and have made some impressive accomplishments, but their achievements remain little-known and have hardly influenced the actual practices of most working programmers.

I wrote this book to break that pattern. This is a popular introduction, intended to demystify formal methods and interpret them for a wide audience. This is a book about *programming* – it shows how Z can help you write programs. It takes you all the way to code, with examples in C.

This is not a conventional textbook. The textbooks provide instruction in writing the Z notation and manipulating Z formulas. But programming is not just formula manipulation. There is much more to developing software than solving symbolic puzzles. My goal is to teach you to apply Z to the novel problems that you are sure to encounter in your work – problems that have never before been expressed formally. I will describe an approach to programming where formal methods can fit in and make sense. Through it all, I never lose sight of the whole point of programming: to create something useful that solves a real problem.

Although this is not a conventional textbook, it is a self-contained introduction to Z and the discrete mathematics on which it is based. It covers most of the notation, including some advanced topics that are not discussed in most textbooks but which I have found to be useful in practical applications of Z. If you are serious about using Z, you will eventually want to get a copy of *The Z Notation: A Reference Manual*, but in the meantime the appendices here contain enough reference material to get you through this book.

My method is to demonstrate the notation through a series of short studies, each just a few pages long. This introduces the essential features of the notation quickly. The examples are drawn from computer graphics, embedded controls, games, safety-critical systems, text processing, artificial intelligence, and databases. Several of the examples are taken from my work in radiation therapy. I present a few of these twice: first in simplified form, then with something nearer to their actual complexity, to show how Z can be scaled up from toy examples to real problems.

This book does not require any prior exposure to Z or formal methods. However, it does require a certain professional maturity. I assume that you have enough experience in real programming projects to appreciate the problems that Z is intended to solve. If you have ever had to make sense of complicated requirements, work from a lengthy prose specification, or figure out an obscure program written by someone else, this book will speak to you. I also assume that you understand certain technical concepts that are used in all modern programming languages, such as Boolean expressions, relational operators, and data types. You should also be comfortable with elementary arithmetic and algebra.

Paper and pencil are all the tools you need to begin using Z, but software can help. Utilities for printing and displaying the Z symbols, and for checking syntax and type correctness, are available for most popular computer systems; some are free. The Z home page (http://www.comlab.ox.ac.uk/archive/z.html) has information on tools and other useful resources.

I have another goal besides just conveying technical information. I want to convince you to try out Z in your own work! Much of this book is devoted to providing motivation and explaining the rationale for using Z.

In my experience, manipulating the notation is not the hard part. Every programming language is a formal language, and Z is simpler than most programming languages. When to use this kind of notation is difficult for newcomers to grasp. Z only makes sense in a programming approach that is very different from the methods many programmers are now using. Language isn't just syntax and semantics; it is culture, too. I've tried to pass some of that culture along in this book so you can learn and enjoy the way of Z.

Acknowledgements

Rob Arthan, Robert Buessow, Norman Delisle, David Garlan, Roger Jones, Bernard Sufrin, Phil Stocks, Jim Woodcock, and especially Mike Spivey patiently answered my questions and greatly enriched my understanding of Z. Bill Bevier suggested the taxonomy of methods for handling concurrency mentioned in Appendix G. Ira Kalet introduced me to serious software development. Ruedi Risler and Peter Wootton taught me about radiation therapy machines. Doug Schuler suggested the case study in Chapter 16. Rosalind Barden, Frank Christopherson, Rob Jasper, Steve Lewis, A.D. McGettrick, Michael Patrick, Simon Plumtree, Gregg Tracton, David Tranah, Jonathan Unger, Lauren Wiener, John Wordsworth, and several anonymous reviewers commented on earlier versions of the manuscript, spotted several technical errors, and suggested many improvements. Lauren Wiener provided useful advice toward getting this book published. Lauren Cowles suggested countless improvements, large and small, and supervised the production of the book.

Jonathan Jacky

He who seeks for methods without having a definite problem in mind seeks for the most part in vain.

— David Hilbert

Part I

Why Z?

1 Formal methods

Formal methods apply logic and simple mathematics to programming. They work best where traditional programming methods don't work very well: problems that are too difficult to solve by intuition or too novel to solve by modifying some existing program or design. They can help you create new programs, or analyze and document programs that are already written. Using formal methods requires creativity and judgment, but once you have created or analyzed a program formally, you can document your work as a sequence of steps that you or anyone else can check. You must be able to do this if you need to convince yourself or others that a program meets requirements for safety, accuracy, security, or any other critical property. It is also worth doing if you simply want to understand how the program works.

1.1   What are formal methods?

Formal methods are methods that use formulas.

A *formula* is a text or diagram constructed from predefined symbols combined according to explicit rules. A good working definition of formula is anything whose appearance or *syntax* can be checked by a computer. According to this definition, *every computer program is a formula*.

It's a little odd for programmers to speak of formal methods as if they were something special – as if formality were an option. If you want to program a computer, you really don't have any choice. Computation *is* formula evaluation.

And yet, formal methods have become something to make a fuss over, something that many programmers are said to be unwilling – or unable! – to use. What distinguishes these formal methods from what programmers already do every day?

The special meaning of formal methods often appears on when we use formulas. When we're doing formal methods, we don't just write the code in a formal notation, we also use formal notations in the stages that come before coding. We express the specification or design in formulas.

Formal methods are also distinguished by what we use the formulas to express: the behavior of programs. Many programmers only know one way to determine the meaning or *semantics* of a formula: execute it on a computer. With formal methods we can determine the meaning of a formula – be it a specification, design, or program – without executing it. The whole point of using formal methods is to be able to predict what a program will do *without running any code* – in fact, without writing any. This means we can discover many errors without having to run any tests. This ability to model behavior distinguishes Z and other formal notations from diagramming methods that can only model program structure.

Formal methods are also distinguished by the choice of notation. The formal notations we use to express specifications and designs are usually different from our programming language – we can use a distinct *specification language*. The specification language need not be executable and may resemble traditional mathematics and symbolic logic more than a programming language. These languages can be more expressive, more concise, and easier to understand than any executable programming language, and they usually come with a lot less syntactic clutter. Z is one of these nonexecutable specification languages (some alternatives are surveyed in Appendix G). We usually call Z a notation rather than a language to emphasize its mathematical nature.

Formal notations such as Z are distinguished from less formal notations such as data flow diagrams because they have a *formal semantics* that assigns a precise meaning to any formula in the notation. Moreover, a formal notation comes with *laws* that enable us to simplify formulas, derive new ones, and determine whether one formula is a consequence of others. This is what most distinguishes mathematical notations such as Z from natural human languages and also from most programming languages. It makes it possible to derive designs and code from a specification, and to check whether code and designs correctly implement a specification. Moreover, since formal notations can be processed by machine, parts of these tasks can be automated.

Formal methods are a kind of *analysis*. Analysis is any activity devoted to understanding software without actually running programs, including reviews, inspections, and walkthroughs – anything that involves reading, discussing, and trying to understand programs without testing. Analysis can be more effective than testing for many purposes, because you can analyze an entire program text, but you can only test a (usually very small) sample of program behaviors. Many studies have found that informal analyses can be more effective than testing for detecting errors and improving software quality [Fagan, 1986; Ackerman, Buchwald, and Lewski, 1989; Russell, 1991; Knight and Myers, 1993]. What we call formal methods are just particular kinds of analyses that employ mathematical notations.

Formal methods can help you create software so that you can understand it before you run it. You shouldn't have to resort to guessing to produce programs. You needn't rely on trial and error to validate and improve them. You still need to test, but it no longer serves as your primary error detection method. You make sure that the code is right by being sure about all the stages leading up to it.

1.2   What formal methods are not

Formal methods are not project management methods. People in computing often use the word *formal* rather loosely, to mean strict, detailed, or methodical. Sometimes formal even connotes a particular style of doing software projects that involves following a lot of written procedures that are enforced by management. In this book, I reserve formal for methods that use logical and mathematical formulas[1]. Management methods are concerned with the process used to create the program, but with formal methods we can assess the program directly.

Another common misconception is that formal methods use one particular modelling technique that is in competition with other popular techniques. This mistake is revealed by questions such as, "Do you use formal methods or object-oriented programming?" Those are not mutually exclusive categories. You can use formal methods with any modelling technique.

1.3   When are formal methods useful?

Formal methods involve writing another formal description of the program, in addition to the code itself. This might seem like extra work and it isn't always useful. Formal methods can help with novel projects, difficult projects, and critical projects.

Novel projects involve building something substantially new, where we can't just take an existing system and make some obvious modifications. We need to compare design alternatives, not just plunge ahead and implement the first idea that comes along. We can't afford to build several versions of the whole system, so we have to analyze models instead.

Projects are difficult when they tackle problems that are profound and deep, or when they present a multitude of intricate details. Difficult projects need not be large; a single page of code can present so many choices that trial-and-error guessing and testing might never converge to a useful solution. We don't have to throw up our hands and complain how incredibly complicated it is. We can use formal methods to derive a solution and check that it is correct.

---

[1] However, the first definition of "formal specification" in an IEEE standard is "a specification written and approved in accordance with established standards" [IEEE, 1987]. A recent book on avionics states, "Formal methods are institutionalized procedures that permit managers, engineers and customers to verify that development is proceeding without major problems" [Neuport, 1994].

Most software is produced with the expectation that users will discover errors that the developers missed, but this is unacceptable for critical projects. Critical projects are those where so much is at stake – safety, security, money – that stakeholders outside the development group demand to be informed about the technical content of the product. These stakeholders might be management, customers, an external quality assurance organization, or government regulators. They are not content to discover how the product behaves in the course of using it; they require a detailed statement of what it will do – and what it will *not* do. They require the developers to show that the promised behavior has been achieved. A formal specification can describe the product behavior, and a formal development can help make the case that the product meets its specification.

Many programming projects are neither novel, difficult, nor critical. In truth, many of these are too tedious to be easy – let's call them *routine*. Experienced programmers can adapt an adequate solution from their files, or their heads. Routine errors arise from fatigue, haste, or simple carelessness, and can be detected by inspection of the code against prose requirements – or implicit understandings that are not even written down. Once the program is running, it is easy to determine if the results are correct, and if they are not they can simply be discarded. In such routine jobs there is no need to use formal methods.

1.4   How can we use formal methods?

We use formal methods in three essential activities: modelling, design, and verification.

1.4.1   Modelling

Models enable us to describe and predict program behavior.

Many programmers believe that the only really accurate description of what a program does is the program text: the code itself. However a mathematical model can describe program behavior accurately and comprehensively, and it is often much shorter and clearer than the code. We can use the model to calculate or infer the behavior of the program before we code it. Modelling makes the behavior of the program predictable – a good property for any program to have, an essential property for a safety-critical system.

Complex systems can have surprisingly simple models. Finding the right model can be the key to a clear design and a compact, efficient program. The chapters in Parts II and IV present a series of models expressed in Z.

A model is a simplified representation. Computing confronts us with a mass of detail; models help us cope. A model leaves something out – it has some of the properties of the system it models, but not all of them. We construct a model to focus on some particular aspect of a system, and we omit all the details that are inessential to that aspect. There can be several models of the same system, each focusing on a different aspect.

For example, a prototype that demonstrates the look and feel of a new system to prospective users is a kind of model because it does not provide all of the functions of the final product. It is a bit like an architect's scale model or an artist's rendering of a new building, because it is intended to convey an aesthetic impression. Sometimes we need a different kind of model, intended to represent the system's functional behavior or internal structure. This is more like the mathematical models that structural engineers use to check that the beams will fit together and bear the loads. Z is used to create this latter type of model.

A mathematical model that represents the intended behavior of a program can be used as a *formal specification*. Programmers sometimes act as if formal specifications were a strange new idea. In fact, we have always used mathematical models in computing.

Here is an example from my own work. In radiation therapy we use computer programs to estimate the radiation dose distribution that would be created in the patient's body by a proposed treatment [Khan, 1984]. Figure 1.1 shows part of the formal specification for our program [Kalet *et al.*, 1993]; the notation is ordinary mathematics. It is supplemented by a picture to help illustrate the definitions of the variables that appear in the formula (not shown here are several pages of prose and formulas that also explain those definitions).

This next example may be more familiar to programmers. Figure 1.2 shows the formal specification for the syntax of numbers in the programming language Pascal. For example, Figure 1.2 permits 1, 0.5, 1E5, and 1.5E-5, but prohibits 1., .5, E5, 1.5E-5.0, and so forth. Figure 1.2 appears in the language reference manual [Jensen and Wirth, 1974] to help programmers understand how to form numbers. However, it can also be considered part of the formal specification for a Pascal compiler. The formal notation is called Backus-Naur Form (BNF). Here again, there is a picture. It illustrates an alternative view of the information presented in BNF. The entire syntax of the Pascal language (which describes every syntactically correct Pascal program) is given in five pages of BNF. Thanks to formal models like this one, writing a correct syntax analyzer for a compiler is a straightforward task. This achievement belies the programmers' complaint that hard problems present too many cases to anticipate. Any compiler can handle a virtually infinite number of distinct cases (program texts), accepting all syntactically legal programs and rejecting every illegal one.

These examples should remind you that using formal specifications is really not such a strange thing to do. *We already use formal specifications in complex applications where we know how to write substantially correct programs that people*

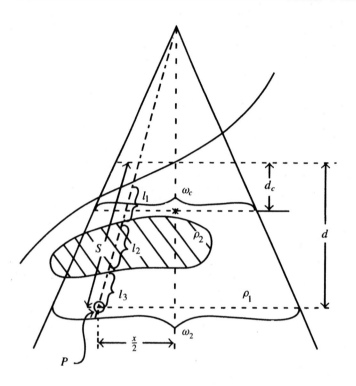

The dose D at a point P inside the patient (see figure 1) due to a single fixed external photon or neutron beam source with a rectangular collimator is calculated by the formula

$$D = \left(\frac{F}{F+m}\right)^2 \cdot D_{cal} \cdot O(w_c) \cdot \left[TPR(w_d, d) \cdot OCR\left(w_1, d, \frac{2x}{w_1}\right) \cdot OCR\left(w_2, d, \frac{2y}{w_2}\right) - B\right] \cdot I \cdot W \qquad (1.1)$$

where D is does per machine unit at point P within the patient.

Figure 1.1: Formal specification for a radiation dose calculation program

can understand. It would be crazy to try to write either of these programs without the formal specification. Can you imagine trying to write a compiler where the syntax was only defined by a lot of prose and examples describing particular special cases? Can you imagine trying to *use* a compiler that was written that way? No competent programmer today would even consider such a thing, and no physicist would begin coding a calculation without the formula close at hand.

These examples also show that a mathematical model does not much resemble a prose description. It is no mere paraphrase of the prose into another notation; it is a different expression of the same behaviors, in a form that is better organized to serve as a guide for programming. Bridging from the users' informal view of the

unsigned number

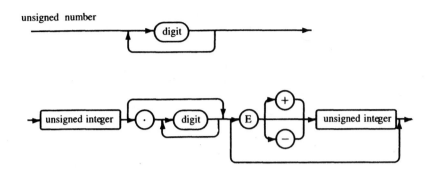

```
<unsigned number> ::= <unsigned integer> | <unsigned real>

<unsigned integer> ::= <digit> {<digit>}

<unsigned real> ::= <unsigned integer> . <digit> {<digit>} |
        <unsigned integer> . <digit> {<digit>} E <scale factor> |
        <unsigned integer> E <scale factor>

<scale factor> ::= <unsigned integer> | <sign> <unsigned integer>

<sign> ::= + | -
```

Figure 1.2: Formal specification for Pascal number syntax.

requirements to the programmers' formal model is one of the central creative tasks in programming. This task is discussed in Chapter 3.

In both examples, the formal model enables us to calculate the results the program should get. We can use the formal model as an *oracle*, an independent standard of accuracy that can tell us what the result of executing the program on any test case should be. We can use the model to help us choose test cases and tell whether the program passed the tests.

An oracle can also help us determine whether we made the right decisions about what the program should do — that is, whether we got the requirements right. Failure to understand the real requirements has been responsible for many software failures and accidents, and these errors can be the most expensive and difficult to fix. Because a formal model enables us to predict program behavior, we can investigate how our program would behave even before we begin design and coding. If we have a formal model, we can apply powerful analytical techniques to confirm that it meets critical requirements such as safety or security. Chapter 15 describes some techniques used in those analyses.

Programmers often try to write complex programs with no formal model; the only formal description is the code itself. As a result the expected system behaviors and the assumptions about the environment cannot be reviewed, criticized, or even examined because they are hidden in the program text itself, usually encoded in some obscure way — they don't call it code for nothing. Such a system is not predictable; the only way to really find out what it does is to experiment with it. This is unacceptable for systems that have requirements for safety, security, accuracy, or any other critical property.

A formal specification can be valuable even when the rest of the development is informal, because it provides an oracle for analyzing requirements and planning tests.

1.4.2   Design

Design means organizing the internal structure of a program.

There are two dimensions to design: *partition* and *refinement*. Partition means dividing the whole system into parts or *modules* that can be developed independently. Refinement means adding detail, going from an abstract model that clearly satisfies the original requirements to a concrete design that is closer to code[2].

Many informal software development methods address design. Most of them teach a particular way to draw and annotate diagrams that you can use to document designs, such as bubble-and-arrow data flow diagrams. Some of these methods are supported by software products called CASE tools to help you produce the diagrams and documents. However, the formal content of many of these methods is weak. They can only represent the structure of a program: what the program's parts are and how they are related to each other. They provide few criteria to determine whether a design is correct, or to choose the best of several plausible designs.

Z is a more powerful design notation because it can also model behavior. Finding the best structure usually depends on understanding the behavior. In Z you can express which components of the system are needed to perform any behavior, down to any level of detail you need (even to individual program variables). This enables you to see how components must be grouped together to provide the behaviors you need. You can find the best way to partition your system into modules.

Z can also support constructive approaches to design. Rather than work *top-down* and partition an abstract specification into modules that we have to implement ourselves, we might achieve savings by working *bottom-up* and assembling our system from prefabricated building blocks or *reusable software components*. In this enterprise — "programming in the large" [DeRemer and Kron, 1976] — the problem shifts to identifying which blocks to use and determining how they should fit together. Z can express precise descriptions of what the blocks do and enable us to calculate how the whole system will behave when the blocks are used in combination. Chapter 15 describes how to infer properties of systems described in Z.

---

[2] In some formal methods literature, refinement is called *reification*.

Z can also help you determine whether your design will work. Mathematics can tie development stages together in a way that is not possible with informal notations. It provides the only way we have to show that an abstract model and a detailed design are two views of the same thing. If we have a mathematical model, we can infer development steps, and then we can check each step by calculation and proof. This means we need not rely solely on intuition to tell whether our designs are correct. We can find and correct design errors without coding and testing a program. Chapters 15 and 26 describe how to check designs.

1.4.3 Verification

Verification means showing that our code will do what we intend.

Verification deals with the final product of our development: code in some executable programming language. One of the products of a formal verification is a *proof*, a convincing demonstration — based only on the specification and the program text, not on executing the program — that the code does what its specification requires. Proof can provide greater confidence than testing because it considers all cases, while testing just samples some of them. Moreover, proof can be more convincing than appeals to intuition because it can be more explicit, easier to check, and therefore less fallible than intuition.

Much of the early research in formal methods concentrated on formal verification. Some even experimented with automating the proofs. This early work was so influential in fixing the image of the field, that when you say formal methods, many programmers still think, "proving the correctness of code," or even "automated proof." This perception is no longer accurate; much recent work concerns modelling and design, in addition to verifying code.

Chapter 27 discusses formal verification and shows that the most efficient way is usually to do the verification in the course of deriving a program from a formal specification.

1.5 Are formal methods too difficult?

Using formal methods can be more difficult than programming in the usual way — because formal methods aim higher. Describing exactly what your program does is more difficult than letting testers or users figure it out for themselves. Making your program do the right thing in every situation is more difficult than just handling some typical cases. Any method that can handle hard problems will sometimes be hard to carry out; only superficial methods can be easy all the time.

Fortunately, most of the mathematics we need for formal methods is not terribly difficult. The discrete mathematics used in this book — and in most practical applications of formal methods — is easier than much of the calculus that students in the sciences and engineering must study.

Formal methods make us confront the hard problems early. The difficulties cannot be escaped, only deferred. Superficial methods put off the hard parts until coding and testing — but then they appear with a vengeance. News stories about stressful projects tell of programmers who work eighty-hour weeks, sleep under their desks, punch holes in walls, have nervous breakdowns, and commit suicide [Markoff, 1993; Zachary, 1994]. Compared to that, formal methods don't seem so difficult after all.

By making difficult issues more visible, formal methods encourage us to seek a more thorough understanding of the problem we are trying to solve. They require us to express our intentions with exceptional simplicity and clarity. They help us resist the usual tendency in programming to make things too complicated and therefore error-prone and difficult to use.

1.6   Formal methods at work

Some programmers still believe that formal methods are too difficult and esoteric for anything but toy problems, but this is no longer true. One recent survey [Craigen, Gerhart, and Ralston, 1993] learned of more than sixty industrial projects that used formal methods, and reported on several large projects that produced important products that are used and work well. These products included microprocessor floating point microcode, embedded programs in electronics instruments, commercial transaction processing software, and safety-critical control systems in railways and power plants. Some of the projects formally specified and verified tens of thousands of lines of code.

The survey reveals that formal methods can be used in many different ways. Some projects used the formal notation to explore new design ideas; others used it to document existing designs. Some used the formal notation for modelling and description, others derived and verified code. Some projects used tools, others were largely paper-and-pencil efforts. Some trained dozens of people in formal methods; others had only a few self-taught enthusiasts. Some projects finished ahead of schedule, others were very late. Some groups believe that formal methods saved them money; others spent more than they expected. Some of the organizations are increasing their use of formal methods, others have abandoned them.

1.7   Formal methods can be practical

Imagine two extremes. At one extreme is trial-and-error hacking: Programmers with no real understanding type in code, make changes, and run tests, hoping to hit on something that works. At the other end is purest formality: Programmers specify, refine, and prove — and finally present their customers with the text of a program they have never bothered to run! Of course, both extremes are caricatures. No one believes they can produce useful software by either method.

Practical development methods lie between these two extremes. Z works well across a wide range on this scale. You can write a few formulas to supplement an informal prose description, or you can derive code from a comprehensive formal specification. Pick the level of formality that makes the most sense for your project.

The realization that computer programs are formulas lies behind all the deep theoretical results in computer science. The same insight can help us with the practical problems we face every day. Skilled programmers have long recognized that good programs share many qualities with good writing — we speak of "programming style" [Kernighan and Plauger, 1978] and "literate programming" [Knuth, 1992]. This literary view is valid and useful; the mathematical view is complementary. Logic and mathematics take advantage of essential qualities of our material. We're writing formulas when we program, so we may as well get good at it.

2 Why Use Formal Methods?

Why study formal methods? This chapter describes the predicament that formal methods were invented to solve and presents a vision of what programming should be.

Software frequently disappoints us. As users, we find that many programs are a poor match to our real needs and frustrate us with unrepaired defects. As programmers, our disappointment is especially keen. We expect to find the joy of creation in our work and the satisfaction of providing something useful. But all too often our expectations are dashed, our joy is spoiled, and our job becomes a dispiriting slog, churning out shapeless code and patching up bugs.

What's wrong? Is there something inherent in the nature of software that makes our troubles as inevitable as bad weather?

I argue that creating software is not intrinsically more difficult than any other kind of engineering. Many of our difficulties result from avoidable mistakes and poor programming practices.

A central problem is that *people feel it is acceptable to create software without fully understanding what they are doing* — they believe they can produce software and then understand it later by running tests and observing users' experience. It is this attitude, rather than any inherent difficulty in the task, that results in so many software problems.

This error can be made at any stage. Designers specify products when they don't fully understand customers' real needs. Programmers write code when they don't fully understand what it will do, and so on. The fundamental error is reliance on *guessing* to produce systems, and *trial and error* to validate and improve them.

We can do much better. We can usually determine much of what is needed in advance and then produce a system that we know will behave as we intend. Our methods aren't perfect, but knowledge and effort pay off. Even modest efforts can produce appreciable improvement.

Conventional wisdom holds that this positive attitude is not realistic, but I argue this conventional wisdom is incorrect and self-defeating. By aiming too low, it makes programming unnecessarily difficult and inflicts inconvenience — and much worse — on the people who use our programs. Here are two true stories that show what we're up against.

2.1 True stories

2.1.1 Money

A man tries to withdraw some cash from an automatic teller machine (ATM). He inserts his card and keys in his number, but the display reads, "Cannot complete, try later." The machine returns his card, but doesn't print anything. Thinking nothing of it, he walks away. A few weeks later the same thing happens. Suspecting something funny is going on, he inserts his card again and checks his balance. The ATM has indeed debited his account, but has not dispensed any cash — and has not given him a printed record of any transaction!

The man complains to his bank. They explain that they cannot reimburse him without "proof" — the card agreement clearly states that a printed receipt from the machine is the only evidence of a failed transaction that the bank must accept. The man is unusually persistent. After several days and many phone calls to his own bank, the bank that housed the ATM machine, and the company that operates the ATMs, he finally gets his money back. After an investigation the bank admits that he was not the only customer who encountered the problem.

It so happens that the man works in computing. He posts an account of his experience in a digest that is circulated by computer network, concluding that he will stay away from the machines and patronize a store where you can show them your card and a human being will give you the money [Denninger, 1988]. A few days later a response from a member of IBM – then the mightiest computer company on earth — appears in the same digest. He writes,

> Electronic banking systems are incredibly complicated. It is impossible to even imagine the number of things that can go wrong, or the number of ways that clever consumers can subvert the system. Go ahead and boycott the machines if you want. However, if you want them to improve, then you have to exercise the system so that the bugs will be found and fixed.

You were expecting an apology? Well, it's only money. The second story is much worse.

2.1.2 Lives

A woman goes to a clinic to get a radiation treatment for cancer. She knows the procedure should be painless, but she feels a searing heat. She complains that she has been burned, but the therapist explains that is impossible; the computer-controlled radiation machine is the most advanced one available. The woman refuses to return to the clinic and they lose track of her. Months later one of her arms is paralyzed, and she is in constant pain.

Almost a year later a man goes to a clinic in another state. He, too, is burned. The clinic and the vendor can find nothing wrong with the radiation machine, so they keep using it. A few weeks later at the same clinic a second man is burned. After days of investigation, clinic staff are able to reproduce the unusual but legitimate sequence and timing of keystrokes that cause the computer-controlled machine to deliver a dose about one hundred times greater than prescribed.

A few months later both men are dead. Their story is reported in the news, and the first woman finally realizes what happened to her. Eventually, investigators find four more cases at other clinics where people were maimed or killed by the same type of machine [Jacky, 1989; Jacky, 1991; Leveson and Turner, 1993; Leveson, 1995].

In a newspaper story on the accidents [Davis, 1987], a quality assurance manager at the company that built the therapy machine was quoted,

> There are too many combinations of features to guarantee that the (radiation) beam won't come on too intensely.

A government agency required the vendor to supplement the machine's computer controls with a nonprogrammable, hard-wired relay safety interlock system.

2.2 Some popular fallacies

The statements quoted in the preceding two stories are symptoms of the problems that Z was designed to solve. In both quotations, the speakers urge their audiences to regard these incidents as inevitable (if regrettable) consequences of some inescapable complexity that is inherent in software. These statements reveal incorrect beliefs that are held by many programmers, including some of the most influential leaders on the computing scene. These beliefs amount to a entire complex of rationalizations and excuses for programs that don't always work. Here is a summary:

Complexity
Software is incredibly complicated. As one manager put it, "the complexity can be of machines like no human has seen before." [1] As a result, "Programmers can

---

[1] Chris Peters of Microsoft. In the same interview, Peters said of his group's spreadsheet program, "I believe that the product I'm working on now is far more complex than a 747 (jumbo jet airliner)" [WGBH, 1992a].

never imagine the countless different ways in which a program can fail, or the many different ways a program can be used." [2]

Testing

Programs are bound to contain errors, because we can never run enough tests to uncover all the mistakes. "You don't have the precision or the reliability to say, well, having built this, we think it works according to the specifications. Instead, you have to exhaustively test it. And there are always particular combinations of circumstances that have somehow eluded the test plan."[3]

Users

Users don't know what they want. The only way to find out is to build something and give it to them to try out. Only then will we discover what we really should have built. The users will be disappointed, but maybe we can do better with the second (or later) versions.

Systems and tools

No matter what we do, our programs will sometimes fail anyway. There are bugs in our compilers, operating systems, window managers, and all the other system software on which we depend. Even the hardware can have problems.

Economics

Producing high-quality software is extraordinarily expensive. The cost is justified only for a very few safety-critical applications. For most applications, the market does not demand high quality. After all, "it *is* only *software*."[4]

Foundations

Computing is still a young science. We can't be expected to produce reliable results in a timely fashion, as if we worked in a mature engineering discipline. "It's different, in that we take on novel tasks every time. The number of times (civil engineers) make mistakes is very small. And at first you think, what's wrong with us? It's because it's like we're building the first skyscraper every time."[5]

These beliefs are self-serving and naive. In fact software usually fails for prosaic reasons that are largely under the control of the people who build it: Not enough

---

[2] Journalist Leonard Lee [1992].

[3] Mitch Kapor, founder of Lotus and author of a phenomenally popular spreadsheet program [Palfreman and Swade, 1991; WGBH, 1992b].

[4] A programmer's response to a customer's complaints about errors in one of his company's products [Gleick, 1992].

[5] Bill Gates, chairman and CEO of Microsoft [WGBH, 1992a].

time or effort is allocated, or knowledge and skills are insufficient, so problems are handled poorly or are simply overlooked. In some cases there is a deliberate decision to release products that are unfinished or known to contain defects in order to meet schedules or save on development costs [Gleick, 1992; Zachary, 1994]. Programmers and customers are encouraged to view this as normal, even inevitable. Software reliability expert and educator Maurice Naftalin [1988] observes,

> The great majority of software workers have been taught in the conventional manner, which can be characterised as encouraging students (or trainee programmers) to produce, as quickly as possible, large programs which they know will contain serious errors.

2.3   Some hopeful alternatives

The beliefs described in the preceding section are all incorrect, but each holds the seed of a truth. Each denial can be turned around into an affirmation.

Complexity
Software shouldn't be too complicated. We can produce a compact description that explains exactly how a program is supposed to behave.

Testing
Software must be made correct by construction, not testing. Testing is *literally* a trial-and-error process. No mature field of engineering or manufacturing relies on testing to reveal design errors. They test to find defects in materials and investigate the effects of wear and other physical phenomenon that programmers do not even have to worry about [Adams, 1991]. Using testing to find mistakes in our own code is a poor use of everyone's time. Testing is inconclusive, and it comes too late to do much good. The proper role of testing is to confirm our understanding of the requirements and check our assumptions about the compiler, operating system, hardware, and other aspects of the environment where our program has to work. When we are done, testing demonstrates to customers and other witnesses that the development was done correctly.

Users
Users do understand the problem they need to solve. What they usually aren't able to do is conceive a detailed computer solution to their problem. That's our job. It takes a lot of time and empathy to appreciate users' needs well enough to provide them with something useful. Many projects skimp on this — they consider learning

the requirements to be just a perfunctory prelude to the real work of programming[6]. In fact it is the single most important task in any project.

Systems and tools

We depend on system software and hardware that aren't perfect, but we can't just pass other peoples' mistakes on to our users. When things go wrong, we must be able to distinguish our own mistakes from the limitations of the systems we have to use. This isn't possible if we program by trial and error, just changing things until the program seems to work. But if we understand our program, we can fix our own mistakes and work around the rest — until we eventually get them fixed or find a better system vendor.

Economics

Coping with mediocre software is extraordinarily expensive. Former software industry leaders have gone out of business after they released defective products and their customers fled to competitors [7]. Moreover, software development *already* costs an extraordinary amount. Microsoft and IBM spend thousands of programmer-years and hundreds of millions of dollars developing complex personal computer software products such as OS/2 and Windows NT [Carrol, 1991; Zachary, 1994]. The costs and effort are as great as we find in large safety-critical engineering projects, like building skyscrapers [Sabbagh, 1990]. But the greatest costs are borne by the customers. Occasionally, horror stories surface where people pay with their lives, or dollars, as in Section 2.1. More often, they pay in time and aggravation for their lost work and the effort they must devote to recovering from problems and improvising workarounds.

Foundations

Computing is a mature science. The electronic computer is about the same age as the jet aircraft engine — to which we routinely entrust our lives. We rarely have to start from scratch; most new software products are refinements of ideas that go back for decades. People were computing long before there were any electronic computers. Programmers are the modern heirs to a legacy of logical ingenuity that reaches back

---

[6] One software engineer quoted by Poltrock and Grudin [1994] speculated, "I think it would be worthwhile if all developers would spend maybe a couple of hours a year seeing how the product is used by customers."

[7] Ashton-Tate was the third largest personal computer software vendor in 1988, when it released dBase IV, a famously buggy version of its flagship product. It spent 18 months working on a corrected version, but it was too late. Its database product line was acquired by another vendor and Ashton-Tate went out of the software business [Keefe, 1990; Lewis, 1990].

to antiquity. The ancient Greeks developed algorithms thousands of years ago that we still use — and proved them correct [8]!

I don't mean to minimize the very real difficulties of programming. Every technology has its unique problems. What I reject is the special pleading that holds computing is so new, so unique, so "incredibly complicated," that it simply defies analysis. We shouldn't have to confess bewilderment, hide behind disclaimers, or conceal our confusion behind a facade of condescending bluster.

Instead, I invite you to consider the opposite view. We can do better. The second group of tenets is our vision of what programming should be. Formal methods — along with a conscientious and systematic approach to our work, and a thorough knowledge of our application — can help us realize this vision.

Our aspirations are tempered by realism. Sometimes it is necessary to release a program that is imperfect and incomplete, because there are times when something is better than nothing. This can be all right if the users are made to understand the limitations in what they are getting. But let's be candid and admit the shortcomings are the result of time pressure and work load, not some inherent problem in computing itself.

I'm not saying it's easy. There is no magic, no method you can follow like a recipe in a cookbook, where merely following the directions will result in a successful project. It takes a great deal of judgment and imagination to make any programming method work. Success does not chiefly derive from the techniques that can be taught in books, which are necessarily devoid of specific guidance for your particular application. Merely selecting a formal notation cannot solve your problem. Your success largely depends on the unique features of your project: the problem itself and the people who join together to solve it. It is up to you to choose a method which is a good match to the problem, and then to express the problem in such a way that the techniques of the method can be brought to bear. These are deeply creative acts that cannot be taught in any very prescriptive way. I can only provide examples and inspiration, and trust in your judgment to apply their lessons to your own work.

---

[8] Euclid taught the algorithm for finding the greatest common divisor of two integers in Alexandria around 300 BC (*Elements*, Book VII) [Dunham, 1990]. We still use Euclid's algorithm because modern cryptography and secure data transmission require an abundant supply of large prime numbers and the algorithm figures in certain primality tests [Schneier, 1994]. Hoare [1987] expresses Euclid's algorithm in several modern programming styles.

3 Formal methods and project management

Formal methods are not project management methods, but some programmers fear that using formal methods would impose a burdensome and inflexible way of working. This chapter should dispel that misconception and reassure you that formal methods are compatible with many different development methods and management styles. This chapter discusses dividing projects into stages, learning users' requirements, translating informal requirements to formal specifications, and validating formal specifications.

3.1 Work in stages

There is one assumption that underlies all formal methods: A programming project is divided into stages, where each stage produces a product that can be examined, reviewed, and assessed for correctness and other qualities.

Three products that must be produced by almost any programming project are the *specification*, which describes the behavior of the product; the *design*, which describes its internal structure; and the *code*, which is executable and is expressed in some particular programming language. Most projects produce other products as well, such as manuals and other materials for instructing users, assurance evidence such as test plans and test results, and so forth.

Working in stages is a central concept in every systematic software development method. Formal methods add these innovations: express the specification and design (not just the code) in a formal notation, and use formula manipulations (such as calculation and proof) to derive the products and check that they are correct.

Experienced programmers are often skeptical of programming methods that proceed in stages. They can draw on a vast mental library of correct solutions to programming problems, which they can adapt to routine situations by *intuition* — that is, without articulating the development steps. Making the stages explicit takes time; writing them down adds work. Why waste time stepping through stages when you can reach a solution in a single leap? These concerns are not unfounded, but the stages don't have to be too onerous.

Working in stages need not be burdensome. In some projects the product of each stage is a heavy document produced with a lot of attention to cosmetic formatting details, but this is not always necessary or even useful. Stages occur in any project, no matter how small. Some projects are so trivial we can do most of the stages in our heads, or we write them down in scribbled notes we throw away; the only product is the code itself. As projects take longer and involve more people, we have to make the stages visible. Our notes get bigger, more public and more permanent — they become "documentation."

The stages need not be steps in a sequence. In most real projects, several stages — or all of them — are in progress at the same time. There is nothing wrong with this, provided we can ensure that the stages are consistent with each other when the project is finished. Sometimes the specification is written last, to record what has been discovered during an exploratory project.

The stages need not be independent of each other. Sometimes it is useful for the specification and design to be independent of the programming language used to code the program and the target computer system where it will run. This kind of independence makes it easier to produce multiple implementations that run on different systems. But sometimes we know in advance that the product will be implemented in a particular programming language and will run on one target configuration. We can take advantage of this knowledge to create a specification and design that are closely matched to the code.

The stages need not imply any division of labor. Sometimes it works best if the same people participate in all stages, so that each staff member assumes full responsibility for a portion of the system, from understanding the users' requirements, through supporting the product in use in the field. This enables each participant to develop a comprehensive appreciation of the whole project that can inform their work on every stage. This can be much more efficient (and more satisfying) than isolating people and forcing them to communicate through documents.

The stages need not connote status. In some organizations, senior programmers (often called "systems analysts," "software engineers," or "scientists") concentrate on specification and design, while junior programmers (called "programmers") are assigned to coding. In fact there is no self-evident scale of difficulty; none of the stages is easy. Each stage applies different kinds of knowledge, emphasizing knowledge about the users and their problem in specification, and knowledge about the programming language and operating environment in design and coding. But the knowledge cannot be too specialized; to perform any stage, you must bridge from one view to another. In this book I use the word "programmer" for anyone involved in the technical work of software production, whether or not they spend most of their time writing code.

It should be clear that the stages are a technical concept, not a management tool. Many books on project management also discuss stages. They often recommend a particular sequence of stages and the activities that should happen in each stage; some even recommend particular formats for documents that should be produced at each stage. You must understand that their stages are idealizations of programming made for the benefit of management. They are not the same stages that I write about. The programmer's stages are not the manager's stages. It is the manager's job to worry about schedules and the expenditure of funds, so the manager wants the stages to be steps in a sequence and see stages get finished! But programmers view the stages as simultaneously evolving aspects of a single thing. Sometimes we can build the best product if we are free to revise all the stages until the last minute.

Sometimes management, customers, or regulators require developers to provide them with the products of development stages. They may require that these products be documented in a particular style or format. You should not allow their reporting requirements (however burdensome they might be) to unduly influence the technical aspects of your project. The format of their documents might suggest a particular way to design the product or organize the the project, but it might not be the best way.

You cannot expect management, customers, regulators, or standards bodies to know how to solve your problem. Solving a problem is a different activity than reporting the solution. Sometimes you have to do both, but do not confuse them. Your management may not understand formal methods and may not require you to report on their use, but they might prove to be very useful to you nevertheless.

3.2   Gathering requirements

There is much more to programming than solving symbolic puzzles. The most important thing of all is to create a program that does something useful. Without this, everything else is wasted. You must understand the users' work and learn the problems they are trying to solve.

I deliberately say "users," not "customers" or "clients." The users are the people who must actually use the program to get their work done. Sometimes the customer — the one who makes purchasing decisions — is the users' manager.

The *requirements* are properties that a system should have in order to succeed in the environment where it will be used [Goguen and Luqi, 1995]. Learning the requirements demands that programmers and other technical specialists devote the time and empathy to understand some job that people do and identify the tasks that are repeatable and well enough understood to be mechanized. It also requires the judgment to determine whether the task is worth mechanizing, or whether bringing in the computer will just make life more complicated and create extra work for people to do.

Getting the requirements right is one of the central problems in computing. It is probably the single most important factor in determining whether a program is useful and effective, yet the vast literature of computer science has surprisingly little to say about it. The issues are deeper than are usually addressed by the user interface or human-computer interaction specialists. The term "user interface" suggests a shell that wraps around some predetermined core of functions; the real requirements problem is to decide what those core functions should be.

Requirements are seldom arbitrary. Many requirements are dictated by nature or by human laws and customs. If the flight control program does not respect the laws of aerodynamics, the airplane will crash. If the computer-aided design program that does integrated circuit layout does not observe the design rules, the circuit will not work. In commercial transactions and funds transfers, the sums must balance. Other requirements are dicated by the interfaces that enable a program to fit into a larger system.

Programmers should participate in gathering the requirements because they appreciate the need for precision and will recognize when users' requests are too vague to be useful. A useful requirement is expressed in a declarative sentence that describes some objective property or occurrence that users can observe. If users say, "make the program easy to use," programmers can work with them to get to something more specific, like "the program will always display a menu of the options that the user can choose." Some users' requests are not software requirements at all: "The program should make our work more efficient." Demands like this concern the larger environment of which the software is only one part; they involve organizational and social issues that are often outside the programmers' control. Nevertheless, programmers can use such requests as opportunities to learn where the real problems are.

Programmers can also help elicit the whole story. Users' requests usually have gaps at cases they haven't considered. Programmers are good at recognizing these gaps, and will take care to meet the users' real needs by covering them properly. It is essential that the users participate in this filling-in process to ensure that important functions are not handled by default or whim.

Programmers also understand that they must negotiate with users to limit the requirements. Projects grow out of control when they try to accommodate too many requests. Some requirements are not very important, and the product would be improved if they were omitted. Users cannot always appreciate how seemingly minor requirements can spoil the clarity of a design and pile on a great deal of extra work. Programmers can advise them on the tradeoffs among features, cost, and development time.

Once we understand the requirements, we should write them down. We almost always need a written statement of requirements. Without it, something is sure to be overlooked or misunderstood.

It is essential that the users themselves understand the written requirements, because they have to review them. They are the only ones who can tell you if the requirements describe a solution to their problem. Therefore, the requirements must be expressed in plain (natural) language in the users' vocabulary, and be liberally provided with figures, tables, and diagrams that they can appreciate. The prose should not describe the problem in computing jargon. If the users are scientists or engineers, some of the requirements might be expressed in formulas, but even in technical applications most of the requirements are expressed in prose and pictures.

3.3 From informal requirements to formal specifications

Formal notations such as Z are designed to help programmers produce software. They are not intended to replace the prose statement of requirements. Writing a formal specification does not come at the beginning of a project. You have to know a great deal about a problem before you can write a useful formal specification.

It is often said that formal specifications are necessary because prose is not precise, but this is not really true. When you are describing the behavior of a system that is designed for some definite purpose, you can write prose that is clear, precise, and free of ambiguity. For example:

The radiation beam cannot turn on unless the therapy room door is closed.

As we shall see in Chapter 10, the meaning of this sentence can be expressed formally:

$$beam = on \Rightarrow door = closed$$

This formula is no more precise than the prose. Its advantages do not derive from precision, but from brevity, ability to guide systematic progression to code, and support for calculation, logical inference, and proof. These advantages are only meaningful to programmers. The formal notation serves no purpose in a requirements document intended for an audience of users.

This little example might suggest that you can translate prose requirements to formal notation one sentence at a time, but that usually does not work. The problem with the prose requirements is not precision, but organization: A good prose description does not map directly into a good formal description. The prose is organized around tasks, problems, and scenarios that users encounter. Much of it is essentially a narrative. The narrative can be repetitious; there may be many operations that work almost the same way. If you try to just translate prose into formulas, you are likely to end up with one of those "incredibly complicated" programs that doesn't always work. A good formal specification is no mere paraphrase of the prose description; it is a different expression of the same behaviors, in a form that is better organized to serve as a guide for programming. Common features can be factored out so they only appear once.

3.4 Validating formal specifications

It is necessary to show that a formal specification expresses the intent of the prose requirements. This is called *validating* the specification. If the requirements are clear, and the formal specification is well organized, much of the specification can be validated by inspection. In cases where it is not so obvious, we can apply the formal reasoning methods taught in Chapter 15. Any meaningful requirement can be expressed in a declarative sentence, and a declarative sentence can be translated to a formula (as in the example in Section 3.3). If this formula is present in the specification, or can be calculated or inferred from the formulas in the specification, the specification is valid for that requirement.

Further reading

Phil Agre [1988] discussed the teller machine incident in a memorable posting to *RISKS*. Nancy Leveson and Clark Turner [1993] wrote the authoritative account of the radiation therapy machine accidents.

There is a vast literature on mishaps involving computers. Lauren Wiener [1993] provides a recent and lively book-length treatment, and I cite some notable incidents in a textbook chapter [Jacky, 1991; Jacky, 1996]. The most systematic compilation is maintained by Peter Neumann, moderator of the ongoing *RISKS FORUM Digest*. Neumann's review and assessment appear in his recent book [Neumann, 1994].[1] Nancy Leveson's book [1995] on system safety and computers reviews many incidents and emphasizes that accidents can only be understood and prevented by considering the whole systems where they can occur.

Even when software does not actually fail, it can make life difficult. Many programs are poorly matched to users' real needs and create extra work for people to do. Thomas K. Landauer's book [1995] describes many examples and suggests some remedies. One school within computer science that does confront the requirements problem is *participatory design*. It has developed techniques for eliciting what the job really is and where the real problems are [Bjerknes, Ehn, and Kyng, 1987; Greenbaum and Kyng, 1991; Schuler and Namioka, 1993].

Matthew Jaffe *et al.* [1991] and Nancy Leveson [1995] show how to analyze requirements for completeness and safety, and Carl Landwehr [1981] reviews work on analyzing security.

The book by David Alex Lamb [1988] and the paper by David Parnas and Paul Clements [1986] are good sources on software design and the technical aspects of

---

[1] Current issues of *RISKS* appear on Usenet news in comp.risks; excerpts and summaries appear in a printed newsletter from the Association for Computing Machinery, *ACM Software Engineering Notes* (for example [Neumann, 1996]). At this writing the *RISKS* ftp archive is at ftp.sri.com and is on the World Wide Web at http://catless.ncl.ac.uk/Risks, but check recent issues for current information.

project management. Parnas [1995] explains the difference between a description, a model, and a specification.

Dan Craigen, Susan Gerhart, and Ted Ralston have done the most thorough survey of formal methods use to date [1993]; it has been summarized in several conference papers and journal articles [Craigen, Gerhart, and Ralston, 1995; Gerhart, Craigen, and Ralston, 1994a; Gerhart, Craigen, and Ralston, 1994b]. Other reviews appear in the paper by Jonathan Bowen and Victoria Stavridou [1993] and the report by John Rushby [1993]. The book edited by Mike Hinchey and Jonathan Bowen [1995] describes many recent projects. C. P. Pfleeger [Pfleeger, 1995] and M. Tierney [Tierney, 1993] review experience with mandated use of formal methods in military secure communications and safety-critical systems.

Many authors have remarked on the attitudes I criticize in Chapter 2. Joseph Weizenbaum's classic *Computer Power and Human Reason* [1976] is usually considered a work of social criticism, but his chapters "Incomprehensible Programs" and "Science and the Compulsive Programmer" are pertinent to my argument.

The quote from David Hilbert appears in the textbook by David M. Burton [1980].

Part II

Introducing Z

4 What is Z?

Z is a set of conventions for presenting mathematical text, chosen to make it convenient to use simple mathematics to describe computing systems. I say computing *systems* because Z has been used to model hardware as well as software.

Z is a mature notation. Conceived in the late 1970s, it developed through the 1980s in collaborative projects between Oxford University and industrial partners, including IBM and Inmos (a semiconductor producer). The first Z reference manual to be widely published benefited from this long experience when it finally appeared in 1989. At this writing a draft Z standard (including a formal semantics) is being considered by the American National Standards Institute (ANSI), the British Standards Institute (BSI) and the International Organization for Standardization (ISO). Z has served as the basis for other notations, including several variants adapted for object-oriented programming.

Z is a *model-based notation*. In Z you usually model a system by representing its *state* — a collection of *state variables* and their values — and some *operations* that can change its state. A model that is characterized by the operations it describes is called an *abstract data type* (ADT). This modelling style is a good match to imperative, procedural programming languages that provide a rich collection of data types, and also to some physical systems (such as digital electronics) that include storage elements. Z is also a natural fit to object-oriented programming. Z state variables are like instance variables, and the operations are like methods; Z even provides a kind of inheritance. However, Z is not limited just to ADTs and object-oriented style; you can also use Z in a functional style, among others.

Z dictates few assumptions about what can be modelled. Z is just a notation, it is not a method; the Z notation can support many different methods. The meaning of a Z text is determined by its authors. It can be understood to model only the behavior of a system: It is an abstract formal specification. Or, the elements of a Z text can be understood to represent structures in code: modules, data types, procedures, functions, classes, objects. In that case the Z model is a detailed design.

Z is not an executable notation. In general, Z specifications cannot be interpreted or compiled into a running program (or prototype or simulation). *Z is not a programming language*. Z texts are not just programs written in very high-level language. What would be the point of writing the program twice?

Z was designed for people, not machines. For years Z was exclusively a pencil-and-paper notation. Z encourages a style where formulas are annotated liberally with prose. Z documents usually include more prose than formal text. Novices can be intimidated by the appearance of Z: a mixture of boxes, text, Greek letters, and invented pictorial symbols. But the notation is easy to learn; once assimilated, its advantages become clear. The boxes and pictorial symbols in Z help your eye grasp the structure of the model even before you read it.

Z actually includes two notations. The first is the notation of ordinary discrete mathematics, expressed in the symbols and syntax described in Part III. The second notation provides structure to the mathematical text: It provides several structuring constructs called *paragraphs*. The most conspicuous kind of Z paragraph is a macro-like abbreviation and naming construct called the *schema*. Z defines a *schema calculus* you can use to build big schemas from small ones. The schema is the feature that most distinguishes Z from other formal notations.

The mathematical notation of Z consists of a small core, supplemented by a larger collection of useful objects and operators called the *Z mathematical tool-kit*. The tool-kit is not software, it is a collection of mathematical theories: definitions and laws concerning objects such as sets, tuples, relations, functions, sequences, and their operators. In Z we use these mathematical objects to model data structures and other components of computing systems. The tool-kit plays somewhat the same role in Z that a standard library of types and functions does in an executable programming language. The portions of the tool-kit used in this book appear in Appendix D.

Z is very powerful, and the notation is used in two rather different ways. First there is a *descriptive* style where we use Z to model some particular system we intend to implement: a text editor or a radiation therapy machine. Then there is an *analytic* style that experts use to define and extend the Z notation itself. Several constructs in Z were put there to support the analytic style and are only rarely used for description. My purpose in this book is to teach the descriptive style. We can take the foundations for granted. We're going to *use* Z.

Z is supported by tools. The notation is defined with sufficient precision that Z texts can be processed by machine. Software tools are available for writing and displaying the special Z symbols and typesetting documents like this book, for checking Z texts for syntax and type errors in much the same way that a compiler checks code in an executable programming language, and even for assisting in proving claims about the behavior of systems modelled in Z. These tools are invaluable for serious work, but you do not need them to begin learning and using Z.

We'll tackle some small examples first. In the next few chapters I'll show you what Z can do, explaining the basics as I go, without a lot of didactic preamble. I'll explain the notation more fully in Part III.

5 A first example in Z

In this Chapter, I describe a well-known function in Z and compare the Z model to code in C. The function is tiny, but not trivial; it reveals in miniature several issues that recur in problems of any size. The Z model describes the behavior of the code without describing its internal structure: It is a *specification*. This exercise demonstrates what a specification is and explains why we need one. It shows how a specification differs from code, and makes it clear why we cannot (in general) expect to compile a useful specification into an executable program. It also provides a first look at some constructs in the Z notation.

Many programmers believe that formal specifications are not useful. They believe that the program text — the code itself — can be the only really complete and unambiguous description of what a program does. This view holds that a formal specification is nothing more than the program written over again in another language. It misinterprets Z to be some kind of very high-level programming language.

This example shows they are wrong. See for yourself: Here is the code in C.

```
int f(int a)
{
    int i,term,sum;

    term=1; sum=1;
    for (i=0; sum <= a; i++) {
        term=term+2;
        sum=sum+term;
    }
    return i;
}
```

The code couldn't be simpler. It is well structured and very brief — in fact it looks trivial. But what does it do? It seems to be adding up a series of numbers — but why? And it returns the counter, rather than the sum — is that a mistake? Try to answer before you turn the page.

I'll give you some hints: Here is the code again with a new name and a comment.

```
int iroot(int a)
/* Integer square root */
{
  int i,term,sum;

  term=1; sum=1;
  for (i=0; sum <= a; i++)
      term=term+2;
      sum=sum+term;
  }
  return i;
}
```

Now I've told you that the code is supposed to compute the integer square root, so you might guess that if you call `iroot` with a set to 4, it should return 2. If you type in the code, write a driver program, and run a little test, you will find that it does.

But the name and the comment are not as helpful as they might seem. Some numbers don't have integer square roots. What happens if you call `iroot` with a set to 3? Negative numbers don't have square roots at all. What if you call `iroot` with a set to -4? Does it return anything, or does it loop forever — or crash? These questions reveal the problem with the name and the comment: They aren't complete. They don't explain how the function behaves for every input. There are a lot of cases, and we don't want to try every one. Can't we come up with a better description?

We need more than just the code. We need a specification. The code describes the computation itself, but a specification describes the *result* of the computation. We start with a definition of square root in English:

> When you multiply the square root of a number by itself, you get the original number back again.

We can say the same thing more concisely in mathematical notation:

$$\sqrt{a} \times \sqrt{a} = a$$

Unfortunately this definition can't serve as the specification for any computer program. Here we confront a difference between the ideal world of mathematics and the real world of the computer: Computers can only represent numbers to some finite degree of precision — they can only carry so many digits. However, many useful numbers — for example $\sqrt{2}$ — cannot be expressed exactly with a finite number of digits. No real computer can represent a number that you can multiply by itself and obtain exactly 2. No matter how many digits you have, there will always be a little error[1]. Our iroot function makes the problem especially obvious because it returns an integer, but the same problem arises no matter how many digits of precision we might have: We must explain how we handle all those numbers with square roots we can't represent exactly. Similar problems arise in most other numerical calculations: It is not possible to compute the exact answer, so we must specify the accuracy.

We can do it easily in Z. Here is a specification for iroot, expressed in a single Z *paragraph* called an *axiomatic definition*:

$$
\begin{array}{|l}
iroot : \mathbb{N} \to \mathbb{N} \\
\hline
\forall a : \mathbb{N} \bullet \\
\quad iroot(a) * iroot(a) \le a < (iroot(a) + 1) * (iroot(a) + 1)
\end{array}
$$

The first thing you will notice is that the Z paragraph is set off from the surrounding prose by lines that suggest a sort of box. Z turns the commenting convention of programming languages inside out: In Z we delimit the formal text, not the prose. There is no way to write informal comments inside a Z paragraph. You are supposed to provide the explanation in the surrounding text, and keep the Z parts brief enough that your readers don't get lost.

Now let's look inside the box. This example shows how Z combines features from programming languages and traditional mathematics. Like many programming languages, Z has declarations and data types. The big horizontal line is a piece of Z syntax that divides the paragraph into parts. The text above the line is the declaration:

$iroot : \mathbb{N} \to \mathbb{N}$

It corresponds to the declaration of the C function:

```
int iroot(int a)
```

Both declarations tell us that iroot is a function that takes an integer argument and returns an integer, but the differences here are not just syntactic. The Z declaration is actually *stronger*: It tells use more. In Z, $\mathbb{N}$ is the symbol for the *natural numbers*, the data type whose members are the nonnegative integers: 0, 1, 2, ...

The $\mathbb{N}$ to the left of the arrow says that the input to the function must be a natural number. This tells us that the behavior of *iroot* is not defined when the input is a negative integer — it might return anything or nothing; it could crash or loop forever. It is up to the caller to ensure that *iroot* is never called with a negative argument.

---

[1] The discovery of such "incommensurable" or "irrational" numbers is another one of those important computer science discoveries that the ancient Greeks made thousands of years ago [Toeplitz, 1963].

The $\mathbb{N}$ to the right of the arrow says that the result returned by the function is also a natural number; *iroot* will never return a negative number. This is tells us that *iroot*(4) will always be 2, never -2 (which would also seem to work, since $-2 \times -2 = 4$). This additional information is necessary because a function must always be defined so that there can be just a single output value for any input value.

The restriction of the input and output of the function to nonnegative integers is not explicit in the C declaration. It is typical for Z declarations to include more information than the declarations in executable programming languages. The collection of data types available in Z is much richer than in any programming language.

Like the code, the Z uses a *dummy variable* or *formal parameter* to define the function. The Z text $\forall a : \mathbb{N}$ corresponds to the C code int a; it introduces the formal parameter a and tells its type (the spot $\bullet$ is just a delimiter). In Z, a is called a *bound variable*; I will explain the $\forall$ ... syntax in Chapter 10.

Now we come to the biggest difference between Z and code. The Z text below the line is called the *predicate*:

$$iroot(a) * iroot(a) \le a < (iroot(a) + 1) * (iroot(a) + 1)$$

The predicate resembles the mathematical definition $\sqrt{a} \times \sqrt{a} = a$, but it says more. It explains what happens when the argument does not have an integer square root: *iroot* returns the *largest* natural number that is *at most* $\sqrt{a}$. When $a = 4$, *iroot* returns 2, but when $a = 3$, *iroot* returns 1, and when $a = 5$, *iroot* also returns 2, and so on. You can plug these numbers into the formula to confirm that they satisfy the specification. It is important that the specification makes this clear because other choices are possible. We might have chosen the predicate with ... $< a \le$ ... instead. This defines a different function that returns the *smallest* natural number that is *at least* $\sqrt{a}$; when a is 4 this function returns 2 just as *iroot* does, but when a is 3 it also returns 2, whereas *iroot* returns 1.

The code that corresponds to the predicate is the *body* of the function:

```
{
   int i,term,sum;

   term=1; sum=1;
   for (i=0; sum <= a; i++)
       term=term+2;
       sum=sum+term;
   }
   return i;
}
```

The code doesn't resemble the specification at all. This is the key difference between Z and an executable programming language: *The predicate in a Z definition describes* **what** *the function does without explaining how to do it; the body of a C function describes* **how** *to compute the function without explaining what the result will be.* The two descriptions are complementary; neither can take the place of the other. We need both.

This example reveals that Z is not a programming language; we cannot expect anyone to produce a compiler that could turn the Z definition into executable code. The Z definition is *nonconstructive*: it is essentially an *acceptance test* that we can use to check whether a candidate *iroot*(*a*) is correct, but it provides no obvious clues how to calculate (or construct) *iroot*(*a*) from *a*. This ability to use nonconstructive definitions is one of the main reasons why specifications in nonexecutable notations such as Z can be so much shorter and clearer than code.

So where *did* the code come from? I have to explain a little about how the code was developed in order to make it clear why we cannot expect anyone to come up with a Z compiler.

As I explained in Chapter 3, you get from a specification to code in stages, adding knowledge at each stage. If you take away the intermediate stages, the results can seem completely mysterious. Usually you apply two kinds of knowledge: knowledge about the application and knowledge about the system where the program must run. In this case the application is mathematics, and it so happens that the system where the program must run is very limited: a tiny embedded controller with a primitive processor and very little memory. We must make our program as small as possible, and we must limit our use of arithmetic to addition and comparison — our processor has no built-in multiply or divide instructions.

To find a solution we must search our store of mathematical knowledge: We look in books or ask an expert. We want a formula that defines square root in terms of addition. The closest one we find is

$$1 + 3 + 5 + \cdots + (2n - 1) = n^2$$

This one will do — it describes squares in terms of addition. It is a *constructive* definition: The quantity of interest n^2 appears by itself on one side of an equation, and the other side only uses operators we have available in our programming language (in this case, addition). We can always translate a constructive definition into an executable program. Chapter 27 explains how the `iroot` code can be derived from this formula.

No compiler could do all of this. There is no algorithm for making the leap from a nonconstructive definition to an executable program. Implementing nonconstructive definitions requires additional knowledge that is specific to each problem. Much of the creative work in programming involves finding this knowledge and figuring out how to apply it.

Creating code from specifications also involves another kind of judgment that cannot, in general, be built into a compiler: choosing tradeoffs in performance. This is essentially an economic judgment. For example in this case we wrote the simplest and shortest code that could compute $iroot(a)$. However, our code is slow. It just counts up to $iroot(a)$, so as a gets larger, it takes longer (technically, we say iroot has complexity $O(\sqrt{n})$). There are more efficient ways to compute $iroot(a)$, but all of them are more complicated than our iroot. If we were not limited to just addition and comparison, the code would look completely different. Our code follows from the knowledge that our implementation requires extreme simplicity instead of speed.

Just as there can be no Z compiler, there is no simplistic Z development method either. There can be no cookbook recipe for getting from Z to code. There are always many different ways to implement a Z specification. It is up to you to choose the best one for your situation.

This freedom to choose from alternative implementations is one of the defining characteristics that distinguishes a specification from code. Describing a system with code can close off alternatives too early and force you to accept a solution that is not the best match to your real needs. This is one of the reasons why a nonexecutable specification is a good thing to have.

Summary

A specification describes the behavior of code without describing its internal structure. A specification can convey information that cannot be expressed directly in code: information about precision, applicability, and exceptional situations. A specification can be nonconstructive: It can express the result that the code achieves without explaining how it works. A nonconstructive specification can be seen as an acceptance test. Nonconstructive specifications achieve expressivity and brevity at the expense of executability; in general they cannot be compiled into code. Therefore they leave the programmer free to choose among different implementation strategies. Functions can be specified in Z paragraphs called axiomatic definitions. The declaration and predicate in a Z axiomatic definition correspond to the declaration and body of a function in an executable programming language.

6 From prose to Z: control console

Here is a first example to illustrate the progression from informal to formal descriptions. I will describe the control program for the therapist's console on a radiation therapy machine (Figure 6.1).

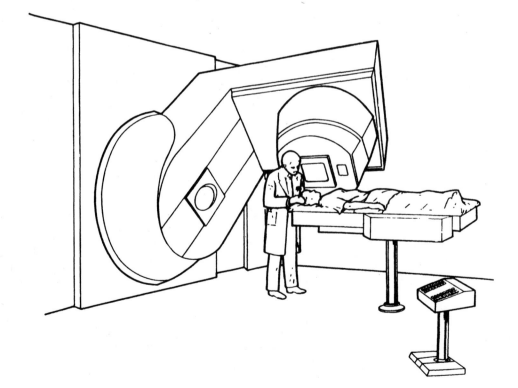

Figure 6.1: Therapy machine.

6.1   Informal requirements

The purpose of this program is to help ensure that patients are treated correctly, as directed by their prescriptions. Many therapy machine settings must be set properly to deliver each prescribed treatment. The console program ensures that the radiation beam can only turn on when the correct settings have been achieved.

The treatment console computer stores a database of prescriptions for many patients. Each patient's prescription usually includes several different beam configurations called *fields*. Each field is defined by many machine settings.

The therapist operates the control program at an ordinary workstation, selecting different console operations by pressing labelled function keys (Figure 6.2). The therapist actually turns the radiation beam on and off by pressing buttons on a separate control panel. These buttons act on directly the therapy machine through nonprogrammable hard-wired controls that are not controlled by the computer. The computer merely senses the condition of these buttons. The therapist sets many machine settings – those involved in positioning the patient and the moveable parts of the therapy machine – at local controls in the therapy room. Again, the control computer can only sense these settings.

The control program is only responsible for checking that the prescribed settings and actual settings agree. There are many other safety conditions that are checked by other computers and nonprogrammable elements. All safety conditions are mediated by relays in a hard-wired *interlock chain*, essentially a chain of switches wired in series. An open switch indicates a potential hazard; a closed switch indicates a safe condition. All switches must be closed to allow the beam to turn on; if any switch opens when the beam is on, it turns off immediately. The console computer indicates that the prescribed settings have been achieved by closing a switch in this chain.

This design expresses a conservative philosophy commonly applied in safety-critical systems: Computers are used only where their complexity is absolutely required; elsewhere, safety is delegated to simpler mechanisms whose trustworthiness can be ensured by time-tested techniques.

When a patient arrives, the therapist presses the SELECT PATIENT key to display the list of patients whose prescriptions are on file and then chooses that patient's identifier from the list (by a method we needn't describe). When the display shows the selected patient, the therapist confirms the selection by pressing ENTER. Then the list of beams on file for that patient appears (Figure 6.3). The therapist chooses one and again presses ENTER. The prescribed settings for the selected field appear (Figure 6.4). Then the therapist enters the treatment room to position the patient and set up the machine.

When all the settings match the prescription, and all safety interlocks are clear, the control program closes its relay in the interlock chain, and the workstation display

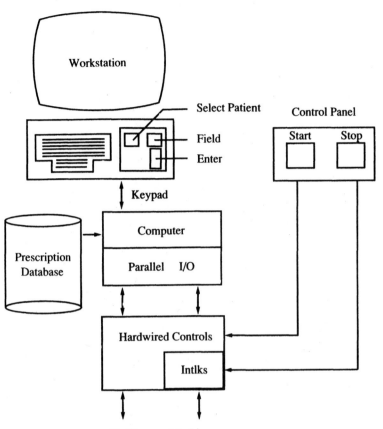

Figure 6.2: Therapy control console block diagram.

indicates that the machine is ready to begin a treatment. Then the therapist presses the START button, and the beam turns on. It usually remains on until the prescribed dose is delivered, and then turns off automatically when a dosimeter opens its relay in the interlock chain. After the beam turns off, it is necessary to repeat some of the setup procedures in order to clear certain interlocks and make the machine ready again.

There can be many exceptions to this usual sequence. The therapist may select a different patient or field at any time, except when the beam is actually on. The therapist can always turn off the beam by pressing the STOP button before the prescribed dose is delivered (for example, if the patient moves). The control program or the hardware safety circuits will open their relays in the interlock chain if they detect any faults. This will also turn off the beam.

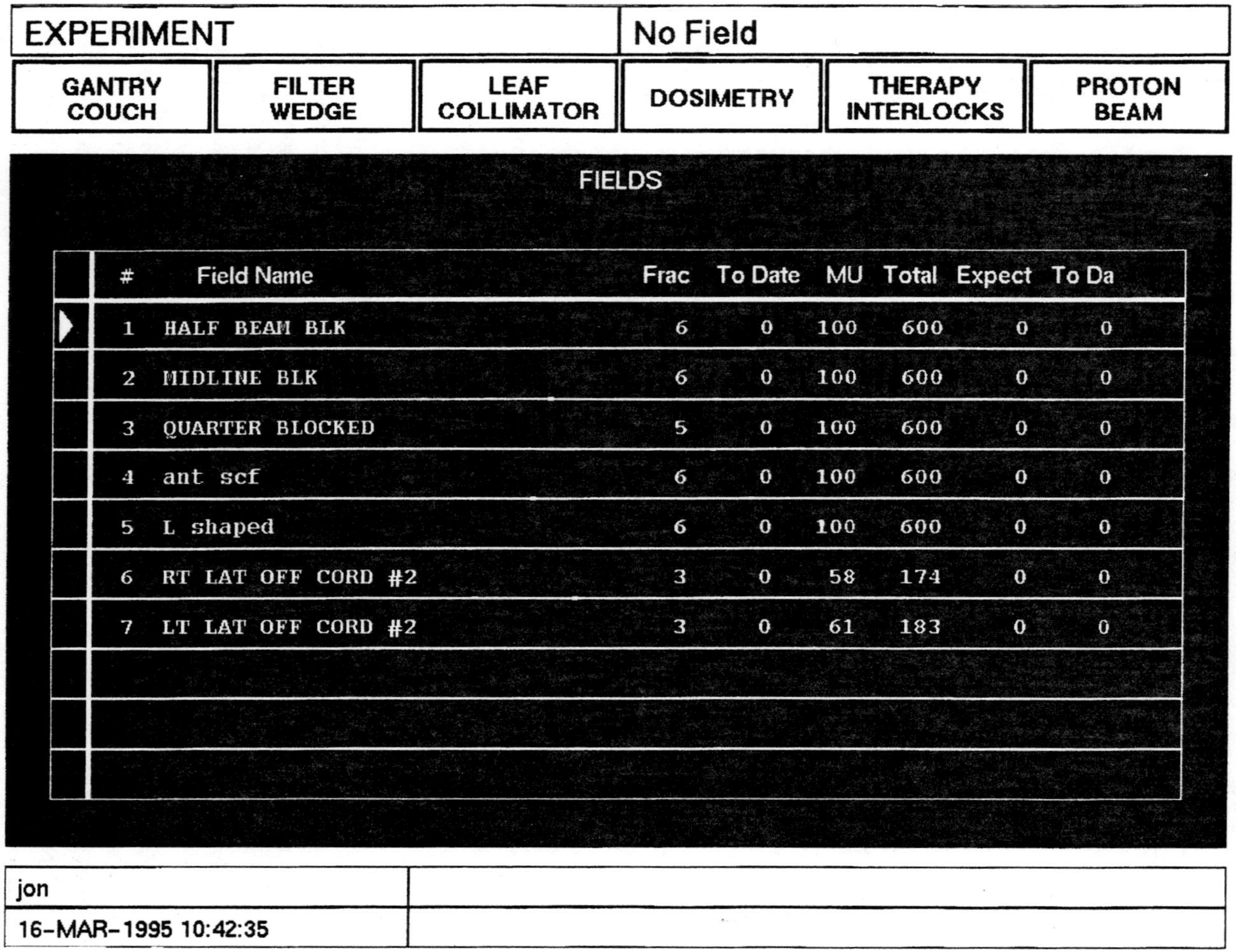

EXPERIMENT | No Field

| GANTRY COUCH | FILTER WEDGE | LEAF COLLIMATOR | DOSIMETRY | THERAPY INTERLOCKS | PROTON BEAM |

FIELDS

#	Field Name	Frac	To Date	MU Total	Expect	To Da
1	HALF BEAM BLK	6	0	100	600	0	0
2	MIDLINE BLK	6	0	100	600	0	0
3	QUARTER BLOCKED	5	0	100	600	0	0
4	ant scf	6	0	100	600	0	0
5	L shaped	6	0	100	600	0	0
6	RT LAT OFF CORD #2	3	0	58	174	0	0
7	LT LAT OFF CORD #2	3	0	61	183	0	0

jon

16–MAR–1995 10:42:35

Figure 6.3: Therapy control console: field selection display.

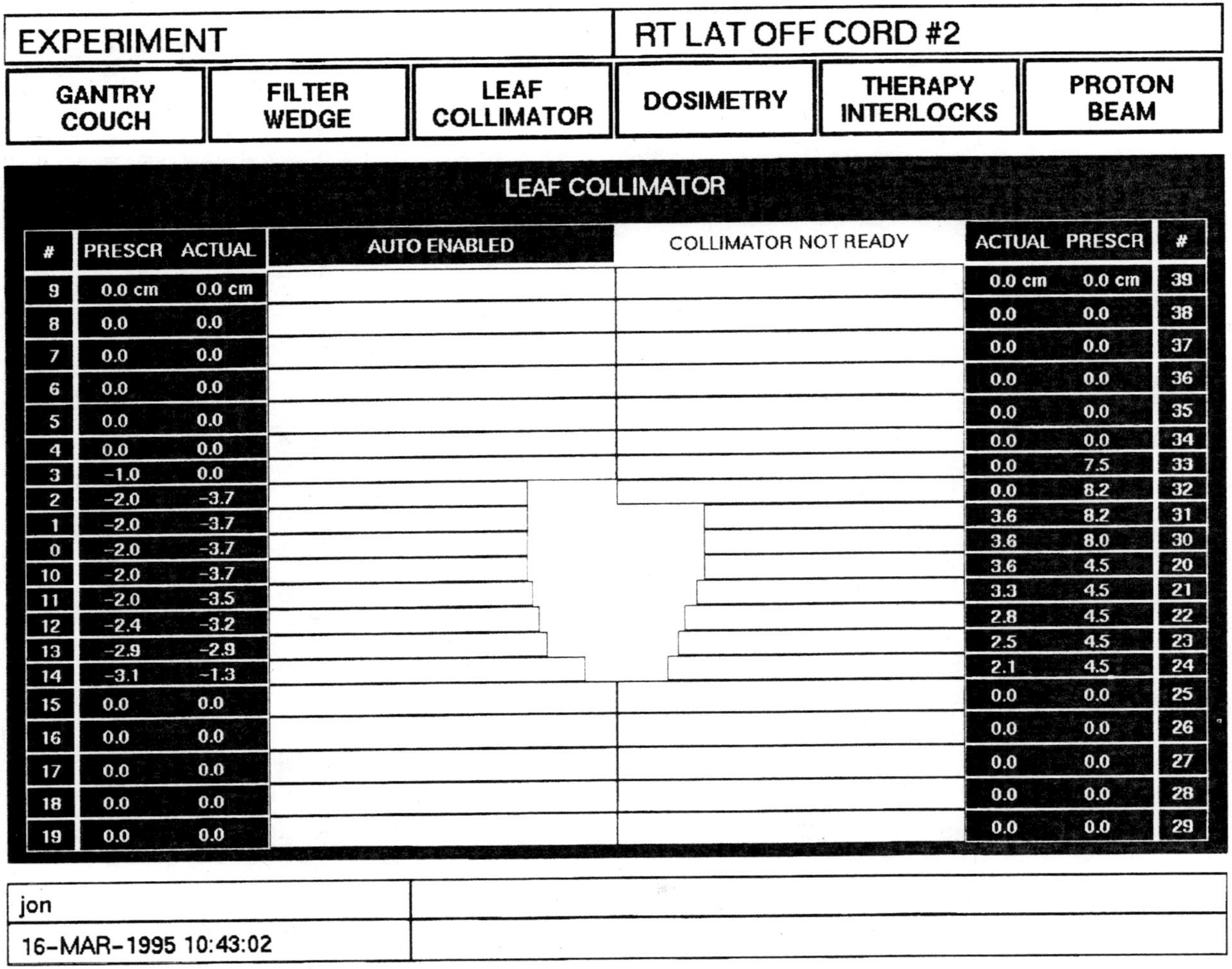

Figure 6.4: Therapy control console: settings display.

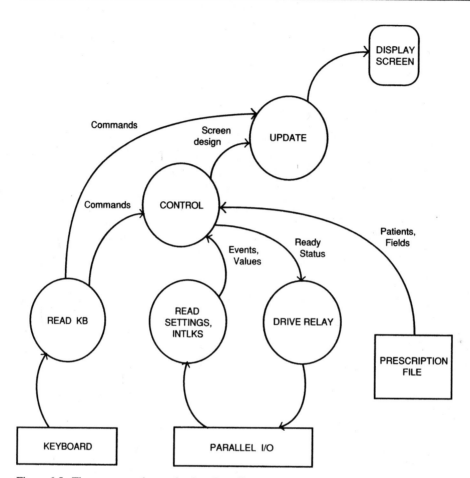

Figure 6.5: Therapy control console: data flow diagram.

6.2 Data flow diagram

Now let's create a model of this control program. First, we try a *data flow* model like the ones recommended in countless books (Figure 6.5).

This diagram describes a way to organize the internal structure of the control program. However, we cannot use it to predict or analyze the behavior of the therapy machine. It has little formal content: merely three symbols (bubbles, arrows, and boxes) and a simple syntax (each arrow has to begin and end on a bubble or box). After checking superficial features — Do all the arrows go someplace? — there is not much we can do formally to help us decide if this diagram describes a good design. Clearly, we need more. We seem to have pushed most of the work into that bubble labelled CONTROL. What's going on in there?

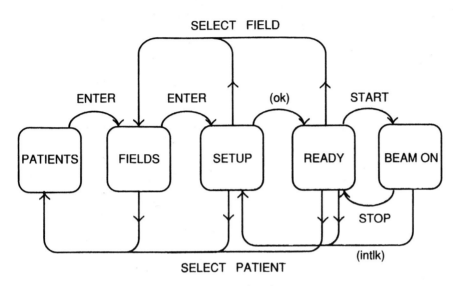

Figure 6.6: Therapy control console: state transition diagram.

6.3 State transition diagram

Next, we draw a *state transition diagram* (Figure 6.6). It doesn't look so different — more bubbles and arrows. But this diagram is much more powerful. It illustrates a completely different kind of model: a *finite state machine* model. It models the behavior of the control program, not its structure.

States are indicated by bubbles, transitions between states by arrows. The arrows are labelled with the events that cause state transitions. Thus, in the PATIENTS state pressing the ENTER key causes a transition to the FIELDS state, but in the FIELDS state pressing ENTER brings you to SETUP.

The key insight here is that the program described in the informal requirements can be modelled by a machine with just a few states. Different screen designs (as in Figures 6.3 and 6.4) correspond to different states; when the machine makes a transition between states, the display updates with a new design. Moreover, the control program's safety relay is closed in the READY and BEAM ON states and is open in all the other states.

We say this diagram is more formal than the data flow diagram because it enables us to infer the behavior of the program, and it can be analyzed. In addition to a simple formal *syntax*, it conveys meaning or *semantics*: We can trace all possible treatment sequences by following the arrows around the diagram. We can say what is and is not supposed to happen in all situations.

	SELECT PATIENT	SELECT FIELD	ENTER	ok	START	STOP	intlk
PATIENTS	—	—	FIELDS	—	—	—	—
FIELDS	PATIENTS	—	SETUP	—	—	—	—
SETUP	PATIENTS	FIELDS	—	READY	—	—	—
READY	PATIENTS	FIELDS	—	—	BEAM ON	—	SETUP
BEAM ON	—	—	—	—	—	READY	SETUP

Figure 6.7: Therapy control console: state transition table.

The state transition diagram says more than the informal requirements. It makes it clear that pressing the STOP button has a different effect than occurs when the dosimeter stops the treatment. After STOP, the system is in the READY state where the treatment can be easily resumed, but after the prescribed dose is delivered, the system is no longer READY. In order to make a formal model, we have to understand the requirements very thoroughly; we often find that the original statement is inadequate.

6.4 State transition table

The state transition diagram is a picture of our state machine model. There are other ways to represent the same model. Figure 6.7 shows the *state transition table*. Entries in the table indicate the next state that is reached when the event indicated by the column heading occurs during the state indicated by the row heading.

This table is a bit more explicit than the state transition diagram because it makes it clear when events are ignored. For example, pressing the SELECT PATIENT key in the BEAM ON mode has no effect (causes no state change); this is indicated by the dash (—) in the table. Including all of these in the diagram would make it too cluttered. As notations grow more formal, they become more explicit and rely less on unwritten assumptions.

Therapy control console

STATE ::= *patients* | *fields* | *setup* | *ready* | *beam_on*

EVENT ::= *select_patient* | *select_field* | *enter* | *start* | *stop* | *ok* | *intlk*

FSM == (*STATE* × *EVENT*) ↛ *STATE*

---

no_change, transitions, control : FSM

---

control = no_change ⊕ transitions

no_change = { s : STATE; e : EVENT • (s, e) ↦ s }

transitions = { (patients, enter) ↦ fields,

  (fields, select_patient) ↦ patients, (fields, enter) ↦ setup,

  (setup, select_patient) ↦ patients, (setup, select_field) ↦ fields,
    (setup, ok) ↦ ready,

  (ready, select_patient) ↦ patients, (ready, select_field) ↦ fields,
    (ready, start) ↦ beam_on, (ready, intlk) ↦ setup,

  (beam_on, stop) ↦ ready, (beam_on, intlk) ↦ setup }

Figure 6.8: Therapy control console: Z specification.

6.5 Z

Finally, we express the state machine model in Z (Figure 6.8). Don't worry about the details of the notation for now. You should be able to see that the function *transitions* models the state transition table in Figure 6.7. For example, the expression (*patients, enter*) ↦ *fields* corresponds to the single transition in the first row of the table: When the *patients* screen is displayed, pressing *enter* displays the *fields* screen. Likewise, (*fields, select_patient*) ↦ *patients*, (*fields, enter*) ↦ *setup* represents the two transitions in the second row of the table.

This is the most explicit version yet. The definition of *no_change* spells out what was left to convention before: In certain states, certain inputs do not cause a state change.

Are we really justified in going to all the trouble to learn this weird notation? I admit it: If all examples were as trivial as this one, we wouldn't need Z.

In fact, this example is very much oversimplified – yet we are already pressing the limits of diagrams and tables. We could easily manage with diagrams and tables that were, maybe, twice as large as these. This example already illustrates two of the most powerful concepts in formal methods: using compact symbolic expressions to represent lots of cases in a little space and using operators to build up complex formulas from simpler ones.

State transition tables are often very sparse: Most of the entries are empty "nothing changes" cells that make the tables large and difficult to read. In Z we don't have to enumerate all the *no_change* transitions as we did in the table — we can do it symbolically; *no_change* is actually a state machine that does nothing. We define a second machine, *transitions*, that includes only the transitions where something actually happens. Then we use the Z *override* operator ⊕ to combine the two. The expression *no_change* ⊕ *transitions* describes the state machine that behaves as *no_change*, except when there is a relevant entry in *transitions*.

More importantly, the diagram and the table are specialized notations that only work for finite state machines. We cannot use them to attack the hard parts of the problem that I left out of this toy example. For example, what really distinguishes the state READY from SETUP? We glossed over this — we merely said the system becomes ready when the *ok* event occurs. This mysterious *ok* event does not come from a key or button; we left it undefined. But we must define it; this transition is the central safety-critical event in the program because it closes the relay that allows the beam to turn on.

In READY, all the settings match their prescribed values; the *ok* event occurs when the system achieves this condition. (In fact, some settings must match exactly, while others are permitted to vary within a tolerance; some settings that don't match can be overridden, while others cannot, and so on.) We cannot represent this with our diagrams or tables because it involves dozens of settings that vary over continuous ranges. We need to model *values* and *relations* between values. We will see how when we develop a more complete model of this program in Chapters 21 and 22.

Exercise 6.5.1   Something very important was left out of our state machine model. What was it? (It can be expressed in terms of the states and events we already defined.)

7 Introducing schemas: text editor

The *schema* is the characteristic construct of Z. Schema boxes distinguish a Z text from any other notation. This chapter describes the schema and introduces most of the other Z paragraphs as well.

We'll model a simple text editor. All you can do with this editor is type in text, move the cursor backwards and forwards through the text, and delete the character in front of the cursor. We will describe some additional features in Chapter 17.

7.1 Basic types and abbreviation definitions

Our editor deals with texts composed of characters. We can express this in two very short Z paragraphs. We declare a *basic type*: the set of all characters. Then we make an *abbreviation definition* to say that a text is a sequence of characters.

[CHAR]

$TEXT == \text{seq } CHAR$

CHAR is our character set. We don't have to say that characters are bytes; they might not be. We don't have to say what the encoding convention is; it might be ASCII, but it needn't be. We don't even have to say which characters are in the set; they needn't include our usual Roman alphabet. These details are not necessary to explain what the editor does. The omission of inessential details is one of the things that distinguishes a model from an executable program.

CHAR is a full-fledged Z data type. In Z we can introduce a new data type just by writing its name inside brackets (see Section 8.1.9). From now on we can use CHAR in declarations, just like $\mathbb{N}$ and all the other predefined data types.

The abbreviation definition introduces another new data type, TEXT, a sequence of characters. We can use seq to define a sequence of any type. Sequences and their operators are defined in the mathematical tool-kit (Section 9.5). The definition symbol $==$ says that *TEXT* is just an abbreviation for seq *CHAR*. Z abbreviations are much like the macros provided in some programming languages. They can save us the trouble of writing out long definitions again and again. But far more important is that they enable us to make our intentions clear by giving meaningful names to our constructions.

Identifers defined in basic type declarations and abbreviations are *global*: They can be used anywhere in the text after their definition.

7.2 Axiomatic descriptions

Our little editor must run in memory on small computers, so we have to say that there is an upper limit on the size of the document it can handle. We know that we are limited to a 16 bit address space at most, and we may have to configure versions that run in even less memory.

We use an *axiomatic description* to express this. We have already used axiomatic descriptions to define functions in Chapters 5 and 6; in Z we use axiomatic descriptions to define constants of any type[1].

$$
\begin{array}{|l}
\hline
\textit{maxsize} : \mathbb{N} \\
\hline
\textit{maxsize} \leq 65535 \\
\end{array}
$$

Here again, the axiomatic description has two parts: the *declaration* above the line says that *maxsize* is a nonnegative integer, and the *predicate* below the line constrains its value. Items declared in axiomatic descriptions are always *constants*, not variables. We have not committed ourselves to a particular value for *maxsize*; it can be any number up through 65,535. However, it still has a constant value, *we just haven't said what that value is*.

Constants declared in axiomatic descriptions are global. This is suggested by the open appearance of the axiomatic description box.

Axiomatic descriptions are also called axiomatic definitions.

7.3 State schemas

All the notation I have presented so far is just a way to write ordinary mathematics. The schema adds something new that we need to model computing systems: storage, that is, memory. The contents of a system's memory are called its *state*. Schemas model states as collections of *state variables* and their values. State variables are also called *components*.

---

[1] In Z, functions such as *iroot* are a kind of constant.

The systems modelled in the preceding chapters have no state: You present them with an input, and immediately you get an output. They behave as if they have no memory: Every time you present them with the same input, you get the same output. Such systems can be modelled by mathematical objects called *functions*. Our *iroot* in Chapter 5 and *control* in Chapter 6 are both functions. In Z we use axiomatic definitions to describe functions, but axiomatic definitions cannot describe states because they provide no way to represent memory[2].

A text editor does have memory: It stores the text you type and the changes you make. The state of our text editor is very simple: We have a document with a cursor. The document is a text (a sequence of characters) that is no larger than our upper limit. We model the document as *two* texts: *left* is the text before the cursor, and *right* is text following it. This turns out to be much more convenient than modelling the document as a single text with an integer index to indicate the cursor position.

Here is our state schema. Its two state variables are *left* and *right*:

$$
\begin{array}{l}
\mathit{Editor} \\
\hline
\mathit{left}, \mathit{right} : \mathit{TEXT} \\
\hline
\#(\mathit{left} \frown \mathit{right}) \leq \mathit{maxsize}
\end{array}
$$

Just as in an axiomatic definition, we declare variables above the line and constrain their values in the predicate below the line. But the schema box looks different from an axiomatic definition. It has a *name*, so we can refer to its contents just by naming it. And the schema box is closed. This is to remind you that the variables declared inside the box are *local*: They can only be used in the schema where they are declared.

The predicate in *Editor* says that the document can hold no more than *maxsize* characters. We use the Z *concatenation* operator $\frown$ to construct the whole text from its two pieces *left* and *right*, and the *size* operator # to count all the characters.

The predicate in a Z state schema is called an *invariant* because it is always true; it describes properties that always hold.

7.4 Initialization schemas

Every system has a special state in which it starts up. In Z this state is described by a schema conventionally named *Init*. For example, we might say that our editor always starts up with an empty document:

---

[2] The *STATE* in the control console example (Chapter 6) was really just an input to the function.

$$
\begin{array}{|l}
\hline
\_Init _____ \\
\; Editor \\
\hline
\; left = right = \langle\rangle \\
\hline
\end{array}
$$

The $\langle\rangle$ in the predicate is the empty sequence.

The *Init* schema *includes* the *Editor* schema in its declaration section. This indicates that all the declarations and predicates in *Editor* apply to *Init* as well, so *Init* can use the local state variables *right* and *left* from *Editor*.

Schemas resemble the *macros* provided by some programming languages. You can use the schema name instead of writing out the whole text of the schema again and again. This preserves your wrists and fingers, makes the Z text shorter, and — most important of all — makes it easier for readers to grasp the structure of your model.

7.5 Operation schemas

We have shown how state schemas can model one of the essential qualities of state: storage. We need to model another aspect of state: change. Our editor starts up empty, but it fills with text as the user types, and its contents change as the user edits. To model this kind of activity, Z provides the *operation schema*.

We want to type text into our editor. Let's define the the *Insert* operation that puts a single character in the document to the left of the cursor. In most editors you invoke this operation by simply typing on any of the ordinary alphanumeric keys on the workstation keyboard. This operation only applies to printing characters, not control characters, so we use an axiomatic definition to define a new constant, the set of printing characters. This axiomatic definition has no predicate because it isn't necessary to say which characters are the printing characters.

$$
\mid\; printing : \mathbb{P}\,CHAR
$$

$$
\begin{array}{|l}
\hline
\_Insert _____ \\
\; \Delta Editor \\
\; ch? : CHAR \\
\hline
\; ch? \in printing \\
\; left' = left \,^\frown \langle ch?\rangle \\
\; right' = right \\
\hline
\end{array}
$$

Here $\Delta Editor$ (pronounced *delta editor*) tells us that *Insert* is an operation schema that changes the state of *Editor*.

This operation schema declares the *input* variable *ch*?, the character to be inserted — that is, the character you just typed. In Z we usually indicate input variables by ending them with a question mark. This is just a naming convention. The question mark is not an operator, it is just another character that we can use to form a variable name.

The predicate tells us how the editor state changes. The unprimed variables *left* and *right* denote the texts to the left and right of the cursor before the *Insert* operation, and the primed variables *left'* and *right'* denote those texts after the operation.

The first line of the predicate, *ch*? $\in$ *printing*, is a *precondition*: It describes what must be true before the operation can occur. Sometimes preconditions are called *entry conditions*. This precondition says that the *Insert* operation can only occur when the input is a printing character; it uses the set membership operator $\in$ (pronounced *in*). The rest of the predicate is a *postcondition*: It describes the state of the editor after the operation. The line *left'* = *left* $^\frown$ $\langle ch? \rangle$ says that the new character is appended to the end of the text preceding the cursor (in other words, it is inserted to the left of the cursor). Here again we use the concatenation operator. The next line *right'* = *right* says that the text following the cursor does *not* change. In Z it is necessary to say when things remain the same. This usually surprises programmers. In specifications this is useful, as we shall see.

Our *Insert* operation works equally well whether the cursor is at the end of the document, at the beginning, or somewhere in the middle. This is why we modelled the editor as two texts. A more obvious model would represent the editor as a single text with the cursor position indicated by an integer: the index of the character before the cursor. But this would make the definition of the *Insert* operation far more cumbersome, because we would have to write formulas to adjust the indices of all the characters to the right of the cursor. What a mess!

7.6   Implicit preconditions

The next operation moves the cursor forward one character. In many editors, the user invokes this operation by pressing the right arrow key $\boxed{\rightarrow}$ on the workstation keyboard. We use an axiomatic definition to declare this *right_arrow* character. We have to include a predicate that uses the set nonmembership operator $\notin$ to say that *right_arrow* is not a printing character; otherwise our editor would try to insert the arrow character into the file, instead of interpreting it as a command.

$$
\begin{array}{|l}
\hline
\mathit{right\_arrow} : CHAR \\
\hline
\mathit{right\_arrow} \notin printing \\
\hline
\end{array}
$$

$$
\begin{array}{|l}
\hline
\underline{\quad Forward \quad\quad\quad\quad\quad\quad\quad\quad\quad\quad\quad\quad\quad\quad\quad\quad} \\
\Delta Editor \\
ch? : CHAR \\
\hline
ch? = right\_arrow \\
left' = left \frown \langle head(right) \rangle \\
right' = tail(right) \\
\hline
\end{array}
$$

Forward uses the *head* and *tail* functions: *head* returns the first element of a sequence, and *tail* returns the sequence with the first element removed. The predicate says that the *Forward* operation removes the first element from *right* and appends it to the end of *left*. This has the effect of moving the cursor forward one character.

There is only one problem with our *Forward* operation: It doesn't always work.

Exercise   Why not?

Solution   Here is the problem: You press the right arrow key when the cursor is at the end of the document, and the editor crashes. It is a typical experience with a shaky new program.

Forward does not work when the cursor is already at the end of the document. The definition breaks because $head(right)$ and $tail(right)$ are not defined when *right* is empty. If we implemented *Forward*, the program's behavior in this situation would be undefined. It might crash, losing all the user's work.

It is crucial that you understand this is not just a coding error. The problem is already evident in our Z model. Our *Forward* operation only makes sense when there is someplace to which to move forward.

We say that *Forward* is a *partial* operation because it only works in some situations; its effects are undefined in others. *Forward* has an *implicit precondition*. An implicit precondition is not written out, as the explicit precondition $ch? = right\_arrow$ is here. Implicit preconditions arise from the interaction between the state invariant and the predicates that are explicit in the operation schema. The implicit precondition of *Forward* is that the cursor is not at the end of the document: $right \neq \langle \rangle$.

We should revise our definition so there are no undefined operations and the precondition is explicit.

```
┌─ Forward ──────────────────────────────────────────
│ ΔEditor
│ ch? : CHAR
├──────────────────────────────────────────────
│ ch? = right_arrow
│ right ≠ ⟨⟩
│ left′ = left ⌢ ⟨head(right)⟩
│ right′ = tail(right)
└──────────────────────────────────────────────
```

It is easy to write operations that have implicit preconditions; failure to recognize them is a frequent source of programming errors. Here we relied on insight and experience to tell us that *Forward* doesn't always work. Must we always depend on our intuition to recognize implicit preconditions? As we shall see, we can calculate the precondition of a Z operation. If we write a formal specification in Z, we can check it systematically for certain kinds of errors and oversights. This is one of the things that distinguishes a formal method from informal ones.

Exercise Does *Insert* have any implicit preconditions? (This exercise is solved in Section 15.4.)

7.7 Schema calculus

Our editor musn't crash. We need to make it robust. We will define a *total* version of *Forward* that works in all situations. We'll define it in pieces, where each piece is a schema. Then we'll use the *schema calculus* to put the pieces together. This is the usual way to define complex operations in Z.

First we define a state schema to describe the *end of file* condition where the cursor is at the end of the document.

```
┌─ EOF ──────────────────────────────────────────
│ Editor
├──────────────────────────────────────────────
│ right = ⟨⟩
└──────────────────────────────────────────────
```

We decide that in this state pressing the right arrow key should not move the cursor or change the contents of the document. In Z it is necessary to say when nothing happens. ΞEditor is the operation on *Editor* that does not change the value of any state variable. We make *right_arrow* into a schema by defining *RightArrow*.

```
┌─ RightArrow ──────────────────────────────────
│ ch? : CHAR
├───────────────────────────────────────────────
│ ch? = right_arrow
└───────────────────────────────────────────────
```

This is necessary so $ch? = right\_arrow$ appears in both disjuncts of the *schema expression* that defines our total operation $T\_Forward$.

$$T\_Forward \mathrel{\widehat{=}} Forward \vee (EOF \wedge RightArrow \wedge \Xi Editor)$$

This formula says that $T\_Forward$ behaves as the *Forward* operation when the cursor is not at the end of the file, but pressing the right arrow key when the editor is in the *EOF* state has no effect.

$T\_Forward$ is also a schema but instead of defining it in box form we write a schema calculus formula on one line. The part of the formula to the right of the definition symbol $\widehat{=}$ is a *schema expression* composed of schema names or *schema references* and *schema operators*. The $\wedge$ operator is pronounced *and*; we use it to combine states and operations together. The $\vee$ operator is pronounced *or*; we use it to separate distinct alternatives. This is the usual Z style for defining total operations in terms of partial ones.

We will study schemas and the schema calculus operators more thoroughly in Chapter 12.

It should be clear how to complete the formal specification of our editor. We still have to define the the *Backward* operation that moves the cursor one character to the left and the *Delete* operation that deletes the character before the cursor. We have to define a total version of each operation. Finally, it is necessary to say how the program handles input characters that are not handled by *Insert*, *Forward*, *Backward*, and *Delete*.

7.8   The Way of Z

As you can see, the Z notation is really quite simple. This little example has revealed most of its features. Let's review some of its lessons.

In Z we use axiomatic descriptions to model constants and functions, and schemas to model states and operations. There is nothing more. Z has no built-in concept of a program or any explicit control structure. In this example the program is defined implicitly by the *top-level* operation schemas that are included in no other operation schemas, such as $T\_Forward$ (*Forward* is not at top level because it is used to define $T\_Forward$). The control structure is determined implicitly by the input variables and preconditions of the top-level operations. Each top-level operation is invoked whenever its input appears and all of its preconditions are satisfied.

Z encourages a modelling method that makes it easy to ensure that specifications are complete. First we determine which operations we need to provide. Then we choose the inputs that should invoke each operation. Then we define the normal or typical case of each operation. Then we think about what might go wrong and consider how to handle inputs in different system states, and augment each typical operation to obtain a total operation. We take care to define a reasonably small number of operations and states so we can do a case analysis to confirm that they cover all possible situations. We identify the states and do the case analysis in Z where it is easy, not in the program code where it is a lot harder. When we write the code, we can preserve the structure of our Z model and take care not to introduce any additional cases.

This example, like many Z specifications, models the program as a state transition system. It is similar in principle to the model of the therapy machine console in Chapter 6, but has many more inputs — all the elements of *CHAR* — and vastly more states — all the possible states in *Editor*. It would be impossible to model a system this large using the diagrams or tables of Chapter 6, but it is not difficult in Z, because we can gather inputs and states together in sets such as *printing* and state schemas such as *EOF*. Unlike a diagram or table, the length of the Z text need not grow in proportion to the number of states. This makes it feasible to model systems that have lots of states.

It is typical for programs to have astronomically large numbers of states, and programmers sometimes complain that this makes programming errors inevitable. In fact the number of states doesn't matter. For each operation in a well-designed system, we can divide the states into a small number of *equivalence classes*. Within a class, every state behaves the same way — it can be handled by the same code. Systems that have huge numbers of states might have only a few equivalence classes for each operation; often there are just two. When we attempt the *Forward* operation, all that matters is whether or not the system is an *EOF* state, and that is easy to test. Of course, we must remember to do it. If we don't think carefully about the states, we can create states with every line of code we write — and we won't know what they are. Programs written that way are usually full of errors.

The key to designing with Z is finding a good model for the system state, because it usually becomes the design for the central data structures in the program. The first attempt often doesn't work out: We have to try defining the same operations with different models of the state, before we find a good one. This exploratory phase can be time consuming but it is worth the effort because it compels us to face the difficult design issues early. *One of the main reasons for making Z models is to explore alternatives so we can reject overly complex designs.* In our editor example, an obvious model represents the document by a single sequence, where the cursor is an integer index into the sequence. If we try it, we find this obvious solution makes the definition of *Insert* overly complicated, because we have to adjust the index of every character to the right of the cursor. This exercise makes it clear that the editor design turns on finding a data structure that makes it easy to insert and delete text in the middle of the document.

Z is not a programming language. The schemas in this chapter are not intended to resemble efficient code. They are intended to be the simplest possible description of the operations that the implementation must provide.

We don't try to do everything in Z. Beginners are often surprised by how much is left out of a Z model, and sometimes feel frustrated because so many details have been deferred. But experienced Z users usually try to find a very abstract model first, then add the details in stages. You can always add detail later, but if you put in the detail at the beginning you might put in the wrong details, or details that bias you towards some particular implementation that isn't the best. This process of adding details is called *refinement* and is the subject of Chapter 26.

Exercises

Exercise 7.8.1   Define the total operations *T_Backward* and *T_Delete*. You may use any functions or operators defined in Appendix D.

Exercise 7.8.2   Define the operation that handles input characters that are not handled by *Insert*, *Forward*, *Backward*, and *Delete*.

Exercise 7.8.3   Our editor would be far more useful if it could read in the contents of a file at the user's demand. Model this in Z.

Exercise 7.8.4   How many distinct states are described by the *Editor* schema? The *EOF* schema? Assume that *CHAR* is implemented by the ASCII character set.

Exercise 7.8.5   Prototype the *Insert* operation in a functional programming language. Investigate the performance of your prototype on sequences of different sizes. (Hint: The Z operators *head*, *tail*, and ⌢ (concatenation) resemble the Lisp functions `car`, `cdr`, and `append`.)

Further reading

The de-facto standard is *The Z Notation: A Reference Manual*, second edition [Spivey, 1992b]. At this writing there is a draft ANSI/ISO standard [Nicholls, 1995]. These documents define the core mathematical notation, the mathematical tool-kit, and the schema calculus.

Some of the early work at Oxford was collected in the first Z book, Hayes' *Specification Case Studies* [1987]; a second edition [1992a] uses the standard notation of Spivey [1992b]. Woodcock and Loomes' textbook *Software Engineering Mathematics* [1990] teaches discrete mathematics using a Z-like notation; a paper by Woodcock [1989b] adds material on schemas in the same style. There are now several introductory textbooks on Z; the most comprehensive are by Diller [1990; 1994], Potter, Sinclair, and Till [1991], and Wordsworth [1992]. The paper by Gravell [1991], the report by Macdonald [1991], and especially the book by Barden, Stepney, and Cooper [1994] offer guidance on Z style, illustrated by many instructive examples.

Among formal notations, Z has perhaps the largest literature of convincing, well-written case studies. My favorites include Morgan's telephone network, and Sørensen and Sufrin's assembler in [Hayes, 1987], Sufrin's text editor [1982], Morgan and Sufrin's Unix file system [1984], Sufrin's make utility [1989], and Bowen's X window system [1992]. Some of the IBM work on its CICS transaction processing system appears in Hayes' paper [1985]. The Inmos work on the IEEE floating point arithmetic standard and the T800 Transputer floating point unit is described in papers by Barrett, and Shepherd and Wilson [1989; 1989; 1990]; Bowen's microprocessor work appears in [1987b; 1990]. Delisle and Garlan [1989; 1990; 1990] model oscilloscopes and other electronic instruments, Spivey [1990] analyzes the operating system kernel for an embedded controller, and Stepney [1993] develops a compiler.

There are annual Z user meetings with published proceedings [Bowen, 1987a; Bowen, 1988; Nicholls, 1990; Nicholls, 1991; Nicholls, 1992; Bowen and Nicholls, 1993; Bowen and Hall, 1994; Bowen and Hinchey, 1995a]. Z has been the subject of two special journal issues [McDermid, 1989; Bowen and Hinchey, 1995b]. An annotated bibliography of the Z literature has been published [Bowen, Stepney, and Barden, 1995].

Woodcock and Loomes [1990] and Spivey [1988] compare Z to other notations in their books. Saaltink offers technical criticism of Z [1991; 1992].

Some notes on the history of Z appear in the paper by Woodcock [1989b] and the annotated bibliography in the first edition only of the textbook by Diller [1990].

There is an unmoderated Usenet newsgroup `comp.specification.z`.

There is a Z home page maintained by Jonathan Bowen on the World Wide Web at `http://www.comlab.ox.ac.uk/archive/z.html`. It includes links to many useful resources, tools, events, people, and documents.

Z tools are available for most popular computer systems, including personal computers. Some are free. For up-to-date information, visit the Z home page.

The integer square root code in Chapter 5 is adapted from an example in Pascal by Alagić and Arbib [1978].

The radiation therapy machine in Chapter 6 is necessarily simplified. For descriptions of real machines, good and bad, see Jacky *et al.* [1990]; Jacky *et al.* [1992]; Leveson and Turner [1993]; Leveson [1995]; and Weinhous, Purdy, and Granda [1990].

The text editor in Chapter 7 is based on Bernard Sufrin's early paper [1982]. Another adaptation appears in Antoni Diller's textbook [1990]. Sufrin's original paper models the appearance of the display as well as the contents of the document.

Part III

Elements of Z

8 Elements

This chapter introduces the three basic constructs that appear everywhere in Z texts: declarations, expressions, and predicates. *Declarations* introduce *variables*. *Expressions* describe the *values* that variables might have. *Predicates* express *constraints* that determine which values the variables actually do have.

8.1 Sets and types, declarations, and variables

The systems that we need to model might contain vast numbers of things. How can we possibly deal with them all? We gather similar objects into collections and treat each collection as a single object in its own right. These collections are called *sets*. Sets are central in Z.

8.1.1 Displaying sets

The obvious way to describe a set is to list or *enumerate* all of its members or *elements*. This is called a *set display*. In Z we follow the ordinary mathematical convention and write sets with braces, separating elements by commas. Here is a display of the set of lamps in a traffic light:

  {*red, yellow, green*}

Elements in a set are not ordered, so the order you write elements in a set display is not significant. Here is another (equally good) display of the same set:

  {*yellow, red, green*}

Sets contain no duplicate elements, and mentioning the same element more than once is redundant but innocuous. So, the same set could even be written

  {*green, red, yellow, yellow, red*}

The set with no elements {} is called *the empty set*. It is usually written $\emptyset$.

Obviously, enumerating elements is impractical for all but the tiniest sets. As we shall see, there are far more powerful ways to describe sets.

8.1.2   Naming sets

When a set contains many members, it is impractical to list them all, so we give sets names. Some sets are used so often that standard names have already been assigned. In particular, there are names for sets of numbers. $\mathbb{Z}$ is the set of *integers*, including negative numbers. $\mathbb{N}$ is the set of *natural numbers*, beginning with zero. $\mathbb{N}_1$ is the set of *strictly positive integers* or *counting numbers*, beginning with one.

We can make up our own names for the sets we define. For example, to write a program that simulates a dice game, we need a set that contains the numbers of spots found on the faces of dice: $\{1, 2, 3, 4, 5, 6\}$. Z does provide notation for a range of consecutive numbers; we can abbreviate this $1 \,..\, 6$ (without braces) pronounced *one up to six*. For the purposes of simulating tosses and scoring a game, a die *is* a number from one up to six, so we choose the name *DICE* for this set. Named sets don't have to be made up of numbers; they can hold anything. We can choose the name *LAMP* for the set $\{red, yellow, green\}$.

8.1.3   Types

In Z we can only form sets from objects that are similar in some way. We say that elements of the same set must have the same *type*; sets in Z are *typed*. So a set can be composed of colors, or numbers, but not a mixture of both. The following text is not Z; it exhibits a *type error* because the elements listed between the brackets have different types:

$\{2, 4, red, yellow, 6\}$ [TYPE ERROR! Elements have different types.]

(There is no standard way to include comments within Z paragraphs; comments should usually appear in the surrounding prose. This example illustrates the convention I use in this book when it is necessary to annotate a single formula: Surround the comment by brackets and right-justify it.)

Types and sets are very closely related. Every type has a *carrier set* that contains all of the objects of that type. For example, the carrier set for the integer type $\mathbb{Z}$ is the set with every integer in it: $\{\ldots, -2, -1, 0, 1, 2, \ldots\}$. We usually say that the type *is* its carrier set[1].

Every type is a set, but not all sets are types. The natural numbers $\mathbb{N}$ are a set, not a type. Natural numbers belong to the type integer, $\mathbb{Z}$, because every natural number

---

[1] The three dots "..." are not Z. They are informal notation that we use to indicate an indefinitely long sequence of numbers.

is also an integer. An object's type is the most inclusive or *maximal* set to which it belongs.

Types are very important in Z, even though only one type is built in: the type integer, appropriately named $\mathbb{Z}^2$. We can define our own types. Most Z texts are largely populated by types invented by their authors. These texts convey a lot of information by their choice of types. This is one of the biggest differences between Z and traditional mathematics. In mathematics there aren't many types, and the type of each object is obvious from context: Mathematicians understand that number theory deals with integers, analysis deals with real numbers, and so on. In Z we typically work with many different types in the same text so we have to be careful to make the type of each object explicit. In this respect Z is more formal than traditional mathematics (that is, more information is expressed in formulas).

8.1.4 Declarations and variables

In order to talk about any object in Z, we have to introduce its name in a *declaration*. Declarations introduce variables and tell to which set each variable belongs. Declarations formalize a kind of language we often find in mathematics: "Let i be an integer . . . ." Here are some Z declarations, along with their meanings:

$i : \mathbb{Z}$ [i is an integer.]

$d_1, d_2 : DICE$ [d_1 and d_2 are two numbers in the range 1 . . 6.]

$signal : LAMP$ [*signal* is one of the colors *red, yellow, green*.]

Each name introduced in a declaration names or *denotes* a single element in the set that appears to the right of the colon. This element is sometimes called the name's *value*. This value may be unknown or undetermined, so the names introduced in declarations are called *variables*. In the preceding declarations, i, d_1, d_2, and *signal* are variables.

Z declarations resemble the declarations found in many programming languages, but they are more flexible. Any set can appear in a declaration — it doesn't have to be a type. Moreover, Z does not require that sets used in declarations have to be referred to by name. Sometimes it is clearer to write out the sets literally instead. The preceding declarations can be written:

$d_1, d_2 : 1 . . 6$ [d_1 and d_2 are two numbers in the range 1 . . 6.]

$signal : \{red, yellow, green\}$ [*signal* is one of the colors *red, yellow, green*.]

---

[2] Rational numbers, real numbers, and complex numbers are not built in, so $\mathbb{Z}$ is the maximal numeric type in Z.

This example illustrates a typical feature of Z: We can usually write the name or object it denotes, whichever we prefer.

Z declarations can express more than the declarations we use in program code. In most programming languages, types and declarations are really about storage: Objects have the same type if they are represented the same way in computer memory, and declarations are primarily used to reserve storage. Z declarations can be more expressive because they can use sets, not just types. You can define sets that are restricted to any elements that you like. As we shall see in Chapter 11, it is easy to define sets like *EVEN*, the set of even numbers, *ODD*, the set of odd numbers, and *PRIME*, the set of prime numbers. We can use them in declarations like these:

$e : EVEN$ [e is an even number.]

$o : ODD$ [o is an odd number.]

$p : PRIME$ [p is a prime number.]

In most programming languages, this would not be possible; all three variables e, o, and p would have to be declared the same way because they all have the same integer type. Z declarations can convey information about the values that variables may take on, not just their types.

8.1.5   Constraining variables, axiomatic definitions

We *constrain* a variable when we say what values it can take on. We have already learned how to write one kind of constraint: Declarations can constrain a variable's value to belong to a particular set. There are many other kinds of contraints besides set membership. In Z we define variables in a construct called an *axiomatic definition* that can include any constraints we wish. The axiomatic definition is a Z *paragraph* that is set off from the surrounding informal prose by an open box. Its general form is:

$$
\begin{array}{|l}
declarations \\
\hline
predicates
\end{array}
$$

The optional predicates are formulas that constrain the variables introduced in the declarations. Here is an axiomatic definition without a predicate. It declares two numbers, d_1 and d_2. They are constrained by the declaration to belong to the set *DICE* (the integers $1 .. 6$):

$$
\begin{array}{|l}
d_1, d_2 : DICE
\end{array}
$$

Now here is an axiomatic definition with a predicate. It declares two numbers in the range $1 .. 6$, but it also constrains them to add up to 7:

$$
\begin{array}{|l}
d_1, d_2 : DICE \\
\hline
d_1 + d_2 = 7
\end{array}
$$

So we might have $d_1 = 1$ and $d_2 = 6$, or $d_1 = 4$ and $d_2 = 3$, and so forth, but not $d_1 = 1$ and $d_2 = 5$, or $d_1 = 4$ and $d_2 = 4$. If we want to add more constraints, we just write them out on successive lines. To say that d_1 must also be less than d_2, we would write

$$
\begin{array}{|l}
d_1, d_2 : DICE \\
\hline
d_1 + d_2 = 7 \\
d_1 < d_2
\end{array}
$$

This still admits $d_1 = 1$ and $d_2 = 6$, but excludes $d_1 = 4$ and $d_2 = 3$.

Variables defined in axiomatic definitions are *global*: They can be used anywhere in a Z text after their definition. This is called *declaration before use*.

Z global variables do not really vary, in the sense of changing value. A Z global variable denotes the same value each time it appears. They are called variables because their (fixed) values may be unknown or undetermined; or we may have a choice of several values. This often surprises programmers because it is so different from program code, where different occurrences of the same variable often have different values, due to the effects of assignment statements[3].

You can think of Z global variables as options or *parameters*: You can choose different values for global variables to describe different configurations. This axiomatic definition defines a global variable named *size* whose value is the size of memory in kilobytes:

$$
\begin{array}{|l}
size : \mathbb{N} \\
\hline
size \geq 640
\end{array}
$$

This declaration says, "You must have at least 640 kilobytes of memory; any size larger than that will work as well." In Z this is called a *loose* definition: It defines not just one configuration, but a whole family of configurations, one for each value of *size* greater than or equal to 640. You can choose any of these configurations that you wish, but then *size* has that same value each time it appears — it wouldn't make sense for *size* to mean 1024 on one page and 2048 on the next.

---

[3] The property that every occurrence of a variable denotes the same value is called *referential transparency*. Referential transparency makes it easier to use certain kinds of reasoning. Z has it; most programming languages don't.

8.1.6   Constants, abbreviation definitions

The strongest constraint you can reasonably make is to allow only a single value[4]. A variable that can only take on one value is called a *constant*. This axiomatic definition makes *size* a constant; it describes a single configuration, the one with two megabytes of memory:

$$
\begin{array}{|l}
\mathit{size} : \mathbb{N} \\
\hline
\mathit{size} = 2048
\end{array}
$$

The Z *abbreviation definition* is a shortcut for defining global constants. It uses the *definition symbol* $==$ to introduce the variable and give its value on one line. This abbreviation definition means exactly the same thing as the preceding axiomatic definition:

$$\mathit{size} == 2048$$

An abbreviation definition does not need to include an explicit declaration, because we can always infer the type of the constant from its value.

Abbreviation definitions are often used to create synonyms for sets and types, in order to make declarations clearer. The names *DICE* and *LAMP* that we introduced informally in section 8.1.2 could be defined formally this way:

$$DICE == 1 \mathrel{..} 6$$

$$LAMP == \{red, yellow, green\}$$

8.1.7   Normalization and signatures

We can deduce the type of any set once we have defined it, so we often write declarations using just sets, as in this axiomatic definition:

$$
\begin{array}{|l}
e : EVEN \\
o : ODD \\
p : PRIME
\end{array}
$$

Sometimes we wish to emphasize the distinction between types and sets. We can write definitions that explicitly reveal the types of the variables. We declare the types in the declaration above the line, and provide additional information about set membership in the predicate below the line. A definition where the types are explicitly spelled out in this way is said to be *normalized*. A *signature* is a declaration that names the

---

[4] You can allow no values at all, but why would you?

type, as we must have in a normalized definition: $e : EVEN$ is a declaration, but $e : \mathbb{Z}$ is a signature.

The following normalized axiomatic definition means exactly the same thing as the preceding unnormalized one. We have to introduce some new Z syntax: $e \in EVEN$ is a predicate that means "e is an element of $EVEN$." The predicate $e \in EVEN$ expresses the same constraint as the declaration $e : EVEN$.

$$
\begin{array}{|l}
e, o, p : \mathbb{Z} \\
\hline
e \in EVEN \\
o \in ODD \\
p \in PRIME \\
\end{array}
$$

Writing the normalized definition makes it clear which variables have the same type. This is an important thing to know because variables that belong to different sets can nevertheless be used together in expressions — as long as they have the same type. We may use a tool called a *type checker* to search for certain kinds of errors in our Z texts. Such tools can check the type of any expression automatically, but it is not possible in general to check set membership automatically.

8.1.8 Set variables

Z variables can name whole collections of objects; that is, they can denote sets. In Z, variables whose values are sets are declared as follows, using the symbol $\mathbb{P}$ (usually pronounced "set of"). This axiomatic definition declares a set of natural numbers named *PRIME* and a set of numbers in the range 1 .. 6 named *toss*:

$$
\begin{array}{|l}
PRIME : \mathbb{P}\,\mathbb{N} \\
toss : \mathbb{P}\,DICE \\
\end{array}
$$

In Z sets are objects in their own right. Every set has a type. The type of a set whose elements have type T is $\mathbb{P}\,T$. So the type of *PRIME* and *toss* is both $\mathbb{P}\,\mathbb{Z}$.

The $\mathbb{P}$ symbol is actually an abbreviation for the mathematical term *power set*, the set of all subsets. If S is the set $\{x, y, z\}$, the power set of S, that is $\mathbb{P}\,S$, is $\{\emptyset, \{x\}, \{y\}, \{z\}, \{x, y\}, \{y, z\}, \{x, z\}, \{x, y, z\}\}$. So $\mathbb{P}\,\mathbb{Z}$ actually means "the set of all subsets of the integers." Any particular set of integers, the prime numbers for example, belongs to this power set. So this form of declaration is really no different: The identifier to the left of the colon denotes one of the elements of the set named to the right.

8.1.9   Defining new types

You may have noticed a chicken-and-egg kind of problem: If each new variable has to belong to a previously defined type, how can we introduce a *new* type that is different from all the others? The numbers come predefined in Z, but from where did the colors *red*, *green*, and *yellow* come?

Z provides two kinds of paragraphs for introducing new types. The first is the *free type* definition. Free types are similar to the enumerated types provided by many programming languages. We define a free type when there aren't too many elements in the type, and we know in advance what they all are. To define a free type, give its name and then, after the definition symbol ::=, list all of its elements. For example, here is the declaration for the free type *COLOR*:

$$COLOR ::= red \mid green \mid blue \mid yellow \mid cyan \mid magenta \mid white \mid black$$

The order here is not significant — no sequence is implied.

The second method is the *basic type* definition. We define a basic type when we do not want to say in advance what all the elements are; this is usual when sets are large. To define a basic type, simply mention its name, enclosed in brackets, as we did for *CHAR* (characters) in Chapter 7. For example, here is the declaration for the type whose elements are all the names that might appear in a telephone directory:

[*NAME*]

Both kinds of declarations introduce new types, not just sets. That means we can't form sets or write expressions that combine elements from different basic types or free types — that would be a type error. We can (and usually do) define new sets made of elements from the basic types and free types that we define.

Sets introduced both ways can be used later to declare variables, just like predefined sets. Here *palette* is a set of *COLOR*, and *subscribers* is a set of *NAME*.

$palette : \mathbb{P}\,COLOR$
$subscribers : \mathbb{P}\,NAME$

Basic types and free types are defined in small paragraphs, but their elements do not have to represent small objects. They need not be simple things like names and numbers. We use basic types whenever we can ignore the internal structure of the elements. You do not need to know the contents of a file to delete it or rename it; you do not need to know the program that a process is running to suspend it or resume it. To model an operating system, we might declare processes and files to be basic types:

[*PROCESS, FILE*]

This example also shows how to declare more than one basic type in one paragraph.

The integer type $\mathbb{Z}$ has no special qualities just because it comes predefined. By convention, it is assumed that this basic type definition precedes any Z text:

$[\mathbb{Z}]$

The useful arithmetic properties of $\mathbb{Z}$ have to be built up in the usual way: by writing axiomatic definitions. Fortunately, these come already written for us in the Z mathematical tool-kit.

Basic sets and free types are usually given names composed of all capital letters, like *NAME* and *COLOR* here. I use capitalized names for other constant sets as well, for example *ODD* and *LAMP*.

8.1.10 Identifiers and layout

By now you have noticed that Z allows great freedom in choosing names. Z identifiers can include symbols besides alphanumeric characters: punctuation marks, as in *in?*, *out!*, and x', subscripts as in y_2, and Greek letters as in $\Delta Editor$. Some identifiers consist of a single pictorial symbol, such as $\oplus$. You can even invent your own pictorial symbols; some Z tools can process symbols that you invent.

Some characters have conventional meanings that I will explain later, but in general there are no restrictions on where you can use nonalphanumeric characters.

Z is case sensitive, so *name*, *Name*, and *NAME* are three distinct identifiers. All three might be used in the same Z text to refer to different things.

You can use semicolons instead of line breaks to separate declarations and predicates. Instead of

$$
\begin{array}{|l}
PRIME : \mathbb{P}\,\mathbb{N} \\
d_1, d_2 : DICE \\
\hline
d_1 + d_2 = 7 \\
d_1 < d_2
\end{array}
$$

you can save a little space by writing

$$
\begin{array}{|l}
PRIME : \mathbb{P}\,\mathbb{N};\; d_1, d_2 : DICE \\
\hline
d_1 + d_2 = 7;\; d_1 < d_2
\end{array}
$$

8.2 Expressions and operators

Expressions describe the *values* that variables might have. So far we have only described two ways to describe values. We can write them out literally, as in 3, *red*, and $\{1, 2, 3, 4, 5, 6\}$, or we can define names that stand for values and then write the names, as in d_1, *signal*, and *DICE*. Clearly, we need more.

Expressions enable us to describe values in terms of names and literals we have already defined. Expressions are formulas where names and literal values appear together with *operators*. Expressions are sometimes called *terms*. The value denoted by an expression is determined by the values of the names and literals it contains, and by the rules or *laws* associated with the operators. In fact a lone name or literal is merely an expression of the simplest kind. So we can say that the value of an expression is determined by the values of the expressions it contains, and its operators.

Mathematics has created an immensely rich collection of operators, but before we can use them in Z, someone must *formalize* them by precisely defining how to express them in Z syntax. The most useful operators have already been formalized for us in the Z mathematical tool-kit. If we need more, it is not too difficult to formalize them ourselves.[5]

Each type has its own repertoire of operators. So far we have only learned two kinds of types: the integers $\mathbb{Z}$ and basic types such as *COLOR* and *NAME*[6].

8.2.1   Arithmetic expressions

The Z mathematical tool-kit defines the usual arithmetic operators addition, subtraction, and multiplication $+$, $-$, and $*$. The tool-kit doesn't provide any way to represent fractions — it doesn't define real or rational numbers — so ordinary division is not available. However, the tool-kit does provide integer division div and remainder or *modulus* mod. For example,

$$12 \text{ div } 5 = 2$$

$$12 \text{ div } 6 = 2$$

but

$$12 \text{ mod } 5 = 2$$

$$12 \text{ mod } 6 = 0$$

---

[5] Some people use familiar mathematical operators such as Σ (the series summation operator) that do not appear in the tool-kit, without bothering to formalize them first. This is fine as long as the meaning is clear to the readers. However, if such texts are analyzed by tools such as syntax analyzers and type checkers, the unformalized operators will be flagged as errors.

[6] It is possible to define free types such as *COLOR* in terms of basic types.

8.2.2 Set expressions

Sets are central in Z, and the tool-kit defines many operators for them. Here are a few of the most important ones. The *union* operator $\cup$ combines sets.

$$\{1, 2, 3\} \cup \{2, 3, 4\} = \{1, 2, 3, 4\}$$

The *difference* operator $\setminus$ removes the elements of one set from another.

$$\{1, 2, 3, 4\} \setminus \{2, 3\} = \{1, 4\}$$

The *intersection* operator $\cap$ finds the elements common to both sets.

$$\{1, 2, 3\} \cap \{2, 3, 4\} = \{2, 3\}$$

8.2.3 Expressions and types

Every expression has a type: the type of the value it denotes. So every arithmetic expression has type $\mathbb{Z}$, and every set expression has type $\mathbb{P}\, T$, where T is the type of the set elements. Each operator works with operands of particular types. The arithmetic operators only work with numbers; the set operators $\cup$, $\cap$, and $\setminus$ only work with sets.

Some operators are *generic*; they can work with different types as long as types are combined correctly. The set operators are generic because they can apply to sets of any type. We can use them with sets of numbers:

$$\{1, 2, 3\} \cup \{3, 4\}$$

or sets of colors:

$$\{red, yellow\} \cup \{yellow, green\}$$

or sets of any type we wish, as long as both operands are sets of the same type.

Some operators take operands of one type and denote values of a different type. For example, the *size* (or *cardinality*) operator # counts the elements of a set. Its operand is a set, but its value is a number:

$$\#DICE = 6$$

$$\#\{red, yellow, green\} = 3$$

In Z we write *#DICE*, not *size(DICE)* or something similar. Z departs from many other notations by having a great many pictorial symbols like this one. They make the formal texts shorter and (after a period of familiarization) easier to read.

8.2.4   Erroneous expressions

Expressions must have the correct appearance or *syntax*. In Z, as in traditional mathematics, most binary operators have *infix* syntax: They appear between their operands, as in $5 + 3$ or $ODD \cup EVEN$. Many unary operators in Z have *prefix* syntax: They appear before their operands, as in $-x$ or $\#DICE$. Using a prefix operator as if it were postfix is an example of a *syntax error*:

> *DICE*#   [SYNTAX ERROR! # is a prefix operator.]

Each operator only works with operands of particular types. It would be nonsense to try to divide a number by a color; this is an example of a *type error*:

> 12 div *red*   [TYPE ERROR! Second operand is not a number.]

The type rules for generic operators are a bit more subtle:

> $\{1, 2, 3\} \cup \{red, green\}$ [TYPE ERROR! Operands are sets of different types.]

Although both operands here are sets, this is a type error because we cannot have numbers and colors in the same set.

Exercise 8.2.4.1   Is this an erroneous expression? Why or why not?

> *{red, green}* $\cup$ *yellow*

Undefined expressions are more subtle. This expression uses proper syntax, and the types are correct:

> d_1 div 0   [undefined expression; second argument is 0]

However, you can't divide by zero, and the definition of div in the mathematical tool-kit explicitly excludes this case. This expression is undefined. It doesn't denote anything; it is nothing but marks on a page. Undefined expressions are not strictly erroneous, but they are meaningless. You probably don't want to write them.

Tools can detect syntax errors and type errors, but it is not possible in general to detect undefined expressions automatically.

8.3   Predicates, equations, and laws

Predicates express *constraints* that determine which values the variables actually do have. So far we have encountered three kinds of predicates: *equations* such as *size* = 2048, *inequalities* such as *size* $\geq$ 640, and *membership predicates* such as $e \in EVEN$. I will say much more about predicates in Chapter 10. In the meantime, here are some essential facts.

Predicates are not expressions; they do not denote values. They are assertions *about* values[7].

We are free to put predicates wherever they will help the reader most. There is no requirement in Z that a predicate which constrains a global variable must appear in the same paragraph as the definition of the variable. In a Z text, a variable denotes the same value wherever it appears, so there is no need to write the constraint near the declaration.

These two examples mean exactly the same thing. In the first example, the predicate appears in the axiomatic definition box where the variable is defined:

$$\begin{array}{|l}
size : \mathbb{N} \\
\hline
size = 2048
\end{array}$$

In this second example, the predicate appears later in the text, long after the axiomatic definition.

$$\begin{array}{|l}
size : \mathbb{N}
\end{array}$$

... formulas that use *size* ...

$$size = 2048$$

When they are separated from declarations in this way, Z predicates do not appear inside boxes.

8.3.1 Equations

We often want to say that two expressions have the same value. There is a symbol for this; of course it is the familiar *equal sign*, =. An *equation* is a predicate where two expressions are joined by an equal sign: $e_1 = e_2$ means that e_1 and e_2 both have the same value. Equations are perhaps the most common predicates. Here are two examples:

---

[7] In many other notations, predicates are just expressions on a *boolean* type that has the two values *true* and *false*; symbols such as =, $\geq$, and $\in$ are just Boolean operators. Z has no Boolean type (see Section 10.7). Z distinguishes predicates from expressions to avoid certain difficulties involving undefined expressions (see Section 10.8.)

$$size = 2048$$

$$\{1, 2, 3\} \cap \{2, 3, 4\} = \{2, 3\}$$

An equation is not an expression; it does not denote a value. It is simply an assertion that the two expressions in the equation have the *same* value, whatever that may be.

Some equations superficially resemble the assignment statements found in many programming languages. This equation

$$size = 2048$$

looks a lot like the assignment statement

```
size = 2048;
```

but equations are not assignment statements. In the preceding example, the assignment statement may cause the value of `size` to change. Occurrences of `size` after the assignment might denote different values than occurrences before, so the location of the assignment in the program is very important — reversing the order of two assignment statements is often a serious error. But the equation does not change the value of *size*. It merely tells what the fixed value of *size* is, each time *size* occurs in the text, so it doesn't matter where the equation occurs.

Moreover, equality (unlike assignment) is *symmetric*: We can reverse the order of the expressions without changing the meaning of the equation. In Z we can write

$$2048 = size$$

but in a programming language `2048 = size;` is a syntax error.

Equations are more expressive than assignment statements because we can put expressions on both sides of the equal sign, not just one. There is no requirement that a single variable must appear by itself on one side. We can write

$$d_1 + d_2 = 7$$

to constrain the relation between d_1 and d_2 without fixing the value of either one.

8.3.2 Laws

Predicates are not just for constraining variables. They are also used to describe the operators themselves. Predicates used in this way are called *laws*. Many laws appear in the mathematical tool-kit. They can help us simplify expressions and compute their values.

For example, this law describes an important property of division that we use all the time in elementary arithmetic calculations. It says we get the same result when we divide after factoring out common factors from the numerator and divisor:

$$(c * n) \text{ div } (c * d) = n \text{ div } d \qquad \text{[where } d \text{ and } c \text{ are not zero]}$$

Obviously, this law is just as valid whether it is written with variables c, d, and n or x, y, and z. The variables that appear in a law are just place-holders. *A law holds no matter what values are assigned to its variables* (subject to side conditions like the one here prohibiting division by zero). The purpose of a law is to describe the operators, not the variables. We will say more about laws when we study formal reasoning in Chapter 15.

9 Structure

We can use objects from discrete mathematics to model *data structures*. This chapter describes them: tuples, relations, functions, and sequences.

9.1 Tuples and records

Sets collect whole groups together, but we often need to associate particular individuals. Every element in a set must have the same type, but we want to create structures composed of dissimilar things. Elements in a set are not ordered, but sometimes order is important. *Tuples* associate particular elements of any type, in a fixed order.

Consider the problem of representing dates, for example July 20, 1969, or November 9, 1989. The obvious solution is to use a data structure with three components, for the day, month, and year. We anticipate doing calculations with dates — for example, to calculate the interval between two dates — so we represent all three components as numbers, even the month (so January is 1, February is 2, etc.). First we name the sets from which the components will be drawn (we allow *YEAR* to take on negative values so we can represent dates from ancient history).

$$DAY == 1 \ldots 31; \ MONTH == 1 \ldots 12; \ YEAR == \mathbb{Z}$$

(Recall that $1 \ldots 31$, pronounced *one up to thirty-one*, is the set of numbers from one up to thirty-one, inclusive.)

Next we have to decide on an order for the components. We choose day, month, year so November 9, 1989, is written (9, 11, 1989). The parentheses distinguish tuples from sets. Order is significant in tuples: The difference between (9, 11, 1989) and (9, 11, 1989) – that is, November 9, 1989 and September 11, 1989 — is quite important. This contrasts with sets, where order is not significant: {9, 11, 1989} and {11, 9, 1989} are the same set.

Tuples are instances of *Cartesian product types*, sometimes called *cross product types*. We define product types using the *cross product* symbol ×. This abbreviation definition introduces a set of tuples named *DATE*.

$DATE == DAY \times MONTH \times YEAR$

Since *DAY*, *MONTH*, and *YEAR* all have type $\mathbb{Z}$, the set *DATE* has the product type $\mathbb{P}(\mathbb{Z} \times \mathbb{Z} \times \mathbb{Z})$.

As you see, tuples can resemble C structures or Pascal records. We can declare Z variables that are tuples:

> *landing, opening* : *DATE*
> _____
> *landing* = (20, 7, 1969)
> *opening* = (9, 11, 1989)

We tried to define *DAY*, *MONTH*, and *YEAR* so that we could only form valid dates, but we were only partially successful. We exclude obviously invalid dates such as November 32, 1989, but the set of valid days actually depends on the month. There is no way to account for this in our definition, so our *DATE* admits invalid dates such as November 31, 1989. A comprehensive solution to this problem requires schemas, as we shall see in Chapter 13.

The components of a tuple can have different types. Consider a database of people who work at a company. The database records several items of information about each person: their name, an identification number (to distinguish different people who have the same name), and the department where they work. Each item belongs to a different type:

[*NAME*]

$ID == \mathbb{N}$

$DEPARTMENT ::= administration \mid manufacturing \mid research$

We can define a tuple that contains all three items:

$EMPLOYEE == ID \times NAME \times DEPARTMENT$

Now we can define variables of this type:

> *Frank, Aki* : *EMPLOYEE*
> _____
> *Frank* = (0019, *frank, administration*)
> *Aki* = (7408, *aki, research*)

9.2   Relations, tables, and databases

We usually work with whole sets of tuples. A set of tuples is called a *relation*. Relations can model tables and databases. You have probably heard of the *relational database*, which is just a database where the data are stored in one or more relations. For example, here is a partial listing of the *Employee* relation from our company database:

ID	Name	Department
0019	Frank	Administration
0308	Philip	Research
6302	Frank	Manufacturing
7408	Aki	Research
0517	Doug	Research
0038	Philip	Administration
⋮	⋮	⋮

This is how we notate it in Z:

$Employee : \mathbb{P}\, EMPLOYEE$

$Employee = \{$

 ⋮

 $(0019, frank, administration),$
 $(0308, philip, research),$
 $(6302, frank, manufacturing),$
 $(7408, aki, research),$
 $(0517, doug, research),$
 $(0038, philip, administration),$

 ⋮

 $\}$

Here the tuples appear in no particular order, to remind you that a relation is just a set of tuples. Sets are unordered; there is no ordering in a relation. (The three vertical dots here are not part of the Z notation, they just indicate that many tuples are not shown, in order to save space.)

9.3 Pairs and binary relations

A particularly common kind of tuple is the *pair*: It has just two components. We can use a pair to associate a name with a telephone extension number, as in (*aki*, 4117). Z provides an alternate syntax for pairs that uses the *maplet* arrow $\mapsto$ to emphasize the asymmetry between the two components. The pair (*aki*, 4117) can also be written *aki* $\mapsto$ 4117.

You can consider the parentheses and maplet arrows to be operators for constructing pairs. Z also provides the *first* and *second* operators for extracting each component from a pair:

$$first(aki, 4117) = aki$$

$$second(aki, 4117) = 4117$$

Operators like these that extract components from structures are called *projection operators*.

A *binary relation* is a set of pairs. Z provides an alternate syntax for declaring binary relations: $\mathbb{P}\,(NAME \times PHONE)$ can also be written $NAME \leftrightarrow PHONE$. Here is a partial listing of the company telephone directory:

Name	Phone
Aki	4117
Philip	4107
Doug	4107
Doug	4136
Philip	0113
Frank	0110
Frank	6190
$\vdots$	$\vdots$

This is how we notate it in Z:

$$PHONE == 0\mathbin{..}9999$$

$$phone : NAME \leftrightarrow PHONE$$

$$
\begin{aligned}
phone = \{ \\
&\quad \vdots \\
&\quad aki \mapsto 4117, \\
&\quad philip \mapsto 4107, \\
&\quad doug \mapsto 4107, \\
&\quad doug \mapsto 4136, \\
&\quad philip \mapsto 0113, \\
&\quad frank \mapsto 0110, \\
&\quad frank \mapsto 6190, \\
&\quad \vdots \\
&\}
\end{aligned}
$$

Note that Doug and Philip share a phone, and Doug might be reached at two different phones (there are also two numbers listed for the names Philip and Frank, but referring back to the *Employee* relation, we suspect those might be for different people with the same name). In general, binary relations can be *many-to-many* relations, as suggested by the symmetric Z relation arrow, $\leftrightarrow$. As we shall see, Z defines special names and arrow symbols for *many-to-one* and *one-to-one* relations.

9.3.1   Domain and range

We sometimes need to speak of the set formed by the first components of all the pairs in a binary relation and the set formed by all the second components. They have names: They are the *domain* and *range*, respectively. The domain of *phone* includes every employee who can be reached by telephone: aki, $doug$, and the others. The range of *phone* includes all the numbers that have been assigned to telephones: 4117, 4017, and so forth. The abbreviations dom (domain) and ran (range) are operators whose argument is a binary relation and whose value is a set. In this example:

$$\mathrm{dom}\, phone = \{\dots, aki, philip, doug, frank, \dots\}$$

$$\mathrm{ran}\, phone = \{\dots, 4117, 4107, 4136, 0113, 0110, 6190, \dots\}$$

(Again, the dots are not part of the Z notation, but indicate that many elements are not shown.)

The domain and range of a relation are not necessarily the same as the sets that appear in its declaration, which are called the *source set* and the *target set*. In this example the source set is *NAME*, and the target set is *PHONE*; the domain and range are subsets of the source and target sets. We declared *phone* : *NAME* ↔ *PHONE*, but there could be many names that do not appear in dom *phone* because they do not have phones in our company, and surely there are many numbers in *PHONE* (that is 0 .. 9999) that do not appear in ran *phone* because they are not assigned to any telephone.

9.3.2   Operators for relations: lookups, queries, updates, and inverses

Relations are more important in computing than in most other applications of mathematics (which tend to emphasize functions instead). Z provides a rich collection of operators for binary relations. We often use binary relations to model tables and databases, and many of the Z relational operators behave like typical database operations.

The *relational image* operator can model table lookup. Its first argument is a relation, its second argument is a set of elements from the domain, and its value is the set of corresponding elements from the range. It is notated in an unusual *mixfix* syntax: Thick brackets (|. . .|) surround the second argument. To look up the numbers for Doug and Philip in the *phone* relation, we use the relational image:

$$phone(\!|\{doug, philip\}|\!) = \{4107, 4136, 0113\}$$

The argument between brackets is not a single individual, it is an entire set, and the value of the image is another set. Z encourages us to think in terms of entire sets and relations.

We often use relations to model databases. The *domain restriction* and *range restriction* operators can model database queries. The domain restriction operator ◁ selects tuples based on the values of their first elements: Its first argument is a set of elements from the domain of a relation, its second argument is a relation, and its value is the matching tuples from the relation. To retrieve all the tuples for Doug and Philip from the *phone* relation, we apply domain restriction:

$$\{doug, philip\} \lhd phone =$$

$$\{philip \mapsto 4107,$$
$$doug \mapsto 4107,$$
$$doug \mapsto 4136,$$
$$philip \mapsto 0113\}$$

The value of this expression is another relation of the same type as *phone*.

The range restriction operator $\triangleright$ selects tuples based on the values of their second elements. Its first argument is a relation, its second argument is a set of elements from the range, and its value is the matching tuples. To retrieve all the tuples that have numbers in the 4000s from the *phone* relation, we apply range restriction:

$$phone \triangleright (4000 .. 4999) = \{$$
$$\vdots$$
$$aki \mapsto 4117,$$
$$philip \mapsto 4107,$$
$$doug \mapsto 4107,$$
$$doug \mapsto 4136,$$
$$\vdots$$
$$\}$$

We can combine domain and range restriction[1]. This expression finds the numbers for Doug and Philip in the 4000s:

$$\{doug, philip\} \triangleleft phone \triangleright (4000 .. 4999) =$$

$$\{philip \mapsto 4107,$$
$$doug \mapsto 4107,$$
$$doug \mapsto 4136\}$$

There are also domain and range *antirestriction* operators $\triangleleft\!\!\!-$ and $-\!\!\!\triangleright$, respectively. $S \triangleleft\!\!\!- R$ is the binary relation R, except without the pairs whose first element is in S, and $R -\!\!\!\triangleright T$ is R without the pairs whose second element is in T.

The *override* operator $\oplus$ can model database updates. Both of its arguments are relations. Its value is a relation that contains the tuples from both relations, except that tuples in the second argument replace any tuples from the first argument that have the same first component. This has the effect of adding new tuples and replacing old ones. For example:

---

[1] The parentheses are needed around $(4000 .. 4999)$ in these examples because the range restriction operator $\triangleright$ binds more tightly than the *up to* operator $..$, so $phone \triangleright 4000 .. 4999$ would be parsed $(phone \triangleright 4000) .. 4999$, which would be a syntax error. See Appendix C.

$$phone \oplus \{heather \mapsto 4026, aki \mapsto 4026\} = \{$$

$$\vdots$$

$$aki \mapsto 4026,$$
$$philip \mapsto 4107,$$
$$doug \mapsto 4107,$$
$$doug \mapsto 4136,$$
$$philip \mapsto 0113,$$
$$frank \mapsto 0110,$$
$$frank \mapsto 6190,$$
$$heather \mapsto 4026,$$

$$\vdots$$

$$\}$$

The *inverse* operator reverses the direction of a binary relation by exchanging the first and second components of each pair. It is a postfix unary operator that is notated as a tilde $\sim$. The inverse of the *phone* relation is a reverse directory from telephone numbers to names:

$$phone^{\sim} = \{$$

$$\vdots$$

$$4117 \mapsto aki,$$
$$4107 \mapsto philip,$$
$$4107 \mapsto doug,$$
$$4136 \mapsto doug,$$
$$0013 \mapsto philip,$$
$$0110 \mapsto frank,$$
$$6190 \mapsto frank,$$

$$\vdots$$

$$\}$$

The examples in this section illustrate the motivation for the pictorial symbols and irregular operator syntax in Z. Newcomers often find them bizarre, but if every operator had a written name and prefix syntax, our example

$$\{doug, philip\} \lhd phone \rhd (4000 .. 4999) = \ldots$$

would have to be rendered as something like:

$$rres(dres(phone, (doug, philip)), upto(4000, 4999))) = \ldots$$

or maybe that should be

$$rres(upto(4000, 4999), dres(doug, philip), phone) = \ldots$$

or perhaps

$$dres(rres(upto(4000, 4999), phone), (doug, philip)) = \ldots$$

You see the problem. The Z pictorial symbols emphasize the asymmetry of the operators to remind us of the correct operand order and work together to make common expressions easy to parse by eye.

9.3.3   Composing relations

When we have several relations that describe the same collection of objects, we can make inferences by forming chains of associations from different relations. *Relational composition* formalizes this kind of reasoning: It merges two relations into one by combining pairs that share a matching component.

For example, you may have noticed that we can infer employees' departments from their telephone numbers. This is possible because each pool of telephone numbers is assigned to a different department, as described by the *dept* relation:

$dept : PHONE \leftrightarrow DEPARTMENT$

$dept = \{$

  $0000 \mapsto administration,$

  $\vdots$

  $0999 \mapsto administration,$

  $4000 \mapsto research,$

  $\vdots$

  $4999 \mapsto research,$

  $6000 \mapsto manufacturing,$

  $\vdots$

  $6999 \mapsto manufacturing\}$

The range of *phone* matches the domain of *dept*, so we can *compose* the two relations: Match up pairs from *phone* and *dept* that contain the same phone number, then form new pairs from these, with just the name and department. For example, we match *philip* $\mapsto$ 0113 from *phone* with 0113 $\mapsto$ *administration* from *dept*, obtaining *philip* $\mapsto$ *administration*. When we perform all such matches, we obtain a new relation with domain *NAME* and range *DEPARTMENT*. The *relational composition* symbol $\mathbin{\S}$ notates this operation:

> *phone* $\mathbin{\S}$ *dept* = {
>
> $\vdots$
>
>   *aki* $\mapsto$ *research*,
>   *philip* $\mapsto$ *research*,
>   *doug* $\mapsto$ *research*,
>   *philip* $\mapsto$ *administration*,
>   *frank* $\mapsto$ *administration*,
>   *frank* $\mapsto$ *manufacturing*,
>
> $\vdots$
>
> }

Z also provides the *backwards relational composition* symbol ∘ which is sometimes used in traditional mathematics. It takes its arguments in reverse order, so *dept*∘*phone* means the same as *phone* $\mathbin{\S}$ *dept*.

Exercise 9.3.3.1   Write a fully formal definition of the *dept* relation that does not use the three dots.

9.3.4   Binary relations and linked data structures

Relations are not just for modelling tables and flat databases. They can model linked data structures as well. Linked data structures are often pictured as *graphs*: networks of *nodes* connected by *arcs*. Data flow diagrams, state transition diagrams, and syntax trees are all examples of graphs. We have already used a kind of binary relation to model the state transition system in Chapter 6.

We can model any graph as a binary relation where both the domain and range are drawn from the same set: the set of nodes in the graph. Each arc in the graph is a pair in the relation. For example, Figure 9.1 shows a simple graph. It is a *genealogy*: Nodes represent family members; arcs connect parent and child. The direction of the arcs is significant: In the drawing, children appear below their parents.

Here is how to notate it in Z. We model the graph with a binary relation on *PERSON* named *child*. The direction of each arc is represented by the order of the corresponding pair: The parent is the first component; the child is second.

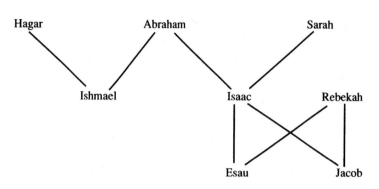

Figure 9.1: A genealogy.

$$PERSON ::= hagar \mid abraham \mid sarah \mid ishmael \mid isaac \mid rebekah \mid esau \mid jacob$$

$$child == \{hagar \mapsto ishmael, abraham \mapsto ishmael, abraham \mapsto isaac,$$
$$sarah \mapsto isaac, isaac \mapsto esau, isaac \mapsto jacob, rebekah \mapsto esau,$$
$$rebekah \mapsto jacob\}$$

All of the relational operators we described with our *phone* example are useful here as well. We can use relational image to find the children of Abraham and Sarah:

$$child(\!|\{abraham, sarah\}|\!) = \{ishmael, isaac\}$$

Ishmael appears here because he is the child of Abraham, though not of Sarah.

The relational notation of Z makes it easy to define linked structures like this one. We do not have to equip the elements of *PERSON* with any links or "pointers" that are used to create linked data structures in many programming languages. In Z, the definition of a linked structure is completely independent of the definition of its nodes. We can put any object into a linked structure without changing its definition, and we can change the shape of a linked structure without changing the contents of any of its nodes.

Exercise 9.3.4.1   Define the *parent* relation: Abraham and Sarah are the parents of Isaac, etc.

9.4   Functions

Sometimes we need to associate a single item with each element in a set. For this we use a special kind of relation, called a *function*. A function is a binary relation where an element can appear only once as the first element in a pair.

We haven't defined any functions yet in this chapter. The *phone* relation is not a function, because some names appear more than once; some people — Doug for example — have more than one telephone number. The *child* relation is not a function either, because some family members have more than one child.

In general, relations are *many-to-many* like *phone* or *child*. A function cannot be many-to-many or even *one-to-many*; a function can only be *many-to-one* or *one-to-one*.

Let's define a function. Imagine that our company announces a new cost-cutting measure: Each employee is allowed only one telephone number. Doug loses his second phone; in fact, he has to share with Philip. There is a new edition of the company phone directory, where each name appears only once, at most. Enforcement of the new policy is so zealous that some people who are unlucky enough to have the same name as another employee find that their phone numbers have disappeared.

We model the new phone directory with the function $phone_F$. Its declaration uses the function arrow, $\twoheadrightarrow$. The arrow suggests the asymmetry of the functional relation: Each employee can only have one phone number, but several employees might have the same number.

$$phone_F : NAME \twoheadrightarrow PHONE$$

$$phone_F = \{$$
$$\vdots$$
$$aki \mapsto 4117,$$
$$philip \mapsto 4107,$$
$$doug \mapsto 4107,$$
$$frank \mapsto 6190,$$
$$\vdots$$
$$\}$$

Another function is suggested by our genealogy (Figure 9.1). A person can have only one mother, so *mother* is a function:

$$mother : PERSON \twoheadrightarrow PERSON$$

$$mother = \{ishmael \mapsto hagar, isaac \mapsto sarah, esau \mapsto rebekah,$$
$$jacob \mapsto rebekah\}$$

Again, the arrow reminds us that each person has one mother, although several people might have the same mother.

Here is another example. Consider a busy office building with several elevators. The elevators and floors can be identified by numbers.

$$\mid \quad n, top : \mathbb{N}$$

$$ELEVATOR == 1 \mathinner{.\,.} n; \quad FLOOR == 1 \mathinner{.\,.} top$$

At any moment, some (perhaps all) of those elevators may be stopped at particular floors. This can be represented by a set of pairs, where the first element in each pair is an elevator, and the second is the floor where it is stopped. In this example, the first three elevators are stopped at the first floor, and the fifth elevator is stopped at the seventh floor:

$$\{1 \mapsto 3, 2 \mapsto 1, 3 \mapsto 1, 5 \mapsto 7, \ldots\}$$

This set of pairs has to be a function because each elevator can only be stopped at one floor at a time. We could declare it this way:

$$\mid \quad floor : ELEVATOR \nrightarrow FLOOR$$

Exercise 9.4.1 The second elevator leaves the first floor and stops at the third floor while all the other elevators remain in place. This new configuration is named $floor'$. Define $floor'$ in terms of $floor$.

9.4.1 Function application

Finding the single item associated with an element by a function is called *function application*. Function application is a special case of relational image. To say that Rebekah is Jacob's mother, we could write

$$mother(\!|\{jacob\}|\!) = \{rebekah\}$$

But we know Jacob can only have one mother, so we don't need to use sets at all. We write function application in prefix syntax:

$$mother(jacob) = rebekah$$

In Z the parentheses are optional; we can often reduce clutter by omitting them:

$$mother\ jacob = rebekah$$

Likewise, we use function application to look up Doug's phone number:

$$phone_F\ doug = 4107$$

As these examples show, it usually works best if the function name suggests the function's range. If e is an elevator, then $floor\ e$ is the floor where e is stopped.

The Z syntax for function application, without parentheses, is uncommon in mathematics but should be familiar to programmers. The shell (command interpreter) languages provided with many popular computer operating systems also omit parentheses, and many shell commands are actually function applications. For example,

```
ls ~doug
```

is a function application whose value is the set of file names in Doug's home directory, and

```
wc structure.tex
```

is a function application whose value is a tuple whose components are the number of lines, words, and characters in the file `structure.tex`. We will see how to specify the `wc` function in Z in Chapter 17.

Function application in Z often surprises programmers who are used to thinking of functions as pieces of executable code. Z functions are often used to model data structures instead; it is best to think of a Z function as a kind of table. Sometimes a function can be implemented by executing an algorithm rather than looking up an entry in a table, but not always. In our elevator example there is no algorithm for determining the floor where a particular elevator might be found; the *floor* function is merely a data structure that holds the set of pairs, subject to the constraint that each elevator only appears once.

In Chapter 11 we will learn methods for describing some functions by rules, instead of explicitly tabulating all of their elements as we do in the small examples in this chapter. But the function is not the rule; the rule is just a convenient way to define the function. The function is the entire set of pairs.

9.4.2 Partial functions and total functions

In our genealogy, we did not name every person's mother. In particular, Hagar, Abraham, Sarah, and Rebekah do not appear in the domain of the function *mother*. The expression *mother rebekah* does not denote anything – it has no value. We say that *mother* is a *partial function*.

The domain of a partial function might not include every element of the source set. Although the declaration says $mother : PERSON \nrightarrow PERSON$, not every $PERSON$ is in the domain of *mother*. Likewise, we have the declaration $phone_F : NAME \nrightarrow PHONE$, but $NAME$ is the set of all possible names, and most names will not appear in the company phone directory. In our elevator example, *floor* is a partial function because some elevators may not be stopped at any floor; they may be in transit between floors.

The mathematics here models a situation we often have to deal with in real programs: Many operations do not apply universally, and we must be sure to handle the exceptional cases. A naive program written to implement the *mother* function (for example, by looking up entries in a table) might crash when called with *hagar* (as the program tries to search past the end of the table). In Z, the stroke through the function arrow $\nrightarrow$ reminds us that we have to be careful to check each argument to make sure that the function application is meaningful.

Some functions are *total functions*: They apply to every element of the source set. Many functions from traditional mathematics are total. For example, the integer square root function we defined in Chapter 5 is a total function: Every natural number has an integer square root. Its declaration *iroot* : $\mathbb{N} \rightarrow \mathbb{N}$ uses the total function arrow $\rightarrow$, without the stroke. In Z, as in life, partial functions are the rule; total functions are special cases.

9.4.3   Injections

Functions are a special kind of relation. Total functions are a special kind of function. Z defines other special functions as well.

Injections are functions that associate each element in their domain with a *different* element in their range: An injection is a *one-to-one* relation. For example, suppose our company changes its telephone directory policy once again. The directory is still functional — each employee only has one number — but now each employee has a *different* telephone number. So Doug no longer has to share with Philip; he gets his own number. The new directory can be modelled by the injection $phone_I$, declared with the injection arrow $\rightarrowtail$:

$$phone_I : NAME \rightarrowtail PHONE$$

$$phone_I = \{$$
$$\quad \vdots$$
$$\quad aki \mapsto 4117,$$
$$\quad philip \mapsto 4107,$$
$$\quad doug \mapsto 4200,$$
$$\quad frank \mapsto 6190,$$
$$\quad \vdots$$
$$\}$$

Injections are reversible in the sense that they can be "run backward" without losing information: The inverse of an injection is another function. Given a telephone number, we can invert $phone_I$ to find the employee who placed the call (perhaps that explains the new company policy).

Besides injections, Z defines several other kinds of functions, each with its own kind of arrow. It is typical Z style to pack a lot of information into declarations and pictorial symbols. We will put some of these special functions to good use in Chapter 18.

9.5 Sequences

Sets are *unordered* collections; it is not meaningful to speak of the first or last element in a set, or whether one element follows another. When we write a set, we have to write down the elements in some order, but the ordering we choose is not significant.

In many situations the ordering of elements is significant. These are modelled by the *sequence*. Sequences can model arrays, lists, queues, and other sequential structures. A sequence of items from set S is declared seq S; sequences are notated inside angle brackets.

The days of the week form a sequence. First we need to declare the names of all the days.

$$DAYS ::= friday \mid monday \mid saturday \mid sunday \mid thursday \mid tuesday \mid wednesday$$

There is no ordering implied by this definition. To express the ordering, we need to define sequences:

$$
\begin{array}{|l}
weekday : \text{seq} \, DAYS \\
\hline
weekday = \langle monday, tuesday, wednesday, thursday, friday \rangle
\end{array}
$$

There are operators for taking apart and putting together sequences. The *head* operator finds the first element in a sequence. Monday is the first weekday:

$$head\ weekday = monday$$

The *concatenation* operator $^\frown$ combines two sequences into one, appending its second argument to its first. Here we use the concatentation operator twice to make the entire week:

$$week == \langle sunday \rangle \frown weekday \frown \langle saturday \rangle$$

We have to use the brackets to make $\langle sunday \rangle$ and $\langle saturday \rangle$ into sequences of one element because both operands of the concatenation operator must be sequences.

Sequences are just functions whose domains are consecutive numbers, starting with one. Another way to write *weekday* is

$$weekday = \{1 \mapsto monday, 2 \mapsto tuesday, 3 \mapsto wednesday, 4 \mapsto thursday,$$
$$5 \mapsto friday\}$$

Since sequences are just functions, operators defined for functions also apply to sequences, including function application itself. The third weekday is Wednesday:

$$weekday\ 3 = wednesday$$

And, since functions are just a kind of set, all the set operators apply as well. There are seven days in a week:

$$\#week = 7$$

9.6 Operators

Most of our operators are just functions that use infix syntax and have symbolic names. For example, addition is a function that is applied to a pair of numbers to yield another number. So

$$2 + 3 = 5$$

is really just a more familiar way of writing

$$(\_ + \_)(2, 3) = 5$$

When you mention an infix function name without its arguments, you must surround its name with underscores to show where the arguments would go. When you write the function name without arguments in an expression, you must enclose it in parentheses. The addition operator is defined in an axiomatic definition that looks something like this:

$$\_ + \_ : \mathbb{Z} \times \mathbb{Z} \to \mathbb{Z}$$

... definition omitted ...

As you can see, in Z the familiar plus sign is really just the name of a set.

$$(\_ + \_) = \{ \ldots, (1, 1) \mapsto 2, (1, 2) \mapsto 3, (1, 3) \mapsto 4, \ldots \}$$

This is an informal description of $(\_ + \_)$ because it uses the three dots, which are just a notational convention that has no formal definition. However some conventions are defined formally in Z. For example the two dots in $1 .. 6$ are actually a function whose name is pronounced *up to*, as in "one up to six." "Up to" is a function from a pair of integers to a set of integers, declared $\_\ ..\ \_ : \mathbb{Z} \times \mathbb{Z} \to \mathbb{P}\,\mathbb{Z}$. The familiar construct $1 .. 6$ is a function application that can also be written in prefix syntax: $(\_\ ..\ \_)(1, 6)$. The full formal definition of $(\_\ ..\ \_)$ appears in the Z mathematical tool-kit (Appendix D). In Z the two "up to" dots are no mere convention; they denote a mathematical object with properties of its own that can be combined in turn with other operators.

Exercise 9.6.1   Fill in the right side of this informal description of "up to": $(_\ ..\ _) = $
. . . .

Exercise 9.6.2   Describe the range of the "up to" function, $\mathrm{ran}(\_\ ..\ \_)$. Propose a use for the object denoted by this expression.

10 Logic

We have described a universe that is richly populated with individuals, sets, tuples, relations, functions, and sequences. We can extend our universe indefinitely by using operators to build up ever more complex structures. But we need something more.

We need a way to *classify* the profusion of structures we can create. We need to divide the wheat from the chaff, the sheep from the goats, the bogus from the *bona fide*. We will make an essentially *binary* distinction between the answer we are looking for — the objects we wish to model — and everything else. Our tool for distinguishing the two is called *logic*. The concept of a purely binary classification may seem crude, but with logic we can express distinctions that are exceedingly fine.

10.1 Basic predicates

The textual unit of logic is the *predicate*. There are just a few kinds of basic predicates. All the others are built up from these.

The simplest predicates are *true* and *false*. We say *true* and *false* are the two *logical constants* or *truth values*. In fact, every predicate has one value or the other, *true* or *false*. There are many rules for simplifying predicates or otherwise inferring whether any predicate, no matter how complicated, is *true* or *false*.

The next basic predicate is *equals*, $=$. The predicate $e_1 = e_2$ is *true* when the two expressions e_1 and e_2 have the same value, and is *false* otherwise.

The remaining basic predicate is set membership, $\in$. The predicate $x \in S$, *x is a member of S*, is *true* when the value of x is one of the elements of the set S.

10.2 Using predicates in Z

In Z we create models by a process of *specialization* or *restriction*. First we make declarations that admit a large number of objects, then we add predicates to allow only the particular objects that we want. Recall the dice game example from Chapter 9. We model the result of throwing two dice with two integer variables. This declaration restricts their values to the range from one to six:

$$| \quad d_1, d_2 : 1 .. 6$$

A Z definition like this one describes a number of *situations*. A *situation* is a particular assignment of values to variables. This particular definition describes thirty-six distinct situations: the one where both numbers are 1, the one where both are 6, and all the rest. We can describe all of the situations in a table. The top and bottom rows enumerate all permissible values of d_1 and d_2, respectively; each column in the table describes a single situation (that is, a particular combination of d_1 and d_2 that is permitted by the predicate).

d_1	1	1	1	1	1	1	2	2	2	2	...	5	5	5	6	6	6	6	6	6
d_2	1	2	3	4	5	6	1	2	3	4	...	4	5	6	1	2	3	4	5	6

(In this table we use the three dots ... to indicate that some columns have been omitted to save space.)

Usually we want to restrict the situations more than we can express in a declaration. In this next definition we add a predicate to admit only situations where the two numbers add up to seven:

$$\begin{array}{|l}
d_1, d_2 : 1 .. 6 \\
\hline
d_1 + d_2 = 7
\end{array}$$

This definition describes the situations where the two numbers are one and six, two and five, and so forth. We say a situation *satisfies* a predicate when it makes the predicate *true*. There are only six situations that satisfy the predicate in this definition:

d_1	1	2	3	4	5	6
d_2	6	5	4	3	2	1

We say this definition is *stronger* than the first one because it it is satisfied in fewer situations.

It is possible to write a predicate that is too restrictive. What if we said the two dice had to add up to thirteen:

$$\begin{array}{|l}
d_1, d_2 : 1 .. 6 \\
\hline
d_1 + d_2 = 13
\end{array}$$

This predicate can't be satisfied in any situation. Here d_1 and d_2 can be no larger than six, so their sum can be no larger than twelve. A predicate that cannot be satisfied is said to be *inconsistent*; its truth value is always *false*. An inconsistent specification cannot be implemented.

10.3   Relations as predicates

Predicates in Z definitions don't have to be equations. This definition says that the value of d_1 must be less than d_2:

$$d_1, d_2 : 1 .. 6$$

$$d_1 < d_2$$

The predicate in this definition is satisfied in these situations:

d_1	1	1	1	1	1	2	2	2	2	3	3	3	4	4	5
d_2	2	3	4	5	6	3	4	5	6	4	5	6	5	6	6

The predicate here uses $<$ (*less than*), a *relation*. Any relation can be used to form a predicate. All of these predicates are based on relations: $odd(x)$, $5 < 12$, k *divides* 12, $S \subseteq T$, *mother*(*ishmael, hagar*), *leap year*. Here *odd* and *leap* take one argument, while the others take two; *odd*, *mother*, and *leap* use prefix syntax, while the others use infix; $<$ and $\subseteq$ come already defined in the mathematical tool-kit, while the others must be defined by their authors.

All this diversity in appearance, syntax, and origins disguises an essential similarity: These are all membership predicates that can be expressed in the form $x \in S$. As we learned in Chapter 9, relations are sets of tuples. *Unary relations* with one argument, such as *odd* and *leap*, are just ordinary sets. So $odd(x)$ means x is a member of the set of odd numbers, and *leap year* means *year* is in the set of leap years.

Binary relations with two arguments, such as $<$, *divides*, $\subseteq$, and *mother*, are sets of pairs. So $5 < 12$ means the pair $(5, 12)$ belongs to the set of pairs of integers where the first component is less than the second, and *mother*(*ishmael, hagar*) (from our genealogy example in Chapter 9) means the pair (*ishmael, hagar*) belongs to the set of pairs of $PERSON$ where the second person is the mother of the first.

Z provides infix syntax and pictorial symbols so that we can use traditional mathematical notation in Z texts: $5 < 12$ looks familiar; $(5, 12) \in less\_than$ could mean the same thing, but it looks bizarre. Prefix syntax is also customary in logic: $odd(x)$ is the common usage, not $x \in odd$.

It is not required that you use prefix or infix syntax; you can use any relation as a predicate. In Chapter 8 we defined ODD, the set of odd numbers. To express that k is odd, you could simply write the membership predicate

$$k \in ODD$$

However, you can define relations that use prefix or infix syntax if you prefer. When you define a prefix relation in Z, or use it in an expression without its arguments, you follow its name with an underscore to show where the argument would go. When you write the relation name without arguments in an expression, you must enclose it in parentheses. So you would define the unary prefix relation *odd* like this:

$$odd\_ : \mathbb{P}\,\mathbb{Z}$$

... definition omitted ...

Now we can express that k is odd this way:

$$odd(k)$$

Prefix binary relations are declared in much the same way:

$$mother\_ : PERSON \leftrightarrow PERSON$$

$(mother\_) = \{(ishmael, hagar), (isaac, sarah), (esau, rebekah),$
$\qquad\qquad (jacob, rebekah)\}$

This enables us to write *mother(ishmael, hagar)* instead of *(ishmael, hagar)* ∈ *mother*.

We often want to use binary relations with infix syntax, so Z makes it easy. Any binary relation can be used in infix syntax when it is underlined. Consider the relation *divides*, the set of pairs of numbers where the first evenly divides the second: 4 *divides* 12 and 6 *divides* 12 are *true*, but 5 *divides* 12 is *false*. We can define *divides* in the usual way:

$$divides : \mathbb{Z} \leftrightarrow \mathbb{Z}$$

... definition omitted ...

Now we can express that 4 divides 12 this way:

$$(4, 12) \in divides$$

or this way:

$$4 \; \underline{divides} \; 12$$

10.4 Logical connectives

We use *logical connectives* to build complex predicates from simple ones. The truth value of a predicate that contains logical connectives is determined by the truth values of its constituent simple predicates. Predicates that include logical connectives can describe situations that are more complex than we can describe by simple equality and set membership.

Some logical connectives are familiar from ordinary English and from programming languages. For example, the connectives *not*, *and*, and *or* in English are not, and, or in Pascal and !, &&, || in C. In our mathematical notation they are ¬ , ∧, ∨.

In the following discussion, p and q are place-holders that stand for any predicate.

10.4.1 Conjunction

The predicate $p \wedge q$, that is, *p and q*, is called a *conjunction*; its components p and q are called *conjuncts*. Conjunction is used to strengthen predicates by combining requirements. A conjunction is only satisfied by situations that satisfy both of its conjuncts: it is *true* only when both of its conjuncts are *true*.

The rule for a logical connective can be expressed by a *truth table* where each row shows a different combination of truth values for the constituent predicates, and the last column shows the truth value for the whole predicate. Here is the truth table for *and*:

p	q	$p \wedge q$
false	*false*	*false*
false	*true*	*false*
true	*false*	*false*
true	*true*	*true*

The predicate in this definition says that the numbers on the two dice add up to seven, and the the first number is less than the second:

$$d_1, d_2 : 1 \mathinner{\ldotp\ldotp} 6$$
$$(d_1 + d_2 = 7) \wedge (d_1 < d_2)$$

It is satisfied in just three situations:

d_1	1	2	3
d_2	6	5	4

Conjunction is used so often in Z that there is a convention for reducing clutter. Successive lines in a predicate are understood to be joined by *and* if no other connective appears. The preceding definition could also be written

$$d_1, d_2 : 1 \mathinner{\ldotp\ldotp} 6$$

$$d_1 + d_2 = 7$$
$$d_1 < d_2$$

10.4.2 Disjunction

The predicate $p \vee q$, *p or q*, is called a *disjunction*; its components are called *disjuncts*. Disjunction is used to offer alternatives. A disjunction is satisfied by any situation that satisfies any of its disjuncts: it is *true* when either, or both, of its disjuncts is *true*:

p	*q*	$p \vee q$
false	*false*	*false*
false	*true*	*true*
true	*false*	*true*
true	*true*	*true*

A disjunction is said to be *weaker* than its disjuncts because it is usually satisfied by a larger number of situations. This disjunct

$$(d_1 + d_2 = 7) \vee (d_1 < d_2)$$

(where d_1 and d_2 are in $1 \mathinner{\ldotp\ldotp} 6$ as declared above) is satisfied in all of these situations

d_1	1	2	3	4	5	6	1	1	1	1	1	2	2	2	2	3	3	3	4	4	5
d_2	6	5	4	3	2	1	2	3	4	5	6	3	4	5	6	4	5	6	5	6	6

We use disjunction to express *case analyses* where situations can be classified into cases and all the situations in a case are handled the same way. For example, below zero degrees on the centigrade scale, water is solid; above one hundred degrees, it is gas; in between, it is liquid. The following definition models this with three cases[1].

$$TEMP == \mathbb{Z}$$

$$PHASE ::= solid \mid liquid \mid gas$$

---

[1] This is a simplified model. Phase actually depends on additional variables besides temperature, and different phases can exist together at the same temperature.

$temp : TEMP$
$phase : PHASE$

$(temp < 0 \land phase = solid) \lor$
$(0 \leq temp \leq 100 \land phase = liquid) \lor$
$(temp > 100 \land phase = gas)$

Notice how conjunction and disjunction work together: *and* combines the conditions that are found together in the same case; *or* separates the cases. This is a very common pattern in Z.

A good case analysis should cover all possibilities, with no overlap where situations can fall into more than one case, and no undefined gaps that are not covered by any case.

Exercise 10.4.2.1   Explain how this predicate differs from the preceding one:

$(temp \leq 0 \land phase = solid) \lor$
$(0 \leq temp < 100 \land phase = liquid) \lor$
$(temp > 100 \land phase = gas)$

These examples show that Z allows a traditional shortcut for writing predicates with infix relations: $0 \leq temp \leq 100$ is an abbreviation for $0 \leq temp \land temp \leq 100$. In general, for infix relation symbols R_1 and R_2, $x \ R_1 \ y \ R_2 \ z$ is an abbreviation for the conjunction $x \ R_1 \ y \land y \ R_2 \ z$.

10.4.3 Negation

The predicate $\neg \ p$, *not p*, is called a *negation*. Negation inverts the truth value of a predicate. The negation $\neg \ p$ is satisfied in all the situations that are *not* satisfied by p. When p is *true*, its negation $\neg \ p$ is *false*; when p is false, $\neg \ p$ is *true*:

p	$\neg \ p$
true	*false*
false	*true*

Exercise 10.4.3.1   Write the table of situations that satisfies this negation:

$\neg \ (d_1 + d_2 = 7)$

10.4.4 Equivalence

The *equivalence* $p \Leftrightarrow q$ is *true* when p and q have the *same* truth value, whether it is *true* or *false*. An equivalence is satisfied in situations that make both of its constituent predicates *true*, and also in situations that make them both *false*.

p	q	$p \Leftrightarrow q$
false	false	true
false	true	false
true	false	false
true	true	true

Equivalence means that two predicates are *true* in the same situations. It plays the same role for predicates that equality does for expressions. The equation $e_1 = e_2$ is *true* when expressions e_1 and e_2 have the same value; the equivalence $p \Leftrightarrow q$ is *true* when predicates p and q have the same truth value. Equivalence expresses that two predicates mean the same thing. Most programming languages use equality (usually $=$, but $==$ in C) to express logical equivalence. Equivalence is sometimes pronounced *...if and only if ....*

Exercise 10.4.4.1 Write the table of situations that satisfies this equivalence:

$$(d_1 + d_2 = 7) \Leftrightarrow (d_1 < d_2)$$

Exercise 10.4.4.2 Consider expressing case analyses using equivalence. Compare this definition of temperature and phase to the previous one. Which logical connective is used to separate cases? What happens at $temp = 0$? At $temp = 100$?

$temp : TEMP$
$phase : PHASE$

$temp \leq 0 \Leftrightarrow phase = solid$
$0 \leq temp < 100 \Leftrightarrow phase = liquid$
$temp > 100 \Leftrightarrow phase = gas$

10.4.5 Implication

The *implication* $p \Rightarrow q$ is *true* in every case *except* when p is *true* and q is *false*:

p	q	$p \Rightarrow q$
false	*false*	*true*
false	*true*	*true*
true	*false*	*false*
true	*true*	*true*

Implication is not provided in most programming languages, and its meaning is difficult to describe in English. For now you can just think of it as an abbreviation for the situations described in its truth table. This turns out to be exactly what we need to describe certain situations. For example, safety requirements can often be expressed as implications.

A *safety requirement* expresses that some unsafe situation must not occur. In a radiation therapy clinic it is necessary that the radiation beam must not turn on when the treatment room door is open, in order to protect staff and visitors from scattered radation. This can be formalized:

$BEAM ::= off \mid on$

$DOOR ::= closed \mid open$

$$\begin{array}{|l}
beam : BEAM \\
door : DOOR \\
\hline
beam = on \Rightarrow door = closed
\end{array}$$

This definition is satisfied in these situations:

beam	*off*	*off*	*on*
door	*closed*	*open*	*closed*

This predicate prohibits a single situation: the one where the beam is on while the door is open. When the beam is off it doesn't matter whether the door is open or closed. The implication arrow suggests this asymmetry.

Implication can express that one predicate follows from another. In the implication $p \Rightarrow q$, p is called the *antecedent*, and q is called the *consequent*. For example in $beam = on \Rightarrow door = closed$, if you know that the beam is on, then you can conclude that the door must be closed. As the implication arrow suggests, the inference only works in one direction: If the door is closed, you cannot conclude that the beam is on.

Implication can be confusing. The implication arrow $\Rightarrow$ is almost too evocative: It suggests cause and effect, or a change of state[2]. It is helpful to view implication

---

[2] In some notations, the symbol for implication is not the arrow, but the hook or horseshoe: $p \supset q$.

this way:

   stronger predicate ⇒ related weaker predicate

For example in

   $beam = on \Rightarrow door = closed$

the first predicate $beam = on$ is stronger, because it is true in fewer situations than $door = closed$ (sometimes the door is closed even when the beam is not on).

Exercise 10.4.5.1   Write the table of situations that satisfies each of these predicates. Would these make reasonable safety requirements?

   $beam = on \Leftrightarrow door = closed$

   $beam = on \land door = closed$

   $beam = on \lor door = open$

   $beam = off \lor door = closed$

Exercise 10.4.5.2   Write the table of situations that satisfies this implication:

   $(d_1 + d_2 = 7) \Rightarrow (d_1 < d_2)$

10.5   Logic and natural language

As you can see from the preceding examples and exercises, it can be quite difficult to translate English statements to formulas in logic. There is an English word or phrase for each logical connective but it can mislead you. The English meaning can be quite different from the logical meaning. For example, the English *and* is sometimes used to enumerate alternatives ("Ladies and gentlemen, boys and girls"), which is closer in meaning to the logical *or*. In English *or* is usually exclusive ("Dinner comes with soup or salad"), but the logical *or* is inclusive. Logical implication $p \Rightarrow q$ is often pronounced *if p then q* but in English this phrase often expresses cause and effect, and is usually intended to convey an unspoken *else* clause: "If it rains for one more day, the river will overflow its banks." Implication does not necessarily indicate cause and effect, and there is no implied *else*; in fact, when p is *false*, the implication $p \Rightarrow q$ is always *true*.

It is not possible to translate natural language requirements into logical formulas by rote or by some mechanical process. It requires deep understanding, and you must review the formulas very carefully to confirm they have the meaning you intend. Attempting a sentence-by-sentence translation from English to predicates usually doesn't work well. It often works better to read all of the requirements, make a table of the situations they describe, and derive the predicates from that.

It is sometimes useful to depict predicates in tabular form and include these *decision tables* as supplementary documentation. However tables become impractical when there are large numbers of variables to consider. Predicates, on the other hand, can be scaled up to handle indefinitely many variables by using *quantifiers*.

10.6 Quantifiers

Quantifiers introduce local variables into predicates. In Chapter 5 we saw this definition of the integer square root function *iroot*:

$$iroot : \mathbb{N} \to \mathbb{N}$$

$$\forall a : \mathbb{N} \bullet$$
$$iroot(a) * iroot(a) \leq a < (iroot(a) + 1) * (iroot(a) + 1)$$

The symbol ∀, *for all*, is the *universal quantifier*. Here it is used to introduce the *bound variable a* into the predicate. This bound variable does not model some particular component of the system we are trying to describe, it is merely a placeholder that stands for any natural number, which we need to explain the meaning of *iroot*. We do not want to clutter up our specification by declaring *a* in an axiomatic definition — that would make it seem far too important. Instead, we use the quantifier to declare *a* right where we need it. Elsewhere, *a* is not defined.

The general form of a universally quantified predicate is

∀ *declaration* • *predicate*

The spot • is just a delimiter. The variables declared in *declaration* are called *bound variables*. This quantified predicate means that *predicate* is *true* for all values of the bound variables that are admitted by the *declaration*. The *scope* of the bound variables is limited to the predicate; outside this scope, the bound variables are undefined. Because bound variables are local to a single quantified predicate, you can declare the same variable names in different quantified predicates if you wish — it is understood that they might refer to different things.

Bound variables in predicates are much like local variables in code. Quantified predicates can also contain global variables, which are called *free variables* when they appear inside a local scope. This example defines a global variable *nmax* and a set of numbers *ns*, where none of the numbers in *ns* exceeds *nmax*:

$$\begin{array}{|l}
nmax : \mathbb{Z} \\
ns : \mathbb{P}\,\mathbb{Z} \\
\hline
\forall i : ns \bullet i \leq nmax
\end{array}$$

The predicate here is pronounced, "For all i in ns, i is less than or equal to $nmax$." In this predicate i is bound and $nmax$ is free. The bound variable i is just a place-holder that stands for any element of ns, but the free variable $nmax$ represents a particular constant in the system we are modelling. (Notice that ns, the range of the bound variable, is a variable; it needn't be a type or a constant set.)

Quantifiers can be combined with other logical connectives to achieve powerful effects. Equivalence expresses that two predicates mean the same thing, so it is useful in definitions. Consider the relation *divides*, the set of pairs where the first number evenly divides the second. We could describe it this way

$$divides == \{\ldots, (5, 10), (10, 10), (1, 11), (11, 11), (1, 12), (2, 12), (3, 12), \ldots\}$$

but this isn't really formal because it uses the three dots. We can write a formal definition by expressing *divides* in terms of remainder or *modulus*, mod: d divides n when the remainder of the division of n by d is zero:

$$\begin{array}{|l}
divides : \mathbb{Z} \leftrightarrow \mathbb{Z} \\
\hline
\forall d, n : \mathbb{Z} \bullet \\
\quad d \ \underline{divides} \ n \Leftrightarrow n \bmod d = 0
\end{array}$$

The bound variables serve as place holders to show how the pattern d *divides* m matches $n \bmod d = 0$, so 4 *divides* 12 means $12 \bmod 4 = 0$, not $4 \bmod 12 = 0$.

So far, most of our predicates have described individuals. A bound variable ranges over every element in a set, so we can write a single predicate that describes every element. Bound variables give us the power we often need to define entire sets, including relations, functions, and sequences.

Exercise 10.6.1 Define the relation $phase_R$ from temperature to phase, consistent with the definitions of *temp* and *phase* in section 10.4.2.

10.6.1 Logic and quantifiers

You can think of the universal quantifier as just a bit of syntax for declaring local variables. In most Z texts, it means nothing more than that. However, you should know that the universal quantifier also has a logical meaning related to *and*.

Let's assume that the set of numbers *ns* in our previous example contains elements n_1, n_2, n_3, and so forth:

$$ns = \{n_1, n_2, n_3, \ldots\}$$

Then the quantified predicate

$$\forall i : ns \bullet i \leq nmax$$

means the same thing as

$$n_1 \leq nmax \wedge n_2 \leq nmax \wedge n_3 \leq nmax \wedge \ldots$$

You can see that the universal quantifier is a sort of abbreviation for a big conjunction that contains indefinitely many *and*s. Notice how the bound variable *i* acts as an index that ranges over all the elements of *ns*. To write the quantified predicate, we do not need to know the names of the elements in *ns*; we do not even need to know how many elements there are. The logical power of quantifiers arises from this ability to compactly express a great many facts. Their power far outstrips what we can express with tables.

The universal quantifier is a generalization of *and*. There is another quantifier which is a generalization of *or*. It is the *existential quantifier there exists*, ∃. The existential quantifier has a similar syntax to the universal quantifier and introduces bound variables in exactly the same way. However the logical meaning of this existentially quantified predicate is different:

$$\exists i : ns \bullet i \leq nmax$$

This predicate is pronounced, "There exists an *i* in *ns*, such that *i* is less than or equal to *nmax*." It means that some – perhaps just one – of the variables introduced in the declaration satisfy the predicate. It is an abbreviation for this disjunction:

$$n_1 \leq nmax \vee n_2 \leq nmax \vee n_3 \leq nmax \vee \ldots$$

Existential quantification appears less frequently in Z than universal quantification, because it cannot be used just to introduce local variables — you always have to consider its logical meaning as well. However, this logical meaning is needed to express certain concepts. For example, an existential quantifier appears in the formal definition of precondition. Notation with quantified predicates is called *predicate calculus*.

10.7 Z and Boolean types

In many formal notations, including some programming languages, *true* and *false* are the values of a *Boolean data type*. Z has no built-in Boolean type. Programmers are often surprised to learn this, but a Boolean type really isn't necessary in Z.

Some notations use Booleans as an all-purpose binary data type. Our radiation therapy safety example would probably look something like this:

$$
\begin{array}{|l}
\hline
beam, door : BOOLEAN \qquad \text{[This is not Z. No built-in Boolean type.]}\\
\hline
beam \Rightarrow door\\
\end{array}
$$

You see the problem: Is the door closed when *door* is *true*, or is it the other way around? In Z we use descriptive binary enumerations instead.

$BEAM ::= off \mid on$

$DOOR ::= closed \mid open$

so we can write

$beam = on \Rightarrow door = closed$

This is much clearer. We don't need a glossary to interpret it.

In languages with boolean data types, relations are usually represented by Boolean functions. The unary relation *odd* would be declared this way, and tests for oddness would be function applications:

$$
\begin{array}{|l}
\hline
odd : \mathbb{Z} \to BOOLEAN \qquad \text{[This is \textit{not} Z! No built-in Boolean type.]}\\
\hline
\end{array}
$$

$odd(3) = true$

$odd(4) = false$

In Z relations are sets, and oddness is represented by set membership:

$$
\begin{array}{|l}
\hline
ODD : \mathbb{P}\,\mathbb{Z}\\
\hline
\end{array}
$$

$3 \in ODD$

$4 \notin ODD$

If you prefer prefix syntax, you can express the same thing this way in Z:

$$
\begin{array}{|l}
\hline
odd\_ : \mathbb{P}\,\mathbb{Z}\\
\hline
\end{array}
$$

$odd(3)$

$\neg\, odd(4)$

In Z *true* and *false* are not the values of a Boolean data type, they are predicates, and predicates and expressions are entirely different things. In many formal notations predicates are just expressions that have Boolean values. Logical connectives like *and* and *or* are functions that take two Boolean arguments and return a Boolean result, and logical equivalance is the same as equality. In Z, predicates are not expressions, and logical connectives are not functions. The formula $odd(3) = true$ is a syntax error in Z because an equation joins two expressions, but *true* is not an expression, it is a predicate.

10.8   Predicates and undefined expressions

The distinction between expressions and predicates differentiates Z from many other formal notations. Why was Z designed this way? Why have two kinds of formulas where it seems that one would do?

Z distinguishes predicates from expressions to address the problem of *undefined expressions*. For example the expression 12 div 0 is undefined because you cannot divide by zero (put more formally, 0 is not in the domain of div). This raises a problem: What is the truth value of a predicate such as $12 \operatorname{div} 0 = 2$? It is tempting to say *false*, but this isn't so obvious because part of the predicate is undefined; 12 div 0 doesn't denote anything. The problem arises frequently because partial functions are common in Z, and we often want to write predicates of the form $f\,x = y$ in contexts where x might not be in the domain of f.

Dealing with undefined expressions is one of the knottiest issues in formal notations; no single widely accepted solution has emerged. Some notations propose rules for determining the truth values of predicates that include undefined expressions; others define a third truth value that means *unknown* or *undefined*.

Z distinguishes predicates from expressions to contain the undefinedness problem. Some expressions have no value; that is inescapable. However, predicates can be handled differently. The *Reference Manual* proposes this solution: Every predicate has a truth value, either *true* or *false*. An equation that contains an undefined expression, such as 12 div 0 = 2, is *undetermined*: Its truth value might be *true* or *false*, but we cannot say which. This sounds like sophistry, but it usually removes the problem. For example we can fix

$$f\,x = y$$

by adding a conjunct that makes the requirement on x clear

$$f\,x = y \wedge x \in \operatorname{dom} f$$

In the case where x is not in the domain of f, the conjunct $x \in \operatorname{dom} f$ is *false*. In that case the truth table tells us that the whole conjuction has to be *false*, regardless of the undetermined truth value of $f \; x = y$. So the entire predicate is *false* when $f \; x$ is undefined, and when $f \; x$ is defined the truth value depends on $f \; x$ and y in the way we expect.

Exercise 10.8.1 What is the meaning of this predicate when $f \; x$ is undefined? When $f \; x$ is defined?

$$x \in \text{dom } f \Rightarrow f \; x = y$$

11 Synthesis

The three basic elements of Z are declarations, expressions, and predicates. Now that we know something about all three, we can begin to do some real work. This chapter describes Z constructs that combine the elements so we can write formal definitions of useful objects. This chapter also describes some notational conventions that make it easier to read and write Z.

11.1 Set comprehensions

Until now we have had to define sets by enumerating all their elements. This is impractical for all but the tiniest sets. To describe large sets, we have had to resort to the three dots, ..., as in our informal definition of the set of odd numbers:

$$ODD == \{\ldots, -5, -3, -1, 1, 3, 5, \ldots\}$$

This is not Z. It is not a formal definition at all because the three dots have no clearly defined meaning — in fact, they mean something different each time they appear. I have been depending on your intuition to infer a reasonable meaning in each case.

We no longer need the three dots. We can use the *set comprehension* to define sets that are as large as we need. Here is a formal definition of *ODD*:

$$ODD == \{i : \mathbb{Z} \bullet 2 * i + 1\}$$

The set comprehension $\{i : \mathbb{Z} \bullet 2 * i + 1\}$ combines the declaration $i : \mathbb{Z}$ with the expression $2 * i + 1$. This means, take every element i from the set $\mathbb{Z}$, substitute its value into the expression $2 * i + 1$ and evaluate, and form the set of results. So 0 from $\mathbb{Z}$ becomes $2 * 0 + 1$ or 1 in *ODD*, 1 from $\mathbb{Z}$ becomes 3 in *ODD*, -2 becomes -3, and so forth. Here i is a *bound variable* that is local to the set comprehension.

A set comprehension has the form

$$\{\ declaration \mid predicate \bullet expression\ \}$$

The value of this set comprehension is the set whose members are all the values taken by *expression* when the variables introduced in *declaration* take all possible values that satisfy *predicate*. The predicate and the expression are both optional; our definition of *ODD* omits the predicate.

When the expression is omitted, it is understood that the set elements take the form of the *characteristic tuple* defined by the declaration. For example in this definition of the points on the line with slope m and intercept b

$$line == \{\, x, y : \mathbb{Z} \mid y = m * x + b \,\}$$

the elements of *line* are tuples of the form (x, y).

Set comprehensions are nothing new; the simpler form

{ *declaration* | *predicate* }

often appears in traditional mathematics texts, usually written as in this example, a definition of the natural numbers:

$$\mathbb{N} = \{\, i \mid i \geq 0 \,\} \qquad \text{[This is not Z – declaration is incomplete.]}$$

Sometimes they even write it backwards, as in

$$\mathbb{N} = \{\, i \geq 0 \mid i \,\} \qquad \text{[This is not Z – syntax is reversed.]}$$

These are not Z because (as is usual in traditional mathematics) the type is implicit — you are supposed to understand that i is an integer. In Z the type must always be spelled out, as in this definition of the natural numbers from the tool-kit:

$$\mathbb{N} == \{\, i : \mathbb{Z} \mid i \geq 0 \,\}$$

Z also uses the definition symbol $==$ rather than the equal sign to indicate that the identifier $\mathbb{N}$ is being defined here.

It is often helpful to think of the set comprehension in this way:

{ *source* | *filter* • *pattern* }

The declaration names a set that is a source of items. The predicate is a filter that selects items that have the desired properties. The expression is a pattern created from every item that passes through the filter. For example, this set comprehension is the set of odd numbers beginning with 11:

$$\{\, i : \mathbb{N} \mid i > 4 \bullet 2 * i + 1 \,\}$$

Let's evaluate this set comprehension. The source is the set of natural numbers:

$$\{\, i : \mathbb{N} \,\} = \{0, 1, 2, 3, 4, 5, 6, 7, 8, \ldots\}$$

Next we add the filter. Only elements larger than four can pass through:

$$\{\, i : \mathbb{N} \mid i > 4 \,\} = \{5, 6, 7, 8, \ldots\}$$

Finally, we add the pattern. Here are the elements transformed:

$$\{\, i : \mathbb{N} \mid i > 4 \bullet 2 * i + 1 \,\} = \{\, 11, 13, 15, 17, \ldots \,\}$$

Exercise 11.1.1   Define the set of right triangles whose sides have integer lengths. The set should not include triangles that are merely reflections or rotations of others in the set.

Exercise 11.1.2   Define the set of points within the rectangular *window* whose lower left and upper right corners are points modelled by pairs of integers (x_l, y_l) and (x_u, y_u), respectively. Then define *segment*, the portion of the previously defined *line* that lies within *window*.

11.2   Lambda expressions

Functions are just sets of pairs, so we could define them using set comprehensions. However functions are so important that there is a special construct for defining them called the *lambda expression*. A lambda expression is just an abbreviation for a set comprehension and retains the same *declaration, predicate, expression* structure:

$$(\lambda \; declaration \mid predicate \bullet expression)$$

The Greek letter *lambda*, λ, alerts us that it is a function which is being defined, not just an ordinary set. The declaration and predicate determine the first element of each pair, and the expression describes the second element.

Here are three definitions of the function *isqr* that associate each integer with its square. The first definition uses set comprehension:

$$isqr == \{\, i : \mathbb{Z} \bullet i \mapsto i * i \,\}$$

The second definition uses a lambda expression:

$$isqr == (\lambda \, i : \mathbb{Z} \bullet i * i)$$

Here the expression is more compact than in the set comprehension because the first element of each pair is left implicit.

Here is a third way, using an axiomatic definition with a quantifier:

$$isqr : \mathbb{Z} \to \mathbb{N}$$
$$\forall i : \mathbb{Z} \bullet isqr\ i = i * i$$

This style is the most verbose, but sometimes it is clearest because it makes the declaration explicit and shows an equation where the function application is written out.

All three definitions mean the same thing:

$$isqr = \{ \ldots, -2 \mapsto 4, -1 \mapsto 1, 0 \mapsto 0, 1 \mapsto 1, 2 \mapsto 4, \ldots \}$$

A lambda expression is just an ordinary expression, so it doesn't have to appear in a definition; we can use it anywhere. If we only need to use a function once, we don't have to define a name for it at all; we can just write the lambda expression in place. Instead of defining $isqr$ and then writing

$$isqr\ 3$$

we can simply write

$$(\lambda i : \mathbb{Z} \bullet i * i)\ 3$$

Obviously, in this example it would be easier to write $3 * 3$ or just 9, but there are situations where lambda expressions are more convenient (section 24.2).

11.3 Some simple formal specifications

A set comprehension includes all three elements of a formal specification. In fact, it *is* a formal specification in miniature. Here are some one-line specifications for the prime numbers. A prime number is an integer larger than 1 that is only divisible by itself and 1. Informally, the primes are:

$$PRIME == \{2, 3, 5, 7, 11, 13, 17, \ldots\}$$

Here the failings of the three dots are painfully obvious: it isn't at all clear how to come up with the rest of the numbers.

Paraphrasing the English definition into mathematical notation, and recalling that $n \bmod m = 0$ means m divides n, we get

$$PRIME == \{\ n : \mathbb{N} \mid n > 1 \wedge \neg\ (\exists m : 2 .. n - 1 \bullet n \bmod m = 0)\ \}$$

This is hard to understand. We have to study the negated, quantified predicate very carefully. Notice how the range of the inner bound variable m depends on the outer bound variable n. Can't we do better?

We observe that a prime number is *not* a product of numbers larger than 1. We can use a set comprehension to form the set of all such products, and then use the *set difference* operator \ to remove all of those products from the entire set of numbers larger than 1.

$$\mathbb{N}_2 == \mathbb{N} \setminus \{0, 1\}$$

$$PRIME == \mathbb{N}_2 \setminus \{\, n, m : \mathbb{N}_2 \bullet n * m \,\}$$

This definition neatly expresses the central idea in the famous *Sieve of Eratosthenes* algorithm for computing the primes: Start with all the numbers, then remove every number that is a multiple of another [Dunham, 1990]. We can often make specifications clearer by moving away from a literal paraphrase of the English, and using set operators instead of negation and quantification.

Exercise 11.3.1   Is our second definition of *PRIME* a constructive definition? Could this definition be translated to an executable program in some suitable language?

11.4   Conveniences and shortcuts

Z provides some additional notational conventions beyond those offered by traditional mathematics. These conventions enable us to abbreviate some common patterns. They make the formal texts less cluttered and easier to read.

11.4.1   Restricted quantifiers

The pattern *declaration | predicate* is very important in Z. We have already seen it in set comprehensions and lambda expressions. We can use it in quantified predicates as well.

Let's extend an example from Section 10.6. Once again we define a global variable *nmax* and a set of numbers *ns*, but this time we stipulate that only the odd numbers in *ns* cannot exceed *nmax*; we don't care about the even numbers.

> $nmax : \mathbb{Z}$
> $ns : \mathbb{P}\,\mathbb{Z}$
> _____
> $\forall i : ns \mid odd(i) \bullet i \leq nmax$

This is pronounced, "For all i in ns where i is odd, i is less than or equal to $nmax$." It is an example of a *restricted quantifier*.

The general form of a universally quantified predicate in Z is:

$$\forall \, declaration \mid p \bullet q$$

where p and q are both predicates. This form is an abbreviation for the unrestricted predicate

$$\forall \, declaration \bullet p \Rightarrow q$$

So our earlier predicate could also be written,

$$\forall \, i : ns \bullet odd(i) \Rightarrow i \leq nmax$$

This reads, "For all i in ns, if i is odd, then i is less than or equal to $nmax$."

Existential quantifiers can be restricted, too. The general form of an existentially quantified predicate in Z is:

$$\exists \, declaration \mid p \bullet q$$

where p and q are both predicates. This form is an abbreviation for

$$\exists \, declaration \bullet p \wedge q$$

Note that the logical connective here is *and* but for the universal quantifier it is *implies*. It turns out that the two different variations are necessary in order to express the intended meaning of restriction in each case. Here is how we say that at least one odd member of ns is less than or equal to $nmax$:

$$\exists \, i : ns \mid odd(i) \bullet i \leq nmax$$

Literally, "There exists an i in ns where i is odd, and i is less than or equal to $nmax$." It means the same thing when we write in the *and*:

$$\exists \, i : ns \bullet odd(i) \wedge i \leq nmax$$

The Z restricted quantifier convention eliminates a logical connective and makes the notation more uniform. It helps make Z easier to read and write than pure predicate calculus.

11.4.2 Local definitions

We have already learned how to declare local variables in quantified predicates, set comprehensions and lambda expressions. In each of these constructs, we declare local variables that range over some set. Sometimes want to introduce a local variable that has one particular value. For this we use **let**[1].

We can use the **let** construct to avoid writing the same expression again and again. In Chapter 5 we used this predicate to define the integer square root *iroot*:

$$\forall a : \mathbb{N} \bullet iroot(a) * iroot(a) \le a < (iroot(a) + 1) * (iroot(a) + 1)$$

This predicate spells out *iroot(a)* four times. With **let** we can abbreviate it with the single letter r:

$$\forall a : \mathbb{N} \bullet (\textbf{let } r == iroot(a) \bullet r * r \le a < (r + 1) * (r + 1))$$

This is shorter, and the structure of the defining inequality is easier to grasp. Notice how the local definition uses the bound variable; this would not be possible in an abbreviation definition because it would lie outside the bound variable's scope.

The general form of a local definition is:

$$(\textbf{let } x == e \bullet s)$$

where x is the local variable, e is an expression, and s is some formula, an expression or a predicate. The first part of the **let** construct has exactly the same form as an abbreviation definition, but the scope of x is limited to s.

This **let** construct is actually an abbreviation for an existentially quantified predicate. Without it, the preceding formula would have to be written this way:

$$\forall a : \mathbb{N} \bullet \exists r : \mathbb{N} \bullet r = iroot(a) \wedge r * r \le a < (r + 1) * (r + 1)$$

This is obscure. You have to study it for quite a while to figure out that r is really nothing more than an abbreviation for *iroot(a)*. The local definition makes a big improvement in readability and provides another reason we don't need to resort to quantifiers. Z provides just a few simple conventions for improving the presentation of predicates, but they make a big difference.

---

[1] The Z community has experimented with several ways to make local definitions. **let** is described in the *Reference Manual*; some earlier sources use a similar **where** construct [Woodcock, 1989b; Macdonald, 1991]

11.4.3 Conditional expressions

Sometimes we wish to assign one or another value to a variable, depending on the truth of some predicate. We can use the *conditional expression* construct **if**... **then**... **else**... to express the two-way case analysis.

For example, the *absolute value* function returns the magnitude of an integer and ignores its sign: The absolute value of 3 is 3, and the absolute value of -3 is also 3. Absolute value is notated using an unusual *outfix* syntax: We write $|-3| = 3$. We can define absolute value this way: If its argument is not negative, just return the argument; otherwise, invert its sign:

$$| \_| : \mathbb{Z} \rightarrow \mathbb{N}$$

$$\forall x : \mathbb{Z} \bullet |x| = \textbf{if } x \geq 0 \textbf{ then } x \textbf{ else } - x$$

The general form of the conditional expression is

if p **then** $e1$ **else** $e2$

where p is a predicate and $e1$ and $e2$ are expressions. It is similar to the conditional expression in C:

```
p ? e1 : e2
```

The conditional expression is an abbreviation for disjunction. Without it we would have to write out the case analysis this way:

$$\forall x : \mathbb{Z} \bullet (x \geq 0 \land |x| = x) \lor (x < 0 \land |x| = -x)$$

This disjunction leaves the function partially undefined if you inadvertently write $x > 0$ instead of $x \geq 0$. The conditional expression is easier to read and ensures that all possibilities are covered.

11.5 Modelling systems and change

Now that we have completed our review of discrete mathematics, we have at our disposal all the expressive power we need to model any computing system. Tuples can model collections of related data. Relations and functions can model changes of state. Who could ask for more?

Let's try an example: an appointment calender. The calender includes the current day, month, and year. We need an operation that advances the date by one day. What could be simpler?

In Section 9.1 we defined a Cartesian product type to represent the date:

$DAY == 1 .. 31$

$MONTH == 1 .. 12$

$YEAR == \mathbb{Z}$

$DATE == DAY \times MONTH \times YEAR$

To compute the next date, usually we can just add one to the day, but the end of each month is a little extra work. We define the *days* function: January, the first month, has 31 days, February, the second month, usually has 28, and so forth. December, the twelfth and last month, has 31 days.

$days == \{1 \mapsto 31, 2 \mapsto 28, \ldots, 12 \mapsto 31\}$

Now let's define the function *next* that takes a *DATE* and returns the next *DATE*.

$$next : DATE \nrightarrow DATE$$
$$\forall d : DATE \bullet next\, d = (\ldots, \ldots, \ldots)$$

You see the problem: The next day, month, and year depend on the components of the current date d, but we have no easy way to get at them. The tool-kit defines functions *first* and *second* that extract components from a pair, but there are no predefined projection functions for extracting components of larger tuples.

There is an alternative: Use pattern matching to get at the components.

$$next : DATE \nrightarrow DATE$$
$$\forall d : DAY;\ m : MONTH;\ y : YEAR \bullet$$
$$(d < days\, m \wedge next(d, m, y) = (d + 1, m, y))\ \vee$$
$$(d = days\, m \wedge m < 12 \wedge next(d, m, y) = (1, m + 1, y))\ \vee$$
$$(d = days\, m \wedge m = 12 \wedge next(d, m, y) = (1, 1, y + 1))$$

This is a good start, but we're still not finished. Our *DATE* tuple admits impossible dates like June 31; shouldn't we exclude them from the domain of *next*? What about the special case that happens on February 28 in leap years? Solving these problems threatens to make the definition a lot more complicated.

We can begin to see the limitations of using ordinary mathematics as a modelling notation. It can be done, but it isn't always convenient. Large tuples can be cumbersome. The logic can get complicated. People complain that the formal specifications are obscure and difficult to understand. It's almost as bad as code!

There is lots of room for improvement: The declarations in the definition of *next* echo the definition of *DATE*, and this text would have to be repeated again and again in every other operation on dates. Wouldn't it be nice if we could abbreviate recurring clusters of declarations, and refer to components by name? Couldn't we make good use of a standard way to notate changes of state? Wouldn't it help if we could express constraints between components that applied to every instance of a data type? Wouldn't it make things clearer if we could define cases separately, then combine them later?

We can have all this: They are all provided by schemas. We will learn more about schemas in the next two chapters.

Exercise 11.5.1   Define the function *month* that extracts the *MONTH* component from a *DATE*.

12 Schemas and schema calculus

Z includes two languages. The first is the language of ordinary discrete mathematics, our subject in the last few chapters. In this chapter we turn to the the new language of schemas.

The schema is the characteristic construct of Z. Schema boxes distinguish a Z text from any other notation. Schemas help us model computing systems because they can represent *state* — memory or storage — and changes of state. Moreover the schema can be used as a powerful macrolike facility to make mathematical texts shorter and easier to read. The *schema calculus* enables us to build up complex schemas from simple ones.

We used schemas to model the text editor in Chapter 7. This chapter explains schemas more fully, introduces a few more examples, and describes the important schema calculus operators. It shows how schema boxes and schema calculus operators can be expressed in ordinary mathematics.

12.1 Inside the schema boxes

This section explains the notation we use to write a single schema box, using our editor example from Chapter 7.

12.1.1 State schemas

We began with this *state schema* to model the editor's state:

$$\begin{array}{l} \underline{\quad Editor\quad} \\ \quad left, right : TEXT \\ \quad\rule{3cm}{0.4pt} \\ \quad \#(left \frown right) \leq maxsize \\ \hline \end{array}$$

This schema says that the *Editor* state consists of two texts named *left* and *right* —
the text before and after the cursor — and the size of the document never exceeds
maxsize.

Schema names usually begin with an initial capital letter followed by lowercase
letters.

12.1.2 Schema inclusion

Next, we defined this schema to define the editor's initial state:

```
┌─ Init ─────────────────────────────────────────────
│ Editor
│ ──────────────
│ left = right = ⟨⟩
└─────────────────────────────────────────────────────
```

This says that the editor starts up with an empty document. The *Init* schema *includes*
the *Editor* schema: Its text includes the name or *schema reference Editor*. This means
that *Init* includes all the declarations and predicates in *Editor*. We can show this by
expanding Init: We replace the included schema reference by its text. Here is how
Init looks when it is expanded:

```
┌─ Init ─────────────────────────────────────────────
│ left, right : TEXT
│ ──────────────
│ #(left ⌢ right) ≤ maxsize
│ left = right = ⟨⟩
└─────────────────────────────────────────────────────
```

This longer version of *Init* means exactly the same thing as the first, shorter
version. Within the predicate of any Z paragraph, successive lines are implicitly
joined by $\land$, *and* (unless a different logical connective is explicitly written in). The
predicate here means the same as

$$\#(left \frown right) \le maxsize \land$$
$$left = right = \langle\rangle$$

or just

$$\#(left \frown right) \le maxsize \land left = right = \langle\rangle$$

Schemas resemble the macros found in some programming languages: You can
write the schema name in place of the schema text. This preserves your wrists and
fingers, makes the Z text shorter, and — most important of all — makes it easier for
readers to grasp the structure of your model.

12.1.3 Operation schemas: Δ, Ξ, and decoration

Z uses *operation schemas* to model changes of state. In Chapter 7 we defined the *Insert* schema to describe what happens when the user types a printing character, and the editor inserts it in front of the cursor.

> $printing : \mathbb{P}\, CHAR$

$$\begin{array}{|l}
\hline
\_Insert_____ \\
\Delta Editor \\
ch? : CHAR \\
\hline
ch? \in printing \\
left' = left \frown \langle ch? \rangle \\
right' = right \\
\hline
\end{array}$$

Insert illustrates several features of Z operation schemas. $\Delta Editor$ tells us that *Insert* is an operation that changes the state of *Editor* (it is traditional in science and mathematics to use the Δ symbol to indicate change). The question mark tells us that *ch?* is the input variable. This is just a naming convention: Variable names that end in ? are understood to model inputs. The question mark is not an operator; it is an example of a Z *decoration*: a character that we put at the end of a variable name to indicate some conventional meaning. The prime ′ is another decoration. It tells us that *left'* and *right'* describe the state after the operation.

We can decorate whole schemas, not just individual variables. Decorating a schema name defines a new schema that is the same as the named schema, except that all the variable names in the new schema are marked with the same decoration as the schema name itself. Decorations are usually punctuation marks (as in S', S'', $S?$, $S!$, etc.) or subscripts (as in S_1, S_2, etc.). The decorated schema name *Editor'* is the name of this schema:

$$\begin{array}{|l}
\hline
\_Editor'_____ \\
left', right' : TEXT \\
\hline
\#(left' \frown right') \leq maxsize \\
\hline
\end{array}$$

A primed schema such as S' or *Editor'* is understood to represent the system state after an operation. There is no prime on *maxsize* because it is a global variable, not a state variable in *Editor*.

The Δ naming convention is just an abbreviation for the schema that includes both the unprimed "before" state and the primed "after" state. The Δ is not an operator;

it is just another character that we can use in a schema name: the capital Greek letter *delta*. $\Delta Editor$ is the name of this schema:

$\Delta Editor$ _____
 Editor
 Editor'

When we expand $\Delta Editor$ we obtain:

$\Delta Editor$ _____
 left, left' , right, right' : *TEXT*

 $\#(left \frown right) \leq maxsize$
 $\#(left' \frown right') \leq maxsize$

In Δ schemas the predicate is always repeated with the primed variables, because the predicate is always true: It holds before and after any operation — it is an *invariant*.

So $\Delta Editor$ is just the name of a schema, and the $\Delta Editor$ in *Insert* is just an ordinary schema inclusion. When we expand *Insert*, replacing the name $\Delta Editor$ with its full text, we obtain:

Insert _____
 left, left' , right, right' : *TEXT*
 ch? : *CHAR*

 $ch? \in printing$
 $\#(left \frown right) \leq maxsize$
 $\#(left' \frown right') \leq maxsize$
 $left' = left \frown \langle ch? \rangle$
 $right' = right$

This is the *Insert* operation fully expanded; it includes no more schema references.

The Ξ symbol indicates an operation where the state does not change (Ξ, the capital Greek letter *xi*, suggests an equal sign). We use Ξ when we only need to read state variables without changing their values, or where the operation exists only to consume inputs or produce outputs.

Ξ is yet another naming convention. $\Xi Editor$ is the name of the operation schema where none of the state variables in *Editor* changes value:

$$
\begin{array}{|l}
\hline
\;\Xi Editor \underline{\hspace{6cm}} \\
\;\Delta Editor \\
\hline
\;\mathit{left'} = \mathit{left} \\
\;\mathit{right'} = \mathit{right} \\
\hline
\end{array}
$$

When we fully expand the $\Delta Editor$ included in $\Xi Editor$ we obtain:

$$
\begin{array}{|l}
\hline
\;\Xi Editor \underline{\hspace{6cm}} \\
\;\mathit{left}, \mathit{left'}, \mathit{right}, \mathit{right'} : TEXT \\
\hline
\;\#(\mathit{left} \frown \mathit{right}) \le \mathit{maxsize} \\
\;\#(\mathit{left'} \frown \mathit{right'}) \le \mathit{maxsize} \\
\;\mathit{left'} = \mathit{left} \\
\;\mathit{right'} = \mathit{right} \\
\hline
\end{array}
$$

We can expand any schema, just as we did with *Init* and *Insert*. In their expanded versions there are no schema names, no Δs or Ξs. Nothing remains but ordinary declarations and predicates, just like we have been using in the last several chapters. (Remember, the primes and question marks are just decorations; *ch?*, *left'*, and so on are just variable names.)

Although we *can* expand any schema, we almost never do — except in discussions like this one, where the purpose is to explain the meaning of the conventions. The whole point of Δ, Ξ, decoration, and the other Z conventions is to free us from having to write such verbose texts.

12.1.4 Vertical and horizontal schema format

Z provides several ways to notate schemas, so we can choose different options to reduce clutter or save space. For example, we can write short schemas on a single line. Here is our *Init* schema in the usual *vertical format*:

$$
\begin{array}{|l}
\hline
\;Init \underline{\hspace{6cm}} \\
\;Editor \\
\hline
\;\mathit{left} = \mathit{right} = \langle \rangle \\
\hline
\end{array}
$$

Here is the same schema in the single-line *horizontal format*. The schema name appears to the left of the definition symbol $\hat{=}$, and the schema body is enclosed within square brackets, with a vertical bar separating the declaration and predicate:

$$Init \mathrel{\widehat{=}} [\ Editor \mid left = right = \langle\rangle\ ]$$

We can join successive lines from the predicate together if we explicitly write in the *and*. We can also write several declarations on the same line if we separate them by semicolons. Here is the *Insert* schema in the usual vertical format:

$$
\begin{array}{|l}
\_Insert \underline{\hspace{6cm}} \\
\Delta Editor \\
ch? : CHAR \\
\hline
ch? \in printing \\
left' = left \frown \langle ch?\rangle \\
right' = right \\
\hline
\end{array}
$$

Here it is with the declarations and predicate each written on one line:

$$
\begin{array}{|l}
\_Insert \underline{\hspace{6cm}} \\
\Delta Editor;\ ch? : CHAR \\
\hline
ch? \in printing \wedge left' = left \frown \langle ch?\rangle \wedge right' = right \\
\hline
\end{array}
$$

It doesn't quite fit in horizontal format:

$$Insert \mathrel{\widehat{=}} [\ \Delta Editor;\ ch? : CHAR \mid ch? \in printing \wedge left' = left \frown \langle ch?\rangle \wedge \ldots\ ]$$

12.2 Schema calculus: conjunction and disjunction

We use the schema calculus to build complex schemas from simple ones. In Chapter 7 we built a total operation from partial ones. *Forward* describes what happens when the user types the right-arrow control character. It is a partial operation because it does not account for all situations; it does not say what happens when the cursor is already at the end of the file. *T_Forward* is a total operation because it describes what happens when the right-arrow characters appear in all possible states.

$$T\_Forward \mathrel{\widehat{=}} Forward \vee (EOF \wedge RightArrow \wedge \Xi Editor)$$

This says that the *T_Forward* operation does the same thing as the *Forward* operation, except when the right-arrow character is typed when the editor is in the EOF state it leaves the editor unchanged. It is a formula in the *schema calculus*; the part to the right of the definition symbol $\widehat{=}$ is a *schema expression* formed from schema names or *schema references* and *schema operators*. The schema operators look the same as the logical connectives from ordinary mathematics that we learned in Chapter 10. As we shall see, their meanings are similar also: We use schema conjunction to combine requirements and schema disjunction to provide alternatives.

Any schema expression can be expressed in a single schema box. The declaration of the combined schema is formed by merging the declarations from all the referenced schemas: The declarations from all of the schemas in the expression appear in the combined schema. Declarations from different schemas that declare variables with the same name and type appear only once; they are not duplicated or renamed. (Schemas that declare variables that have the same name but different types are not *compatible*: They cannot be combined in schema expressions.) The predicate of the combined schema is formed by joining the predicates from each of the referenced schemas, using the logical connectives in the schema expression. What could be simpler?[1] The examples in the following sections should make it clear.

12.2.1 Schema conjunction

Schema conjunction combines the predicates using the logical connective *and*, ∧. We use schema conjunction to combine requirements.

To explain how schema conjunction works, we'll take a little detour away from our editor and consider an arithmetic problem. What if the tool-kit did not define integer division and modulus div and mod, and we had to define them ourselves? Both functions deal with integers related as numerator, divisor, quotient, and remainder, so it seems like a good idea to package up the definitions in a schema. To make things a little simpler, we'll limit our definitions to natural numbers instead of integers.

This is what division means: We divide a number n by a nonzero divisor d and obtain quotient q and remainder r. The quotient times the divisor, plus the remainder, should equal the original number: For example, 12 divided by 5 yields quotient 2 and remainder 2, because $2 * 5 + 2 = 12$. It seems simple enough:

Quotient
$n, d, q, r : \mathbb{N}$

$d \neq 0$
$n = q * d + r$

---

[1] Actually, we really have to normalize all the schemas, merge the signatures (not the declarations), and combine the predicates taking into account any predicates contributed by the declarations. Then we can move predicates back into the declarations if we wish. In most cases this is the same as the simpler procedure described in the main text.

As soon as we write it down we see that this isn't strong enough: We can always make the predicate *true* by setting the quotient q to zero and setting the remainder r equal to the original number n: We could say 12 divided by 5 gives quotient 0 and remainder 12, because $0 * 5 + 12 = 12$. This is not what we wanted at all! We also have to say that the remainder is *less* than the divisor:

┌─ *Remainder* ─────────────────────────────────────
│ $r, d : \mathbb{N}$
│ ───
│ $r < d$
└───

Now we can form the complete specification using the *schema conjunction* operator *and*, $\wedge$:

> *Division* $\hat{=}$ *Quotient* $\wedge$ *Remainder*

This is typical Z style: Define requirements separately, then use the schema conjunction operator to combine the requirements. Written out as a single schema box, *Division* is:

┌─ *Division* ──────────────────────────────────────
│ $n, d, q, r : \mathbb{N}$
│ ───
│ $d \neq 0$
│ $r < d$
│ $n = q * d + r$
└───

The declaration of *Division* includes all the declarations from *Quotient* and *Remainder*; the variables r and d that are declared in both appear only once in *Division*. The predicate of *Division* is formed by joining the predicates of *Quotient* and *Remainder* with the logical connective *and*, $\wedge$. Separate lines in a schema predicate are implicitly joined by $\wedge$, so the predicate of *Division* could be written out

$$d \neq 0 \wedge r < d \wedge n = q * d + r$$

We'll use the *Division* schema to define our division function in Section 12.3.

Obviously, we cannot implement *Division* just by implementing *Quotient* and *Remainder* separately. Schema conjunction is far more powerful than any combining operator we have in programming languages. This is one of the reasons why there can never be a Z compiler.

The other schema calculus operators work in much the same way as conjunction. We always merge the declarations in the same way, but we combine the predicates differently, depending on the schema operator.

12.2.2 Schema disjunction

Schema disjunction combines the predicates using the logical connective *or*, ∨. We use disjunction to handle separate cases, especially errors and other exceptional conditions.

Our *Division* schema is partial: It doesn't say what happens when the divisor d is zero. Let's define a total version *T_Division* where q and r are defined in this case. For lack of any better alternative, we simply set q and r to zero also:

```
┌─DivideByZero────────────────────────────
│  d, q, r : ℕ
├──────────────────────────────────────
│  d = 0 ∧ q = 0 ∧ r = 0
└──────────────────────────────────────
```

Now we join the normal and exceptional cases to describe the total operation:

$$T\_Division \mathrel{\widehat=} Division \lor DivideByZero$$

Expressed as a single schema box, *T_Division* is:

```
┌─T_Division──────────────────────────────
│  n, d, q, r : ℕ
├──────────────────────────────────────
│  (d ≠ 0 ∧ r < d ∧ n = q * d + r) ∨
│  (d = 0 ∧ r = 0 ∧ q = 0)
└──────────────────────────────────────
```

Here we have written in the *or* connective ∨, so this time the lines in the predicate are not implicitly joined by *and*. It is clear that the two cases joined by *or* are mutually exclusive.

12.2.3 Combining conjunction and disjunction

Now we can understand our *T_Forward* operation from Chapter 7. It uses both conjunction and disjunction:

$$T\_Forward \mathrel{\widehat=} Forward \lor (EOF \land RightArrow \land \Xi Editor)$$

When we expand the three schema references in *T_Forward* we obtain:

```
┌─ Forward ─────────────────────────────────────────────
│ left, right, left′, right′ : TEXT
│ ch? : CHAR
├───────────────────────────────────────────────────────
│ ch? = right_arrow
│ right ≠ ⟨⟩
│ #(left ⁀ right) ≤ maxsize
│ #(left′ ⁀ right′) ≤ maxsize
│ left′ = left ⁀ ⟨head right⟩
│ right′ = tail right
└───────────────────────────────────────────────────────
```

```
┌─ EOF ─────────────────────────────────────────────────
│ left, right : TEXT
├───────────────────────────────────────────────────────
│ #(left ⁀ right) ≤ maxsize ∧ right = ⟨⟩
└───────────────────────────────────────────────────────
```

```
┌─ RightArrow ──────────────────────────────────────────
│ ch? : CHAR
├───────────────────────────────────────────────────────
│ ch? = right_arrow
└───────────────────────────────────────────────────────
```

```
┌─ ΞEditor ─────────────────────────────────────────────
│ left, right, left′, right′ : TEXT
├───────────────────────────────────────────────────────
│ #(left ⁀ right) ≤ maxsize
│ #(left′ ⁀ right′) ≤ maxsize
│ left′ = left ∧ right′ = right
└───────────────────────────────────────────────────────
```

Merging the declarations, combining the predicates, and simplifying[2], we obtain:

---

[2] We factor the invariant about *maxsize* and the equation with *ch?* out of the disjunction by applying the *distributive* law: $(p \wedge q) \vee (p \wedge r) \Leftrightarrow p \wedge (q \vee r)$.

$\underline{\quad T\_Forward\,}$
$left, right, left', right' : TEXT$
$ch? : CHAR$

$\#(left \frown right) \leq maxsize$
$\#(left' \frown right') \leq maxsize$
$ch? = right\_arrow$
$((right \neq \langle\rangle \wedge left' = left \frown \langle head\ right\rangle \wedge right' = tail\ right) \vee$
$(right = \langle\rangle \wedge left' = left \wedge right' = right))$

This is easier to read if we reintroduce $\Delta Editor$:

$\underline{\quad T\_Forward\,}$
$\Delta Editor$
$ch? : CHAR$

$ch? = right\_arrow$
$((right \neq \langle\rangle \wedge left' = left \frown \langle head\ right\rangle \wedge right' = tail\ right) \vee$
$(right = \langle\rangle \wedge left' = left \wedge right' = right))$

Here again, we write in the *or*. It is clear that the two disjuncts cover all possibilities.

So a schema expression can always be written as a schema box, and a schema box can always be expanded to ordinary mathematical formulas. We can regard schemas and the schema calculus as nothing more than conveniences; we can explain them without introducing any new mathematical concepts. But the convenience is invaluable; compare the clarity of the schema expression for *T_Forward* with the clutter of its expanded version.

The notational conventions in Z are simple, but they enable us to write mathematical texts that are dramatically smaller and clearer. Z makes it practical to use ordinary mathematics to model computer systems.

12.3   Schemas everywhere

Schema references aren't just for defining new schemas. We can use them like macros to make mathematical texts shorter and easier to read. A schema reference can appear wherever we find a declaration, a predicate, or the common pattern *declaration | predicate*. This pattern is called a *schema text*. It occurs in set comprehensions, lambda expressions, and quantified predicates.

For example, let's use a set comprehension to define the natural number division function *ndiv*. Our new *ndiv* function works much like the integer division function div from the tool-kit: Its argument is a pair of integers, and it returns an integer, but its domain is limited to the natural numbers. For example $ndiv(12, 5) = 2$, or 12 *ndiv* $5 = 2$. Here is the definition:

$$ndiv == \{n, d, q, r : \mathbb{N} \mid d \neq 0 \wedge r < d \wedge n = q * d + r \bullet (n, d) \mapsto q\}$$

The declaration and predicate here contain exactly the same formulas as our *Division* schema, so we can write

$$ndiv == \{Division \bullet (n, d) \mapsto q\}$$

Division is not a function at all; it is just a state schema whose variables are constrained to be related as numerator, divisor, quotient, and remainder. The expression in this set comprehension arranges the variables in the proper pattern or *syntax* to define a function. Notice that the remainder *r* does not appear in the expression at all, but it is still needed in the definition.

Schema texts also appear in quantified predicates. This predicate expresses a fact about division: When the remainder is zero, the quotient and the divisor are factors of the numerator:

$$\forall n, d, q, r : \mathbb{N} \mid d \neq 0 \wedge r < d \wedge n = q * d + r \bullet r = 0 \Leftrightarrow n = q * d$$

It's much shorter written with the schema reference

$$\forall Division \bullet r = 0 \Leftrightarrow n = q * d$$

Schemas can also serve as predicates. *Factor* expresses that the two numbers *n* and *d* are factors of *n*:

```
┌─ Factor ─────────────────────────────
│ n, q, d : ℕ
├──────────────────────────────────────
│ n = q * d
└──────────────────────────────────────
```

Now we can write the preceding predicate this way:

$$\forall Division \bullet r = 0 \Leftrightarrow Factor$$

Here *Factor* appears where syntax demands a predicate. This is permitted; a schema reference can be used as a predicate, provided it is inside the scope of a declaration that declares all of its state variables. The necessary declarations are provided here by *Division*.

Interesting system properties can often be expressed entirely in schemas. When the *Editor* starts up, the cursor is at the end of the (empty) file:

$\forall\, Editor \mid Init \bullet EOF$

To paraphrase, "For every *Editor* in the *Init* state, the predicate of the *EOF* state holds."

Schema references are often used as predicates below the line in schema definitions. We can augment our *T_Division* schema with a status value that indicates an error when the *DivideByZero* condition occurs:

$STATUS ::= ok \mid error$

```
__S_Division _____
 T_Division
 status : STATUS
 _____
 DivideByZero ⇔ status = error
```

Exercise   Expand $\forall\, Editor \mid Init \bullet EOF$.

Exercise   What does *S_Division* say about *status* when the *DivideByZero* condition does not occur?

12.4   Other schema calculus operators

Schema conjunction and disjunction are the most useful schema calculus operators, but there are several others.

12.4.1 Schema composition and piping

A few schema operators are not based on logical connectives. The *schema composition* operator ⨾ derives from relational composition: $S \,⨾\, T$ is the operation that begins in an initial state of S and ends in a final state of T. Obviously, this only makes sense when the final state of S matches an initial state of T. For example, we could use schema composition to define a new editor operation *ForwardTwo* that moves the cursor forward two characters:

$ForwardTwo \,\widehat{=}\, Forward \,⨾\, Forward$

Schema piping is useful for combining operations that communicate through input and output variables. For example we might wish to model the low-level interface to the console keyboard from which our editor receives its input. The *Get* operation on the *Console* state has one output, the character which was most recently pressed on the keyboard:

```
┌─ Get ──────────────────────────────────────────────
│ ΔConsole
│ ch! : CHAR
├────────────────────────────────
│
│ . . .
└────────────────────────────────────────────────────
```

Then we could form a new operation *G_Insert* by piping the output of *Get* to the input of *Insert*:

$$G\_Insert \mathrel{\widehat{=}} Get \gg Insert$$

This is almost like *Get* $\wedge$ *Insert* except the pipe operator $\gg$ ensures that the output and input variables *ch*! and *ch*? are merged as well.

Schema composition and piping can resemble sequences of instructions in an executable programming language. Sometimes they can be implemented that way, but it is important to understand that in Z they do not denote sequences of operations. A schema expression can only define a single operation. *ForwardTwo* is one operation that jumps the cursor forward over two characters; there is no state here where the cursor rests between the characters; likewise, *G_Insert* is a single operation. Z is not a programming language.

Exercise 12.4.1.1 What is the precondition of *ForwardTwo*?

12.4.2 Schema negation

The logical negation operator *not* gives rise to *schema negation*. I have to warn you that it is not very useful. It often means something quite different from what you might expect.

In Chapter 7 we defined the state schema EOF to describe the editor states where the cursor is at the end of the file. You might expect that $\neg EOF$ describes the editor states where the cursor is not at the end of the file, but it doesn't mean that at all.

To negate a schema, we expand all the included schemas, normalize, and then negate the predicate of the normalized schema. Let's work it through. Here is the definition of EOF:

```
┌─ EOF ────────────────────────────────────────
│ Editor
│ ───────────
│ right = ⟨⟩
```

Explanding the included reference to *Editor* we obtain:

```
┌─ EOF ────────────────────────────────────────
│ left, right : TEXT
│ ───────────
│ #(left ⌢ right) ≤ maxsize
│ right = ⟨⟩
```

Next we must normalize. Recall that *TEXT* is an abbreviation for seq *CHAR*. This sequence is a function from natural numbers to characters, so its type is $\mathbb{P}(\mathbb{Z} \times CHAR)$. We obtain:

```
┌─ EOF ────────────────────────────────────────
│ left, right : ℙ(ℤ × CHAR)
│ ───────────
│ left ∈ seq CHAR
│ right ∈ seq CHAR
│ #(left ⌢ right) ≤ maxsize
│ right = ⟨⟩
```

Now we negate the predicate of EOF. Remember that the lines in the predicate are implicitly joined by *and*. When we negate the predicate these become *or* because we have to apply *DeMorgan's Law*: $\neg (p \wedge q) \Leftrightarrow \neg p \vee \neg q$[3]. Here is $\neg EOF$[4].

```
┌────────────────────────────────────────
│ left, right : ℙ(ℤ × CHAR)
│ ───────────
│ left ∉ seq CHAR ∨
│ right ∉ seq CHAR ∨
│ #(left ⌢ right) > maxsize ∨
│ right ≠ ⟨⟩
```

---

[3] Moreover, ∉, >, and ≠ are the negations of ∈, ≤, and =, respectively. That is, $x \in S \Leftrightarrow \neg (x \in S)$, etc.

[4] This schema box has no name because it is the expansion of the unnamed schema expression $\neg EOF$.

There are four ways to satisfy the predicate of $\neg\ EOF$. Only one of them, $right \neq \langle\rangle$, means that the cursor is not at the end of the file. Then $\#(left \frown right) > size$ means that the file is larger than the invariant of *Editor* allows, and the other two predicates mean that the state is not a seqence of characters at all!

Negating the predicates implicit in declarations often adds meanings that you do not intend. For this reason schema negation is not very useful. It is usually better to define a new schema that says just what you want:

$$NotEOF \mathrel{\widehat{=}} [\ Editor \mid right \neq \langle\rangle\ ]$$

$NotEOF$, unlike $\neg\ EOF$, includes the declaration and invariant of *Editor*.

13 Schema types and bindings

This chapter shows how to use schemas to define new data types. It also explains the mathematical meaning or *semantics* of schemas. This will help you use schemas expressively and reason about Z texts.

13.1 Schema types

So far we have treated schemas as nothing more than macros that we can use to abbreviate blocks of mathematical text. In this view, schemas and the schema calculus are just conveniences: They save us a lot of writing, but they don't introduce any new concepts. This modest view provides practical benefits — but it isn't very ambitious.

Schemas are more than just abbreviations. They are objects in their own right. Schema definitions declare new data types called *schema types*. The instances of schema types are objects called *bindings*. Schema references denote *sets of bindings*. Schema types and bindings are new kinds of mathematical objects.

So far we have defined only three kinds of fundamental data types — all of the others are built up from these: *basic types*, declared as in [X], whose instances are individuals; *set types*, declared as in $\mathbb{P}\, X$, whose instances are sets; and *Cartesian product types*, declared as in $X \times Y$, whose instances are tuples. Schema types and their instances, *bindings*, are the fourth (and last) kind of data type in Z.

A binding is the formal realization, in Z, of what we have been calling a *situation* or a *state*: an assignment of particular values to a collection of named variables. A binding resembles a tuple in that it is a composite object whose components can have different types. But the components of a tuple are distinguished by position, while the components of a binding are distinguished by name. Schema types are much like structure types in C and record types in Pascal.

Let's define a *Date* schema that models any date as three numbers: the day, month, and year. We tried to accomplish something like this with the *DATE* tuple in Chapter 9, but we had no way to rule out impossible dates such as June 31 or February

29, 1995. With a schema we can do better: We write a predicate that describes the valid dates.

First we must define the *days* function that associates each month with the number of its days: January, the first month, has 31 days; February, the second month, usually has 28 days, and so forth.

$$days == \{1 \mapsto 31, 2 \mapsto 28, \ldots, 12 \mapsto 31\}$$

A typical valid date has no more days in it than the *days* function allows. We can express this by including the constraint *day* ≤ *days month* in the predicate part of the schema. In February, *month* = 2 so the value of the function application *days month* is 28, and the predicate requires *day* ≤ 28, but in January and December we get *day* ≤ 31, and so forth. This ability to constrain the relation between components of every instance of a data type is one of the most important features of Z. It makes the schema much more powerful than the tuple.

```
┌─ TypicalDate ─────────────────────────────────
│ day : 1 . . 31
│ month : 1 . . 12
│ year : ℤ
│──────────────────────────
│ day ≤ days month
└───────────────────────────────────────────────
```

TypicalDate defines a new schema type that is written this way, with special brackets:

$$⦉day, month, year : ℤ⦊$$

The components of a schema type are distinguished by name, not position, so the order of the *day*, *month*, and *year* components in the schema type isn't significant (we often list components in alphabetical order, to make them easier to find). The type of *day* and *month* in the schema type is ℤ, not the integer ranges 1 . . 31 and 1 . . 12, because these ranges are sets, not types; the type of both of these sets is ℤ.

The types of the components in the schema type can be found by *normalizing* the schema: Rewrite the schema so that the declarations of all its components are expressed in terms of their underlying types, and move the predicates specializing the declarations into the predicate part of the schema. This is how *TypicalDate* looks when it is normalized:

```
┌─ TypicalDate ──────────────────────────────────────────────
│ day, month, year : ℤ
├────────────────────────────────────────────────────────────
│ day ∈ 1 .. 31
│ month ∈ 1 .. 12
│ day ≤ days month
└────────────────────────────────────────────────────────────
```

Here *day, month, year* : ℤ is the *signature* of *TypicalDate*; *day* : 1 .. 31, and so forth, is its *declaration*.

The *TypicalDate* schema does not describe every valid date. There is a special case: In leap years there is an extra day, February 29. We solve this problem in the usual Z way: Define another schema to cover the exceptional case; then use schema disjunction to combine the cases. We define the prefix unary relation *leap_* so that *leap year* is *true* when *year* is a leap year. Our *leap_* is just a set of years: Leap years occur every four years, excluding only centuries not divisible by 400 (2000 is a leap year, though 1900 was not).

$$(leap\_) == \{\ y : ℤ \bullet 4 * y\ \} \setminus (\{\ y : ℤ \bullet 100 * y\ \} \setminus \{\ y : ℤ \bullet 400 * y\ \})$$

```
┌─ Feb29 ────────────────────────────────────────────────────
│ month, day, year : ℤ
├────────────────────────────────────────────────────────────
│ month = 2
│ day = 29
│ leap year
└────────────────────────────────────────────────────────────
```

Feb29 looks different from *TypicalDate*: Its components appear in a different order, its *month* and *day* belong to ℤ rather than integer ranges, and the predicate is different. Nevertheless, *Feb29* has exactly the same schema type as *TypicalDate*: ⟨|*day, month, year* : ℤ|⟩.

The schema types are the same because *TypicalDate* and *Feb29* both have components with the same names and types — they have the same signature. The order of the components, the particular sets named in the declarations, and the schema predicate do not affect the schema type.

The instances of schema types are objects called *bindings*. Bindings resemble structures in C and records in Pascal. Here is one of the many bindings that belongs to the schema type of *TypicalDate* and *Feb29*:

⟨*day* ⇒ 30; *month* ⇒ 2; *year* ⇒ 1996⟩

(The arrows ⇒ indicate binding, not logical implication.) This particular binding represents the impossible date February 30, 1996; the schema type includes bindings that are not constrained by any predicate.

Schema references denote *sets of bindings*. The set *TypicalDate* contains all of the bindings in the schema type ⟨*day* : $\mathbb{Z}$; *month* : $\mathbb{Z}$; *year* : $\mathbb{Z}$⟩ that satisfy the predicate of *TypicalDate*[1]. Here are some of the bindings from *TypicalDate*:

$$\vdots$$
$$\langle day \Rightarrow 27; \ month \Rightarrow 2; \ year \Rightarrow 1996 \rangle,$$
$$\langle day \Rightarrow 28; \ month \Rightarrow 2; \ year \Rightarrow 1996 \rangle,$$
$$\langle day \Rightarrow 1; \ month \Rightarrow 3; \ year \Rightarrow 1996 \rangle,$$
$$\vdots$$

Here are some of the bindings from *Feb29*:

$$\vdots$$
$$\langle day \Rightarrow 29; \ month \Rightarrow 2; \ year \Rightarrow 1992 \rangle,$$
$$\langle day \Rightarrow 29; \ month \Rightarrow 2; \ year \Rightarrow 1996 \rangle,$$
$$\langle day \Rightarrow 29; \ month \Rightarrow 2; \ year \Rightarrow 2000 \rangle,$$
$$\vdots$$

Now we can describe any valid date, and only valid dates, by combining our two schemas using disjunction:

$$Date \ \hat{=} \ TypicalDate \ \lor \ Feb29$$

Expanding *Date* (not forgetting to normalize *TypicalDate*) we get:

__*Date*_____
day, *month*, *year* : $\mathbb{Z}$

$(day \in 1 \mathinner{.\,.} 31 \land day \le days \ month \land month \in 1 \mathinner{.\,.} 12) \ \lor$
$(day = 29 \land month = 2 \land leap \ year)$

Schema references denote sets of bindings, and so do schema expressions. *TypicalDate* $\lor$ *Feb29* contains every binding that belongs to *TypicalDate* or *Feb29*: all valid dates, in fact. Here are some of them:

---

[1] Z provides different ways to write down the set denoted by the schema *S*. In a declaration we simply write *S*. In set comprehensions and other contexts where we want to emphasize that we are naming a set, we can write {*S*}.

$\vdots$

$\langle day \Rrightarrow 27;\ month \Rrightarrow 2;\ year \Rrightarrow 1996 \rangle,$
$\langle day \Rrightarrow 28;\ month \Rrightarrow 2;\ year \Rrightarrow 1996 \rangle,$
$\langle day \Rrightarrow 29;\ month \Rrightarrow 2;\ year \Rrightarrow 1996 \rangle,$
$\langle day \Rrightarrow 1;\ month \Rrightarrow 3;\ year \Rrightarrow 1996 \rangle,$

$\vdots$

Schema types and bindings provide a new kind of meaning or *semantics* for schemas. Our new *denotational semantics* encourages a view of schemas that is much richer than merely regarding them as abbreviations for blocks of formulas[2]. *Editor* is no longer just an abbreviation for the string *left, right : TEXT* | #(*left* ⌢ *right*) ≤ *maxsize*, it actually denotes a collection of record-like data structures — you can almost touch them. Now the predicate ∃ *Editor* • *Init* has a more vivid interpretation: "Take a look at all the *Editor* data structures — you can find one that satisfies the predicate of *Init*."

13.2 Using schema types and bindings

Schema references denote sets, so we can use them in declarations to define record-like variables that have schema types. We access the components of these variables using the *selector* dot — exactly the same syntax we use for selecting members of structures in C and fields of records in Pascal. Here we define the variable *landing*, a member of *Date*, and constrain its value to be July 20, 1969:

> *landing* : *Date*
> ___
> *landing.day* = 20
> *landing.month* = 7
> *landing.year* = 1969

Now I have to warn you that the notation for schema types and bindings is not part of Z. It seems that we should be able to define *landing* this way, explicitly writing out the schema type and the binding:

> *landing* : ⦇*day, month, year* : $\mathbb{Z}$⦈
> ___
> *landing* = ⟨*day* ⟹ 20, *month* ⟹ 7, *year* ⟹ 1969⟩

---

[2] In a *denotational semantics*, the meaning of a formula is the object it represents or *denotes*. In our denotational semantics of Z, schemas denote sets of bindings.

This would closely resemble our definition using a tuple (Section 9.1):

$$landing : DAY \times MONTH \times YEAR$$

$$landing = (20, 7, 1969)$$

However, our second definition of *landing* is not permitted in Z as it is defined in the *Reference Manual* and taught in most textbooks. This does not limit the expressiveness of Z, because we can always resort to the style of our first definition. However, the absence of explicit notation for schema types and bindings can be regarded as missing syntax that makes the Z notation irregular[3].

Schema references can appear in declarations anywhere we use types. This can help us write definitions that are quite compact. Let's define the *weekday* function that tells us the day of the week for any date (for example, July 20, 1969, was a Sunday). We represent the days with numbers; so Sunday is 0, Monday is 1, and so forth (it turns out to be more convenient to start with zero). You can guess the shape of this function, because there are only seven values in the range, and the *weekday* of a given day of the month advances one day each year, and an additional day on leap years[4].

$$weekday : Date \rightarrow 0 .. 6$$

$$\forall d : Date \bullet weekday(d) = (d.day + d.year + d.year \text{ div } 4 + \ldots) \text{ mod } 7$$

In fact we can write an even shorter definition. All the variables we need are defined in the schema *Date*, so we can omit the bound variable *d*. There is only one problem: Now that we no longer have the bound variable *d*, what is the argument of *weekday* in the predicate? It is tempting to say *Date*, but that would be type error. *Date* is a whole set of bindings, but the argument of *weekday* is a single binding.

To solve this problem Z provides the *binding formation* operator θ (the Greek letter *theta*, perhaps because it suggests the English word *the*). Then $\theta Date$ (sometimes pronounced *the Date*) refers to the (otherwise anonymous) member of *Date* that is currently in scope. So we write:

$$weekday : Date \rightarrow 0 .. 6$$

$$\forall Date \bullet weekday(\theta Date) = (day + year + year \text{ div } 4 + \ldots) \text{ mod } 7$$

---

[3] The *Reference Manual* does use $\langle\!|\ldots|\!\rangle$ and $\Rightarrow$, but only in discussions about Z semantics; they are not included in the definition of the Z notation itself. The draft Z standard [Nicholls, 1995] proposes to include a standard notation for schema types and bindings.

[4] A complete formula for *weekday* appears in many sources, for example Rosen [1993].

Now we can refer to the state variables *day* and *year* directly, because they are in the scope of the declarations in *Date*.

We often find θ in schema predicates. For example the usual way to write the definition of $\Xi Editor$, the operation where the before and after states are the same, is

```
┌─ ΞEditor ──────────────────────────────────
│  ΔEditor
│ ────────────────────────────
│  θEditor′ = θEditor
└─────────────────────────────────────────────
```

Without θ we have to explicitly write out the equality of each component: *left′* $=$ *left* $\wedge$ *right′* $=$ *right*. This becomes tedious for large schemas.

Here is another way to use θ. You have probably noticed that an operation schema is much like a relation: It relates before states and after states. It is often easier to define a schema, but sometimes we would prefer relation syntax instead. We can have both. The binding operator makes it easy to define the relation corresponding to any operation schema. This schema defines what it means for one date to precede another:

```
┌─ Precedes ─────────────────────────────────
│  ΔDate
│ ────────────────────────────
│  (year < year′) ∨
│  (year = year′ ∧ month < month′) ∨
│  (year = year′ ∧ month = month′ ∧ day < day′)
└─────────────────────────────────────────────
```

Here we use Δ as a convenient way to declare pairs of related state variables such as *year* and *year′*. We do not always have to interpret Δ as a change of state.

This set comprehension defines the relation *precedes*. We use the binding operator twice to separate the before and after state variables into the two components of a pair:

$$precedes == \{\ Precedes \bullet (\theta Date, \theta Date')\ \}$$

Now we can write definitions like this one

```
┌─ Biography ─────────────────────────────────────────────
│ name : NAME
│ birth, death : Date
│ . . .
├─────────────────
│ birth precedes death
│ . . .
└────────────────────────────────────────────────────────
```

Exercise 13.2.1 Define the operation *Next* that advances a *Date* by one day.

We can use schemas in declarations wherever we can use sets — even inside other schemas. This makes it easy to define complex structures.

For example, let's define a more powerful editor. We would like to work on several files at once in different workspaces or *buffers*. Each buffer has a name — usually the name of the file where we will save the buffer's text. The buffer we are currently working in is called the *active* buffer. Every buffer, including the active buffer, has its own text and cursor position, so we can model each one as an instance of our previously-defined *Editor*. The state of our multibuffer editor is a function from names to editor instances, with the active buffer distinguished:

```
┌─ MultiEditor ───────────────────────────────────────────
│ active : NAME
│ buffer : NAME ⇸ Editor
├─────────────────
│ active ∈ dom buffer
└────────────────────────────────────────────────────────
```

In this chapter we have seen that schema references can be used as expressions whose values are sets of bindings. A schema reference can appear where syntax demands a set, for example in a declaration. In section 12.3 we learned that schemas can be declarations or predicates; now we know that they can be expressions as well!

14 Generic definitions and free types

It isn't possible to do justice to all of Z in an introductory book like this one. This chapter mentions a few features that are not discussed elsewhere. You should know that they exist.

14.1 Generics

Z provides *generic* constructs that enable you to write definitions that apply to any type.

We have already used many generic operators. In our editor example we used several functions from the Z mathematical tool-kit to operate on sequences of characters called *TEXT*. For example we used the concatenation operator $\frown$ to join texts together: $left' = left \frown \langle head\ right \rangle$. You might infer that the concatenation operator must be defined something like this:

$$
\_\frown\_ : TEXT \times TEXT \to TEXT
$$

$$
\dots
$$

But this cannot be right — we defined *TEXT* ourselves, but concatenation came already defined in the mathematical tool-kit. In fact this definition would be far too restrictive, because it only applies to texts. The concatenation operator ought to work on any kind of sequence. Of course it does, because the actual Z concatenation operator is defined in a *generic definition*. Turning to the tool-kit in the *The Z Notation* we find:

$$
\begin{array}{|l}
\llcorner [X] \rule{4cm}{0.4pt} \\
\quad \_\,^\frown\,\_ : \mathrm{seq}\ X \times \mathrm{seq}\ X \to \mathrm{seq}\ X \\
\rule{3cm}{0.4pt} \\
\quad \ldots
\end{array}
$$

Here X is a *formal generic parameter* that stands for any type. In our editor we *instantiate* this function by providing the *actual generic parameter CHAR*, so seq X becomes seq *CHAR* — which is the same as *TEXT*.

The double bar and the parameter at the top of the box alert you that the definition is generic. Generic defintions are global, even though they appear inside a box.

Abbreviations can also be generic. The left side of an abbreviation definition need not be a single identifier. It can be an entire pattern including formal generic parameters. This is how the tool-kit defines the binary relation symbol $\leftrightarrow$:

$$X \leftrightarrow Y == \mathbb{P}(X \times Y)$$

The Z mathematical tool-kit largely consists of such generic definitions and abbreviations. You can write your own; this is a very powerful way to extend the Z notation. In this book we concentrate on using Z rather than extending it, so we don't find it necessary to use generic definitions here.

Z also provides *generic schemas*. This example from the *Reference Manual* defines a generic resource manager named *Pool*. There can be different instantiations of *Pool*, where the generic parameter *RESOURCE* is supplied with an actual parameter that might represent any resource, for example memory pages, disk blocks, or processors.

$$
\begin{array}{|l}
\llcorner Pool\ [RESOURCE] \rule{4cm}{0.4pt} \\
\quad owner : RESOURCE \nrightarrow USER \\
\quad free : \mathbb{P}\,RESOURCE \\
\rule{5cm}{0.4pt} \\
\quad (\mathrm{dom}\ owner) \cup free = RESOURCE \\
\quad (\mathrm{dom}\ owner) \cap free = \emptyset
\end{array}
$$

In *Pool*, the set *free* models the pool of available resources, and the function *owner* associates the resources that have been allocated with the users that own them. The predicate says that every resource either belongs to some owner or is free, and no free resource belongs to anyone.

14.2   Free types

Free type definitions are not just for introducing enumerations. They can also be used to define recursive data types that include several kinds of distinct elements. One application of free types is to write syntax definitions, similar to the definition of programming language syntax in Chapter 1. Here is a definition of the syntax of simple arithmetic expressions on natural numbers, such as $2 + 3$ and $(12 \text{ div } (2 + 3)) - 7$:

$$OP \quad ::= plus \mid minus \mid times \mid divide$$

$$
\begin{aligned}
EXP ::= \; &const\langle\!\langle \mathbb{N} \rangle\!\rangle \\
\mid \; &binop\langle\!\langle OP \times EXP \times EXP \rangle\!\rangle
\end{aligned}
$$

Here the first free type definition is a simple enumeration that introduces the binary operators. The second definition says that an expression is a numeric constant, or a pair of expressions joined by a binary operator.

Free types also provide an alternative to the method of Section 9.3.4 for modelling linked data structures.

Free types are just a notational convenience; the meaning of any free type definition can be expressed using only basic types and axiomatic definitions.

15 Formal reasoning

So far we have been using Z to name objects, describe their structure, and state some of their properties. For each property of an object, we added another formula to the description. But this is not always necessary. We don't have to spell out each property explicitly. Once we have stated a few properties, we can infer many more by using *formal reasoning*. This ability to infer new facts by applying simple rules is one of the distinguishing features of a formal method.

Reasoning enables us to use a formal model as a *nonexecutable prototype* or *oracle*. Formal reasoning plays somewhat the same role for mathematical models that testing does for code. Just as you can experiment with code by running it, you can investigate the behavior of a nonexecutable prototype by reasoning. You can check important system properties before you write a single line of code. Moreover, an exercise in formal reasoning often establishes the behavior for a whole class of situations, not just a single test case.

We can use formal reasoning to *validate* a mathematical model against requirements. A model is valid if its properties satisfy the intent of the requirements. Requirements are usually not expressed formally, but we can translate almost any reasonable requirement to a predicate. We can then attempt to determine whether this predicate follows from the predicates in our model. If it does, the model is valid with respect to that requirement.

Formal reasoning provides a systematic way to check for certain kinds of errors and oversights. In this chapter we will learn how to investigate *preconditions*. Misunderstandings about preconditions can cause programming errors.

Formal reasoning can also show how one model is related to another. It can show that a detailed design is a correct refinement of a more abstract specification, and it can verify that code implements its specification.

An exercise in formal reasoning is sometimes called a *proof*. In this chapter we will learn how to do formal reasoning in Z and write simple proofs.

15.1   Calculation and proof

Formal reasoning means reasoning with formulas. An exercise in formal reasoning is a kind of calculation. The arithmetic calculations you learned in school are examples of formal reasoning. Here is a simple one:

A train moves at a constant velocity of sixty miles per hour. How far does the train travel in four hours?

To solve this problem, you calculate the distance by multiplying velocity and time. We can express the problem in Z:

$$distance, velocity, time : \mathbb{N}$$
$$\overline{}$$
$$distance = velocity * time$$
$$velocity = 60$$
$$time = 4$$

The problem is to find *distance*, which is implicit in the other predicates. We calculate the solution in steps. Here is the solution written out in full detail:

$$distance = velocity * time \qquad\qquad\qquad [Definition]$$
$$= 60 * time \qquad\qquad\qquad [velocity = 60]$$
$$= 60 * 4 \qquad\qquad\qquad [time = 4]$$
$$= 240 \qquad\qquad\qquad [\text{Arithmetic}]$$

This calculation is a formal proof of the predicate $distance = 240$ (miles). We do not have to include this predicate in the Z axiomatic description because it can be inferred from the other predicates.

This proof applies two principles: We can *substitute* equals for equals, and equality is *transitive*: from $a = b$ and $b = c$, we can conclude $a = c$. The proof is written out in a format that makes it easy to check. Each step is written on a separate line annotated with its justification, and the vertical layout makes it clear that the solution follows from the transitivity of equality.

Each step in our proof is a formula, but not only that; the entire proof is also a formula! The proof *is* a predicate. Written out in the usual way it is

$$distance = velocity * time = 60 * time = 60 * 4 = 240$$

Without the annotations, our proof is just an ordinary Z predicate (it uses the Z convention that $a = b = c$ is an abbreviation for $a = b \wedge b = c$).

A proof can be any predicate; it need not be an equation. Let's change the problem statement slightly to say that the train is moving at less than sixty miles per hour: $velocity < 60$. Then the proof becomes:

$distance = velocity * time$ [Definition]

$\qquad\quad < 60 * time$ [$velocity < 60$]

$\qquad\quad = 60 * 4$ [$time = 4$]

$\qquad\quad = 240$ [Arithmetic]

Written out on one line, this is

$distance = velocity * time < 60 * time = 60 * 4 = 240$

This time we obtain the inequality $distance < 240$ because we can infer $a < d$ from $a = b < c = d$.

Exercise 15.1.1 Equality $=$, greater than $>$, and less than $<$ are all transitive. Is inequality $\neq$ transitive as well?

Calculations need not be arithmetic. This example uses set membership $\in$ and the subset relation $\subseteq$. Organizations are modelled as sets of people, and organizational hierarchy is modelled as subset relations. Philip works on the adhesives team in the materials group, which is part of the research division.

> $philip : PERSON$
> $adhesives, materials, research, manufacturing : \mathbb{P}\,PERSON$
>
> ----
>
> $adhesives \subseteq materials$
> $materials \subseteq research$
> $philip \in adhesives$

Intuition tells us that Philip must work in the research division. We don't have to write a formula to say that because it is easy to show:

$philip \in adhesives$ [Definition]

$\qquad\quad \subseteq materials$ [Definition]

$\qquad\quad \subseteq research$ [Definition]

This is a formal proof of the predicate $philip \in research$. It uses the transitivity of the subset relation: From $S \subseteq T \subseteq U$ we can infer $S \subseteq U$. The proof is trivial but it can save us a great deal of writing. Without it we would have to include the predicates *philip* ∈ *materials* and *philip* ∈ *manufacturing* in the definition — and so on for every other employee. Now that we can do the proof, we don't have to include these facts; we can infer them when they are needed. If the company is reorganized — for example, *materials* is moved from *research* to *manufacturing* — we only need to change a single line.

In the preceding proofs, each line shows an expression which is joined to the expression on the preceding line by an equal sign or a relation symbol. We can also build proofs where the lines are predicates joined by logical connectives. The connective is often equivalence, which plays much the same role for predicates that equality does for expressions. Here is a formalization of the little algebra problem: find x, given $2x + 7 = 13$.

$$
\begin{array}{|l}
x : \mathbb{Z} \\
\hline
2 * x + 7 = 13
\end{array}
$$

We simply solve for x

$$
\begin{aligned}
2 * x + 7 &= 13 && \text{[Definition.]} \\
\Leftrightarrow 2 * x &= 13 - 7 && \text{[Subtract 7 from both sides.]} \\
\Leftrightarrow 2 * x &= 6 && \text{[Arithmetic.]} \\
\Rightarrow (2 * x) \operatorname{div} 2 &= 6 \operatorname{div} 2 && \text{[Divide both sides by 2.]} \\
\Leftrightarrow x &= 6 \operatorname{div} 2 && \text{[Division on left side, algebra]} \\
\Leftrightarrow x &= 3 && \text{[Division on right side, arithmetic]}
\end{aligned}
$$

This completes our proof of the predicate $2 * x + 7 = 13 \Rightarrow x = 3$.

15.2 Laws

A proof is sound or *valid* only when every step is justified. We try to write our proofs so the validity of each step is self-evident, but we need an authority we can consult to confirm that every step is justified. That authority exists. It is a collection of formulas called *laws*.

A law looks just like an ordinary predicate, but the identifiers have a different meaning: They are not variables, they are *place-holders*. This distinction is important: A variable always denotes a particular value, but a place-holder represents *any* expression of the appropriate type. A predicate may be *true* or *false* depending on the values of its variables, but a law is always *true* when a place-holder is replaced by any expression of the appropriate type. Predicates usually express facts that are particular to some specific situation, but laws express rules that are universally applicable. For example

$$2 * n = 6 \qquad\qquad\qquad \text{[This is an ordinary predicate.]}$$

is a predicate with one variable, n. This predicate is really just a roundabout way of saying $n = 3$; it is *true* when $n = 3$ and *false* otherwise. In contrast

$$0 * n = 0 \qquad\qquad\qquad\qquad \text{[This is a law.]}$$

is a law that is *true* for any integer expression we can write in place of n. It expresses a fundamental property of arithmetic: Multiplication by zero always results in zero. Likewise

$$n = d * q + r \qquad\qquad\qquad\qquad\qquad \text{[Predicate]}$$

is a predicate that includes the variables n, q, d, and r. This predicate is *true* when $n = 7, q = 2, d = 3$, and $r = 1$, and in many other situations as well, but it is *false* when $n = 7, q = 2, d = 3$, and $r = 0$, and in many other situations besides that. In contrast

$$d \neq 0 \Rightarrow n = d * (n \text{ div } d) + (n \text{ mod } d) \qquad\qquad \text{[Law]}$$

is a law that is *true* for any integer expressions we might write in place of the place-holders n and d (notice how the implication takes care of division by zero). This law expresses the definitions of integer division div and remainder mod.

In some laws the place-holders do not just stand for expressions; they stand for whole predicates. For example

$$p \vee \neg\, p \qquad\qquad\qquad\qquad\qquad \text{[Excluded middle]}$$

is a law. It is always *true*, for any predicate we might substitute for the place-holder p. This is the famous *law of the excluded middle*, which says that in our logic, a predicate is either *true* or *false*. There are many laws like this one that describe the properties of the logical connectives. For example *DeMorgan's Law* explains how to negate a conjunction: Form the disjunction of the negated conjuncts.

$$\neg\, (p \wedge q) \Leftrightarrow \neg\, p \vee \neg\, q \qquad\qquad\qquad \text{[DeMorgan]}$$

We used DeMorgan's law to calculate the schema negation in section 12.4.2. We used this *distributive* law to simplify the predicate of *T_Forward* in section 12.2.3.

$$(p \wedge q) \vee (p \wedge r) \Leftrightarrow p \wedge (q \vee r) \qquad\qquad \text{[Distributivity]}$$

Where do laws come from? The short answer is: They are written down in books. All the laws can be derived from just a few, but I can simplify this book enormously by taking the laws as givens and stating them without justification. The laws used in the book are collected in Appendix E. It is possible to create new laws from the ones we already have in much the same way we prove ordinary predicates.

Exercise 15.2.1   The proof of $2 * x + 7 = 13 \Leftrightarrow x = 3$ in Section 15.1 used informal justifications such as "divide both sides by two." This style of reasoning is formally justified by *Leibniz' Law*, which says that equality is preserved by function application: $x = y \Rightarrow f\ x = f\ y$ (where f is a function and x is in the domain of f). Find each step in the proof where Leibniz' law is applied, and identify the functions used in those steps.

Exercise 15.3.1   Leibniz' Law is an implication, not an equivalence. When is $x = y \Leftrightarrow f\ x = f\ y$ true?

15.3   Checking specifications

We can use formal reasoning to check our work for certain kinds of errors and oversights. This is one of the most important qualities that distinguishes a formal method from informal ones.

In the course of writing a complex specification it is not difficult to write formulas that conflict. This error is called *inconsistency*. There are systematic ways to apply formal reasoning to discover certain kinds of inconsistencies.

For example, every system has a special state in which it starts up, which is usually named *Init*. If the specification is consistent, this initial state must statisfy the state invariant, so the predicate $\exists\ State \bullet Init$ must be *true*. This predicate is called the *Initialization Theorem*. It seems obvious, but errors involving initial states are not uncommon; programs that are supposed to manage a collection of files sometimes crash when all of the files are absent or empty. For our editor example this requirement becomes

   $\exists\ Editor \bullet Init$

which can be read, "There exists an *Editor* that satisfies the predicate of *Init*." It expands to

   $\exists\ left, right : TEXT \mid \#(left \frown right) \leq maxsize \bullet left = right = \langle\rangle$

This can be paraphrased, "There exist two texts whose combined length does not exceed *maxsize*, and both texts are empty." This is obviously true; our initial state is consistent with our state invariant. In this simple example there is no need for any further formal investigation, but in Section 15.4 we will learn some techniques that would enable us to prove this predicate formally.

15.4 Precondition calculation

Many actual program failures occur because programmers did not account for all the *preconditions* — the conditions that must be satisfied before an operation can be invoked. In the text editor study in Section 7.6 our first attempt to define the operation that moves the cursor forward was inadequate because it failed to account for the situation where the cursor is already at the end of the file. If we had implemented that first version, we might have produced a faulty program that could crash, losing all the users' work. In Chapter 7 we discovered the precondition by experience and insight. In fact, we don't have to depend on intuition: We can can calculate the precondition of any operation defined by a Z schema.

The precondition of an operation is a predicate that describes all the starting states in which the operation is defined. Therefore the precondition only contains unprimed "before" variables and input variables, but no primed "after" variables or output variables. Sometimes the precondition is explicitly written out in the operation schema, and we can find it by inspection. For example, here is the second version of the *Forward* operation from Section 7.6:

$$
\begin{array}{|l}
\hline
\_Forward\_\rule{4cm}{0pt}\rule{4cm}{0pt}\\
\Delta Editor\\
ch? : CHAR\\
\hline
ch? = right\_arrow\\
right \neq \langle\rangle\\
left' = left \frown \langle head(right)\rangle\\
right' = tail(right)\\
\hline
\end{array}
$$

Here the precondition is simply the predicate that defines the input variable and the uprimed state variable:

$$ch? = right\_arrow \wedge right \neq \langle\rangle$$

An operation is total when the predicates in the precondition that define the "before" state variables cover all possibilities; that is, when they are equivalent to *true*. Clearly *Forward* is not a total operation because $right \neq \langle\rangle$ doesn't cover the case where $right = \langle\rangle$. We defined an augmented operation *T_Forward* to account for that case. Here is the expanded version of *T_Forward* from Section 12.2.3:

$\boxed{\begin{array}{l} \underline{\;T\_Forward\;}\rule{6cm}{0pt} \\ \Delta Editor \\ ch? : CHAR \\ \rule{8cm}{0.4pt} \\ ch? = right\_arrow \\ ((right \neq \langle\rangle \wedge left' = left \frown \langle head\ right\rangle \wedge right' = tail\ right) \vee \\ (right = \langle\rangle \wedge left' = left \wedge right' = right)) \end{array}}$

Extracting the predicates where the "before" variables are defined, we obtain:

$$(right \neq \langle\rangle) \vee (right = \langle\rangle)$$

The *T_Forward* operation is total because this disjunction covers all possibilities. This example illustrates a common pattern in Z: Preconditions are disjunctions where each disjunct models a different case; the cases are supposed to cover all possibilities, so the disjunction should be equivalent to *true*. It is often possible to check this by inspection. In this example we can easily confirm our inspection formally: The disjunction is equivalent to *true* because it matches the law of the excluded middle, $p \vee \neg p$.

Sometimes the precondition of an operation is implicit; we cannot easily find it by inspection. This situation arises when the predicate in the operation definition interacts with the state invariant. Consider the *Insert* operation that puts a character into the text buffer to the left of the cursor. Here is our definition from section 12.1.3:

$\boxed{\begin{array}{l} \underline{\;Insert\;}\rule{7cm}{0pt} \\ \Delta Editor \\ ch? : CHAR \\ \rule{7cm}{0.4pt} \\ ch? \in printing \\ left' = left \frown \langle ch?\rangle \\ right' = right \end{array}}$

Does this operation always work, or does it have some preconditions that aren't obvious? Let's calculate the precondition.

The precondition of an operation describes all the initial states where the operation is defined. The precondition of operation schema Op on state schema S is described by the schema expression $\exists S' \bullet Op$: "There exists a final state that satisfies the predicate of the operation schema." In our example this becomes

$$\exists Editor' \bullet Insert$$

Recall from section 12.1.1 that *Editor* is the text editor's state schema.

```
┌─ Editor ──────────────────────────────────────────────
│ left, right : TEXT
│ ─────────────────────
│ #(left ⌢ right) ≤ maxsize
└──────────────────────────────────────────────────────
```

To express the schema expression $\exists\, Editor' \bullet Insert$ as a predicate, we write all the formulas in *Editor*, remembering to prime all the state variables and then write the predicate only of *Insert* (section 12.1.3).

$$\exists\, left', right' : TEXT \mid \#(left' \frown right') \leq maxsize \bullet$$
$$ch? \in printing \land left' = left \frown \langle ch? \rangle \land right' = right$$

In this predicate the primed variables *left'* and *right'* from the final state are bound, and the input variable and the unprimed variables from the initial state are free. It is understood that these free variables satisfy the declarations in *Insert*.

Now this is just an ordinary predicate with all the Z schema calculus removed, so we can use any of the laws of ordinary discrete mathematics and logic to simplify it. We recall from Chapter 11 that restriction in an existentially quantified predicate is an abbreviation for conjunction. This can be expressed by a law

$$(\exists\, d \mid p \bullet q) \Leftrightarrow (\exists\, d \bullet p \land q) \qquad \text{[Restricted } \exists \text{-quantifier]}$$

Applying this law, we obtain

$$\exists\, left', right' : TEXT \bullet$$
$$ch? \in printing \land \#(left' \frown right') \leq maxsize \land$$
$$left' = left \frown \langle ch? \rangle \land right' = right$$

We can eliminate the existential quantifier because the predicate contains equations that assign fixed values to the bound variables. This is expressed formally by a law called the *One-point rule*:

$$(\exists\, x : T \bullet x = e \land p) \Leftrightarrow p[e/x] \qquad \text{[One-point rule]}$$

The notation $p[e/x]$ means p with e substituted for x. Applying the one-point rule with the equations $left' = left \frown \langle ch? \rangle$ and $right' = right$, we obtain

$$\#ch? \in printing \land ((left \frown \langle ch? \rangle) \frown right) \leq maxsize$$

Now the primed variables have disappeared, and the predicate only contains input variables and unprimed variables from the initial state — just as we would expect for a precondition.

To review our progress so far we express the steps in our standard proof format, using *pr* to abbreviate *ch*? ∈ *printing*.

$\exists\, Editor' \bullet Insert$ [Definition of precondition]

$\Leftrightarrow \exists\, left', right' : TEXT \mid \ldots \bullet \ldots$ [Expand schemas]

$\Leftrightarrow \exists\, left', right' : TEXT \bullet \ldots \wedge \ldots$ [Restricted ∃-quantifier]

$\Leftrightarrow pr \wedge \#((left \frown \langle ch?\rangle) \frown right) \leq maxsize$ [One-point rule]

Now the calculation proceeds quickly. We apply some laws about sequences: $\#(s \frown t) = \#s + \#t$ (the length of a sequence is the sum of the lengths of its components) and $\#\langle x\rangle = 1$ (the length of a singleton sequence is one).

$\Leftrightarrow pr \wedge \#((left \frown \langle ch?\rangle) \frown right) \leq maxsize$ [see above]

$\Leftrightarrow pr \wedge \#left + \#\langle ch?\rangle + \#right \leq maxsize$ $[\#(s \frown t) = \#s + \#t]$

$\Leftrightarrow pr \wedge \#left + 1 + \#right \leq maxsize$ $[\#\langle x\rangle = 1]$

$\Leftrightarrow pr \wedge \#left + \#right < maxsize$ [Arithmetic]

This completes the calculation. The precondition of *Insert* is *ch*? ∈ *printing* ∧ *#left* + *#right* < *maxsize*. When the input is a printing character, the number of characters to the left and right of the cursor must be less than the buffer size. In other words, the buffer must have room for at least one more character, or the *Insert* operation won't work. To make our editor robust, we have to define a total version of the insert operation that handles the full buffer case somehow. Perhaps it should just discard *ch*? and leave the buffer contents unchanged.

Perhaps the precondition in this example is obvious, but many software failures result from errors that seem obvious in retrospect. This precondition concerns a *resource limitation*: What happens when the editor runs out of memory? Many failures are examples of resource limitations. When real-time programs run out of time, they miss a deadline; when calculations run out of numbers, they overflow.

What is important in this example is that the calculation did not depend on our intuitions about buffers becoming full; it used a general technique that can be applied to any operation. In this example the precondition was just what we expected, but in more complicated examples, the calculation sometimes reveals unexpected preconditions.

15.5 Formal reasoning and intuition

Most reasoning is informal, even in "logical" subjects like science, mathematics, and computing. Most proofs in textbooks and journals are informal: They contain formulas, but the proofs themselves are not formulas. Informal reasoning draws on all kinds of knowledge and reaches conclusions without making the steps explicit. Perhaps there are no steps; the conclusions come in a flash of intuition.

In formal reasoning the steps are explicit. Moreover, the validity of a formal proof depends only on the *syntax* (shape or appearance) of the formulas. A formal proof in the format of this chapter is valid if every pair of successive lines matches a law. The proof does not depend on the *semantics* (meaning or denotation) of the formulas at all. It does not matter what the symbols in the proof represent. Your knowledge of the application and your intuitions about what the symbols mean may help you discover a formal proof, but they have no bearing on the validity of the proof itself. In this sense formal proof is profoundly counter-intuitive.

The uncommon sense of formal reasoning is valuable exactly because it works so differently from ordinary reasoning. It can act as an independent check on intuition. Programming problems can be very intricate and intuition can fool you. And sometimes when intuition fails and you are stumped, the shape of a formula can suggest a solution you might have overlooked.

15.5.1 A caution

Most proofs involve a few insights and a lot of details. Authors try to present the insights and gloss over the rest, instead of listing every step in mind-numbing detail (in our precondition example we didn't bother to prove that the length of the singleton sequence is one, $\#\langle x \rangle = 1$). It is a matter of judgment when the proof is complete, a consensus decision by the authors and their audience. The reviewers' main job — after checking for outright errors — is to determine whether the level of formal detail is appropriate.

Because it depends on judgment and consensus, proof is a social process. Like any social process, it is fallible. Eliding details achieves brevity but incurs a risk of error. There are many cases where published proofs by distinguished experts were found to be invalid [Gerhart and Yelowitz, 1976; DeMillo, Lipton, and Perlis, 1979; Rushby and von Henke, 1991].

15.6 Machine-checked proof

A formal proof is a kind of formula, so it can be analyzed by a machine. The little proofs in this chapter (when stripped of annotations) are ordinary predicates that can be processed by any Z type checker. One can imagine a more ambitious program that checks each step in a proof to ensure that it matches a law; it might relieve the author of some tedium and help reviewers overcome the fallibility of the social process. Such programs exist; they are usually called *theorem provers* because most can generate some proofs automatically. However, it is not possible to construct an algorithm that can prove every predicate in a notation as expressive as Z[1]. Proof demands creativity and invention, and practical theorem provers all require guidance by an expert who must often develop the proof to greater detail than many human reviewers would demand.

Enlisting the computer to help check proofs of very difficult algorithms — such as synchronizing multiple processors in the presence of faults — has revealed errors in published proofs that were developed and reviewed by distinguished human experts. "A mechanical theorem prover ... (acts) as an implacable skeptic that insists on all assumptions being stated and all claims justified." [Rushby and von Henke, 1991]

A new technique called *model checking* provides another way to automate the analysis of formal specifications. In contrast to the purely syntactic techniques discussed thus far, a model checker constructs and then checks a representation (or "model") of all the conditions described by the formulas. For example if the formulas describe a state transition system, a model checker constructs a representation of its state transition diagram. Judicious assignment of conditions into equivalence classes can make it feasible to use model checking on systems that have a great many states [Jackson, 1994; Jackson and Damon, 1996].

---

[1] This famous result was established by Alan Turing in the 1930's [Mackenzie, 1995].

Further reading

An innovative approach to the material covered here in Chapters 9, 10, and 15 is explored by Gries and Schneider in *A Logical Approach to Discrete Math* [1993]. They emphasize formal proof throughout and give detailed instruction in techniques of symbolic (as opposed to merely arithmetic) calculation.

The textbook by Newton-Smith [1985], the monograph by Van Gasteren [1990], and the paper by Ohlbach [1985] are particularly good on the subtleties and pitfalls of expressing English statements in formal logic.

The prime number examples in Chapter 11 are from a paper by Gravell [1991].

Jim Woodcock's tutorial paper "Structuring Specifications in Z" [1989b] provides many examples that illustrate the versatility of schemas.

According to the brief history in Woodcock's paper, schemas evolved gradually. They began as simple macros for naming and abbreviating chunks of mathematical text. Only later did people realize they could represent states and operations. The notion that schemas introduce a new kind of type and denote sets of bindings emerged later still.

A denotational semantics for Z based on sets of bindings is developed by Mike Spivey in his book, *Understanding Z: A Specification Language and its Formal Semantics* [1988]. A similar semantics is proposed in the draft Z standard [Nicholls, 1995]. The draft also proposes standard notation for schema types and bindings.

The best explanations of genericity and free types are in Spivey's *Reference Manual* and also *Understanding Z*. The free type example in Chapter 14 comes from the manual for a typesetting and type-checking tool [Spivey, 1992a]. An example in Diller's textbook [1990] uses free types to describe the syntax of predicates, in order to specify a theorem prover. Several other examples appear in the book by Barden, Stepney, and Cooper [1994].

The *Reference Manual* also provides more complete explanations of schema composition and piping, and defines a few additional schema operators that are not discussed in this book.

The proof style taught in Chapter 15 is called the *equational* style (even though it isn't just for equations). This style is used by Van Gasteren [1990], Cohen [1990], Kaldewaij [1990], and Hehner [1993], and is central in the textbook by Gries and Schneider [1993]. Hehner observed that a proof in this style is just an ordinary predicate.

Woodcock's paper [1989b] includes many equational proofs about Z specifications, and another paper presents a larger investigation of a memory management system [Woodcock, 1989a]. A calculation by Spivey [1990] reveals a potentially hazardous deadlock in the kernel of the real-time operating system for an X-ray machine. Jonathan Unger and I report some proofs from a programming project in our paper [1995].

Most Z textbooks use equational proof but also teach different proof systems called *natural deduction* and *sequent calculus* (see the texts by Woodcock and Loomes [1990], Diller [1990], Potter *et al.* [1991], and Wordsworth [1992]). Proofs in these systems are not just predicates; it is necessary to introduce additional formal notation to present them. Gries and Schneider [1993] compare natural deduction to the equational style.

In addition to the mathematical tool-kit in the *Reference Manual*, there are large collections of laws (in slightly different syntax) in the books by Morgan [1994], Hehner [1993], and Gries and Schneider [1993]. Gries and Schneider and also Cohen discuss Leibniz' law.

The *Reference Manual*, Woodcock's paper, and all the Z textbooks discuss precondition calculations.

You need a technique called *induction* to prove many properties of integers, sets, sequences and linked data structures. A chapter in Paulson's textbook [1991] illustrates induction with many examples involving data structures much like those we use in Z.

Mackenzie provides a historical review of theorem provers [1995], and Paulson develops a small prover in a textbook chapter [1991]. Popular provers include NQTHM (the Boyer-Moore prover) [Boyer and Moore, 1988], HOL [Gordon and Melham, 1993], EVES [Craigen, 1995] and PVS [Owre *et al.*, 1995]. Extensions for handling Z formulas have been added to EVES [Meisels and Saaltink, 1995] and HOL [Bowen and Gordon, 1995].

Jackson [1994] and Jackson and Damon [1996] have applied model checking to Z specifications. Wing and Vaziri-Farahani [1995] proved some properties of a distributed file system by model checking.

Part IV

Studies in Z

16 Document control system

In this chapter we'll model a simple document control system in Z. People who work together need to share their work, but there are many opportunities for misunderstandings and confusion. Errors can be introduced when two people working on the same thing — a file of program code, for example — make changes that conflict with each other. We can enlist the computer to help prevent such errors: This is the purpose of a document control system. Real examples include SCCS (source code control system) and RCS (revision control system) [Tichy, 1982].

Here is an excerpt from the informal description:

> If a user wants to check out a document in order to change the document and the user has the permission to change it, and nobody else is changing it at the moment, then that user may check the document out.
> As soon as a user has checked out a document for editing everyone else is disallowed from checking it out (of course people with read permission can read it).
> When the user is done editing the document, it should be checked in, allowing another user to check it out.

Here is the Z model. We begin by introducing two basic sets that hold everything of interest in this universe, namely people and documents:

$[PERSON, DOCUMENT]$

Some people have permission to change particular documents. We can model that as a relation on documents and people:

$permission : DOCUMENT \leftrightarrow PERSON$

This relation is just a set of pairs of the form $(document, person)$. For example, Doug can change the specification, Aki and Doug can change the design, and Aki and Phil can change the code.

$$doug, aki, phil : PERSON$$
$$spec, design, code : DOCUMENT$$

$$permission = \{(spec, doug), (design, doug), (design, aki), (code, aki),$$
$$(code, phil)\}$$

The state of the system is merely another relation of the same type, this one saying which documents are actually checked out to whom. The central requirement is that a document can only be checked out to one person at a time, so in this case the relation is a function: It associates each object in the domain with a single object in the range.

```
┌─ Documents ──────────────────────────────
│ checked_out : DOCUMENT ↦ PERSON
│
│ checked_out ⊆ permission
└───────────────────────────────────────────
```

Note that *checked_out* is a partial function, indicated by the stroke through the arrow ↦. This means that some documents might not be checked out to anybody. The predicate says that documents can only be checked out to people who have permission to change them.

A possible state of our system occurs when Doug has checked out the specification and design, and Phil has checked out the code.

$$checked\_out = \{(design, doug), (spec, doug), (code, phil)\}$$

We need two operations that change the state, *CheckOut* and *CheckIn*. Here is *CheckOut*. It has two input parameters, the person $p?$ and the document $d?$.

```
┌─ CheckOut ──────────────────────────────
│ ΔDocuments
│ p? : PERSON
│ d? : DOCUMENT
│
│ d? ∉ dom checked_out
│ (d?, p?) ∈ permission
│ checked_out' = checked_out ∪ {(d?, p?)}
└───────────────────────────────────────────
```

CheckOut has two preconditions. They are the predicates that contain no primed "after" variables. First, document $d?$ can't already be checked out: It can't be in the domain of *checked_out*. Moreover, the person doing the checking out needs permission: $(d?, p?)$ must belong to *permission*. If the preconditions are satisfied we add the pair $(d?, p?)$ to *checked_out*; this prevents anyone else from checking out $d?$.

We must account for cases where the preconditions are not satisfied. There are two preconditions, so there must be two such cases. *CheckedOut* says that the document is already checked out: $d? \in$ dom *checked_out*. *Unauthorized* expresses that the person does not have permission: $(d?, p?) \notin$ *permission*. In both cases nothing gets checked out and the state of the system does not change: Ξ *Documents*.

$$CheckedOut \; \hat{=} \; [\; \Xi Documents; \; d? : DOCUMENT \mid d? \in \text{dom } checked\_out \;]$$

$$\begin{array}{l}
\underline{\text{Unauthorized}} \\
\Xi Documents \\
p? : PERSON \\
d? : DOCUMENT \\
\hline
(d?, p?) \notin permission \\
\end{array}$$

The total operation $T\_CheckOut$ covers all three possibilities.

$$T\_CheckOut \; \hat{=} \; CheckOut \vee CheckedOut \vee Unauthorized$$

This concludes our presentation. This little study illustrates some typical features of Z models:

You can ignore details in order to focus on the aspects of the problem in which you are interested. Here we concentrated on permissions and keeping track of who has checked out what. We did not model actually copying documents back and forth between the central repository and users' local directories. We modelled the collections of documents and users as fixed sets, and the permissions as a constant. A real document control system would have to provide some way to enter new documents into the system and delete old ones, and there would also have to be a way to assign and change permissions. If we wished to model all that in Z we could represent people, documents, and permissions as variables in the state schema instead of basic types and global constants.

Models should be simple. If you find yourself writing complicated functions and quantified predicates, it is usually a sign that you are on the wrong track. Let the basic properties of sets, relations and functions do the work for you. The requirement that only one person at a time can check out a document can be neatly expressed by a function.

The requirements about permissions can be represented by letting the *checked_out* function be a subset of the *permission* relation. In Z, functions are relations and relations are sets, so operators defined for sets also apply to relations and functions, and you can put them all together in the same expressions. This is an advantage of Z that you don't find in every formal notation.

Exercise 16.1   Define the normal *CheckIn* operation, and a total *T_CheckIn* operation that accounts for the exceptional cases.

17 Text processing

This chapter continues our investigations into text processing. In Chapters 7 and 12 we modelled the state of a simple text editor as nothing more than a sequence of characters. In this chapter we add a little more structure: words and lines. This will enable us to model a word counting utility and format operations such as filling paragraphs.

17.1 Breaking a text into words

Once again we begin by defining a set of characters. A text is just a sequence of characters. Certain characters are *blanks*. Spaces, line breaks, and tabs are certainly blanks, but we might also choose to include punctuation marks and other special characters. In fact, we define a *word* to be a sequence of nonblank characters, so a blank is any character that might separate two words. A *space* is a sequence of blank characters.

$$[CHAR]$$

$$blank : \mathbb{P}\, CHAR$$

$$TEXT == \text{seq}\, CHAR$$
$$SPACE == \text{seq}_1\, blank$$
$$WORD == \text{seq}_1 (CHAR \setminus blank)$$

TEXT includes the empty sequence, but *SPACE* and *WORD* must have at least one character, so we declare them to be seq_1 (nonempty sequences).

Our word counting and formatting utilities are based on a function called *words*. The *words* function returns the sequence of all the words in a text. For example,

$$words \langle H, o, w, \ , a, r, e, \ , y, o, u, ? \rangle = \langle \langle H, o, w \rangle, \langle a, r, e \rangle, \langle y, o, u \rangle \rangle$$

Clearly *words* is a total function from a *TEXT* to a sequence of *WORD*. To define *words*, we consider all possible patterns of words and spaces, and write an equation for each.

$words : TEXT \to \text{seq}\, WORD$

$\forall s : SPACE;\ w : WORD;\ l, r : TEXT \bullet$
   $words \langle\rangle = \langle\rangle \wedge$
   $words\ s = \langle\rangle \wedge$
   $words\ w = \langle w \rangle \wedge$
   $words\ (s \frown r) = words\ r \wedge$
   $words\ (l \frown s) = words\ l \wedge$
   $words\ (l \frown s \frown r) = (words\ l) \frown (words\ r)$

As you can see, there really aren't so many patterns. When the text is empty, the result is empty. When the text is nothing but space, the result is empty too. When the text is a single word, the result is a sequence that contains just that word. When the text begins or ends with a space, you can strip it off; the result is the same. Wherever the interior of the text contains a space, you can discard the space and break the text in two. That's it.

This example illustrates several Z techniques that can make definitions shorter and clearer than code. The function is applied to *patterns* like $l \frown s \frown r$ that reveal the internal structure of their arguments. If you think in terms of code that has to work its way through the text from beginning to end, you can't use patterns in this way. The definition is *recursive*: The function being defined can appear on both sides of an equation. (The definition is not circular: By repeatedly applying the equations to any text, we will eventually arrive at the simple cases.) Finally, the last equation is *nondeterministic*: It doesn't tell us where to begin breaking between words; any space is as good as another. We don't need to assume that the text will be scanned in order from beginning to end.

The definition might seem obvious, but it includes cases that are often forgotten. Published programs that purport to fill paragraphs break down when presented with an empty file or a text that ends with a series of blank lines. The errors are not just coding bugs; they reveal a failure to understand the problem fully. Writing formal definitions encourages us to think carefully about all the cases. We don't have to complain, as some programmers do, that there are so many possibilities we can't consider them all.

17.2 A word counting utility

The number of words in text t is simply $\#(words\ t)$. We can define a function similar to *words* that breaks a text into lines. We consider a line break to be a special blank character named *nl* (for new line).

> $lines : TEXT \rightarrow \text{seq}\ LINE$
> ――――――――
> ... definition omitted ...

Now we have everything we need to write a formal specification for the Unix word counting utility *wc*. This popular utility is actually a function whose argument is a file name, and whose result is a tuple whose components are the number of lines, words, and characters in the file. A typical application looks like this:

```
% wc structure.tex

110 559 4509
```

Here is the definition of *wc*:

> $wc : TEXT \rightarrow (\mathbb{N} \times \mathbb{N} \times \mathbb{N})$
> ――――――――
> $\forall file : TEXT \bullet$
> $\qquad wc\ file = (\#(lines\ file), \#(words\ file), \#file)$

Or, if you like to be more terse

$$wc == (\lambda\ file : TEXT \bullet (\#(lines\ file), \#(words\ file), \#file))$$

17.3 Filling paragraphs

Almost any text editor provides a *fill* operation. The fill operation transforms raggedy-looking text with lines of different lengths into nicely formatted text with lines nearly the same length.

For example, you can type in something that looks like this:

```
Almost any text editor provides a fill
operation. The fill operation transforms raggedy-looking text
with lines of
different lengths into nicely formatted text with lines
nearly the same length.
```

and then you can use the fill operation to turn it into this:

```
Almost any text editor provides a fill operation.  The
fill operation transforms raggedy-looking text with lines of
different lengths into nicely formatted text with lines
nearly the same length.
```

Let's define the fill operation in Z. We observe that fill is just one example of a *format* operation that changes the appearance of a text by breaking lines in different places and expanding or contracting the spaces between words, subject to the constraint that no line exceeds the page width. Moreover, a format operation must not change the content of the text: It preserves the same words in their original order.

$$\mid width : \mathbb{N}$$

$$
\begin{array}{|l}
\underline{\;Format\;\rule{8cm}{0.4pt}} \\
\; t, t' : TEXT \\
\hline
\; words\ t' = words\ t \\
\; \forall l : \text{ran}\ (lines\ t') \bullet \#l \leq width \\
\end{array}
$$

The fill operation is a format operation that satisfies an additional constraint: The lines should be filled as much as possible. There are many different ways to express this, and each one results in a slightly different appearance to the text. Perhaps the simplest rule is to require that the filled text occupy the fewest possible lines.

$$
\begin{array}{|l}
\underline{\;Fill\;\rule{8cm}{0.4pt}} \\
\; Format \\
\hline
\; \#(lines\ t') = min\ \{t' : TEXT \mid Format \bullet \#(lines\ t')\} \\
\end{array}
$$

This definition says that *Fill* is essentially a *minimization* operation: It is the specialization of *Format* that minimizes the number of lines. The schema is a little tricky because *Format* is used in two different ways and different occurrences of t' represent different things. The t' on the left of the equal sign is the final state of *Fill*. The t' inside the set comprehension is different: It is a bound variable that ranges over all final states of *Format* that can be reached from the initial state of *Fill*. Inside the set comprehension, *Format* is used as a predicate. The t in this *Format* is free: It is the initial state of the enclosing schema *Fill*.

Fill is nondeterministic. There are usually many different ways to place line breaks and spaces that achieve the same minimal number of lines. In specifications, nondeterminism is usually a good thing. We should only ask for what we really want. Nondeterministic definitions are often shorter and clearer because they can omit unimportant details. When we come to implementation, they give us the freedom to make choices that can increase efficiency or convenience. Moreover, nondeterministic definitions enable us to build up specifications by a process of increasing specialization. Just as *Fill* is a specialization of *Format*, we can define specializations of *Fill* to achieve different effects such as justified right margins or minimal spaces between words. Z was designed to support this style of definition by specialization. It makes the formal texts easy to understand and enables us to reuse general definitions.

Exercise 17.3.1   Does *Format* have any preconditions?

Exercise 17.3.2   Define *Justify*, the specialization of *Fill* that produces justified right margins. (The last character in every line is aligned at a fixed right margin.)

18 Eight queens

We have already learned how Z can be used to describe data structures. Sometimes the solution to a problem is just a data structure that has some particular properties. In that case, the description of the data structure is the central element in the whole specification. A well-known example is the problem of the eight queens.

Many books on programming show how to solve the problem of the eight queens (for example, see Wirth [1976]). Here is the problem statement in English:

> Eight queens must be placed on a chessboard so that no queen attacks any others. A chessboard is a square grid with eight columns, or *files*, and eight rows, or *ranks*. When a queen is placed on a square, it attacks any other queen that sits on the same rank, file, or diagonals.

Figure 18.1 illustrates one solution to the problem.

This is not a problem of great practical significance, but it does illustrate some common difficulties of prose specifications: They usually turn out to be imprecise and incomplete. The English problem statement is usually considered sufficient because "everybody knows what it means." When we write real specifications, usually everybody does *not* know what is needed. When we write the program, we can't appeal to visual impressions and intuitions. Could you explain the eight queens problem to somebody who had never seen a chessboard? What if you had to communicate by telephone and couldn't refer to a picture? What exactly *is* a "diagonal" anyway?

We can do it in Z. We'll build a model of the chessboard using numbers and arithmetic. We begin by numbering the files and ranks from one to eight, starting with the lower left square. Then the solution shown in Figure 18.1 becomes:

$$\{ 1 \mapsto 8,\ 2 \mapsto 4,\ 3 \mapsto 1,\ 4 \mapsto 3,\ 6 \mapsto 2,\ 7 \mapsto 7,\ 8 \mapsto 5 \}$$

In this form it is clear that the solution is a mathematical structure, not a picture. What is it about this particular structure that makes it a solution? It should be possible to express that in mathematics as well.

Q							
						Q	
			Q				
							Q
	Q						
		Q					
				Q			
		Q					

Figure 18.1: A solution to the eight queens problem.

We begin by defining some synonyms to make our specification easy to read.

$SIZE == 8$

$FILE == 1 .. SIZE$

$RANK == 1 .. SIZE$

$SQUARE == FILE \times RANK$

Every solution is a set of *SQUARE*. We begin to write a schema, using the predefined functions *first* and *second* to extract the elements of each pair:

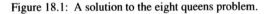

```
┌─ Queens ─────────────────────────────────────────────
│ squares : ℙ SQUARE
├──────────────────────────────────────────────────────
│ #squares = SIZE
│ ∀ s1, s2 : squares | s1 ≠ s2 •
│       first s1 ≠ first s2 ∧ second s1 ≠ second s2
│ ...
└──────────────────────────────────────────────────────
```

The complicated predicate here merely says that there are eight queens, and no two of them can occupy the same file or the same rank. What a long-winded mess! We really don't need all this formal text — the situation it describes is so common that it is already defined in the standard Z tool-kit. It is a *bijection*, a function that maps every element of its domain to every element of its range, in one-to-one correspondence. Z provides a special symbol for bijections, and the declaration becomes

$$squares : FILE \rightarrowtail\!\!\!\!\twoheadrightarrow RANK$$

This declaration conveys everything we need to say about the files and ranks, so we needn't mention them again in the predicate.

Next, I'll describe the diagonals. For now, it helps to look at a picture (Figure 18.2). This is just to help us get started; when we have completed our Z specification, we won't need the picture anymore.

Each square sits on two diagonals: One slants up, the other, down. Each diagonal can be identified by the number of the rank where it intercepts the left edge of the board (we have to imagine the board extending up and down). We can calculate the intercept of any diagonal by using the equation of a line:

$$rank = slope \times file + intercept$$

The slopes are just 1 and -1 for the up and down diagonals, respectively, so we get:

$$up = rank - file$$

$$down = rank + file$$

We define functions that, given any square, return the up and down diagonals that pass through it:

$$DIAGONAL == 1 - SIZE .. 2 * SIZE$$

$$
\begin{array}{|l}
up, down : SQUARE \rightarrow DIAGONAL \\
\hline
\forall f : FILE;\ r : RANK \bullet \\
\quad up\,(f, r) = r - f \ \wedge \\
\quad down\,(f, r) = r + f
\end{array}
$$

Now we have all the pieces we need to complete the problem statement in Z. We know better than to start writing some complicated predicate with quantifiers and such. Instead, we look in the tool-kit for something suitable. We want to say that when the domain of the function *up* is restricted to the *squares* occupied by queens, each square is mapped to a different diagonal; the function is an *injection*. The tool-kit defines symbols for domain restriction $\lhd$ and injective functions $\rightarrowtail$. Function signatures

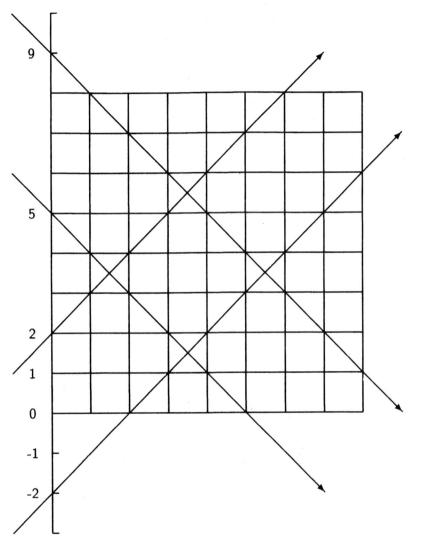

Figure 18.2: Numbering the diagonals for the eight queens problem.

such as *SQUARE* $\rightarrowtail$ *DIAGONAL* can appear in predicates as well as declarations, and we can use *expr* $\in$ *TYPE* to say that an expression has all the properties of a type in addition to any properties entailed by the declarations of its components:

$$\text{squares} \lhd \text{up} \in \text{SQUARE} \rightarrowtail \text{DIAGONAL}$$

The same can be said of *down*. We can eliminate repetition by collecting the two functions into a single set:

Eight queens

Eight queens must be placed on a chessboard so that no queen attacks any others. A chessboard is a square grid with eight columns, or *files*, and eight rows, or *ranks*. When a queen is placed on a square, it attacks any other queen that sits on the same rank, file, or diagonals.

$SIZE == 8$

$FILE == 1 .. SIZE$

$RANK == 1 .. SIZE$

$SQUARE == FILE \times RANK$

$DIAGONAL == 1 - SIZE .. 2 * SIZE$

$up, down : SQUARE \rightarrow DIAGONAL$

$\forall f : FILE;\ r : RANK \bullet$
$\quad up\,(f,r) = r - f \wedge$
$\quad down\,(f,r) = r + f$

___Queens_____
$squares : FILE \rightarrowtail\!\!\!\rightarrow RANK$

$\{\ squares \vartriangleleft up,\ squares \vartriangleleft down\ \} \subseteq SQUARE \rightarrowtail DIAGONAL$

Figure 18.3: Eight queens.

___Queens_____
$squares : FILE \rightarrowtail\!\!\!\rightarrow RANK$

$\{\ squares \vartriangleleft up,\ squares \vartriangleleft down\ \} \subseteq SQUARE \rightarrowtail DIAGONAL$

This completes the formal specification (Figure 18.3). The formal text is not much longer than the English problem statement, but it says much more, such as what a "diagonal" is. We don't need the picture any longer.

Our formal specification is much shorter and easier to understand than any program that could solve the problem. The solution shown in Figure 18.1 is just one of many; our specification describes all of them. The set of bindings *Queens* is the collection of all solutions to the problem. The formal model doesn't bias us toward any particular strategy for designing the program. Instead, it presents all the facts we would need to program a solution in any language — and nothing more.

Exercise 18.1   The eight queens problem models a single board position. A real chess game is a series of *moves*. In most moves, a single chess piece moves from one square to another, according to certain rules. For example, the queen can move to any square which lies on the same rank, file, or diagonals as the square that the queen occupied before the move.

Model the queen's moves in Z. You may assume that none of the potential destination squares is occupied by another piece.

Exercise 18.2   The knight's tour is another familiar computing problem inspired by chess. The knight moves in an L-shaped pattern (consult a chessplayer, or a book, for the exact rule). Model the knight's tour: a sequence of legal moves where a knight visits every square on the board exactly once.

19 Computer graphics and computational geometry

Z can describe data structures. In this chapter we'll use Z to define the fundamental objects of computer graphics and computational geometry: points, line segments, contours, and polygons.

Consider the distinction between a *contour*, which is any sequence of connected line segments, and a *polygon*, which is a closed contour that has an inside and an outside (Figure 19.1)[1]. Your eye can see the difference immediately, and the distinction is vital for many computations of great practical importance.

Figure 19.2 is a computer graphic that shows a view of a patient's anatomy and radiation beam geometry, used to plan this patient's radiation treatment for cancer. Cross-sections of anatomical structures must be polygons, not just contours, and the physics calculations that compute the radiation dose depend on this. If some contours are not closed, or cross over themselves, the dose calculations may be incorrect.

The difference between contours and polygons is vital, but there is no way to express this distinction in most programming languages: You have to represent both as mere sequences (arrays or lists) of points. Data types in programming languages correspond closely to the way data are represented in computer memory: If two objects are stored in the same format, they belong to the same data type. Z is far more expressive because we can distinguish data types based on their values and constraints between the values of their components. This enables us to define data types that capture such requirements as "a closed contour that doesn't cross over itself."

First let's define *contour*. A contour is a sequence of points. A point is represented in the usual way, as a pair of (x, y) coordinates. It works well enough to let the coordinates range over the integers, the only numeric type that comes already defined in Z. You can think of the integer coordinates as representing pixels on a display screen, rather than locations in real space. We define separate identifiers for the

---

[1] In some computer graphics literature our contour is called a *polyline*.

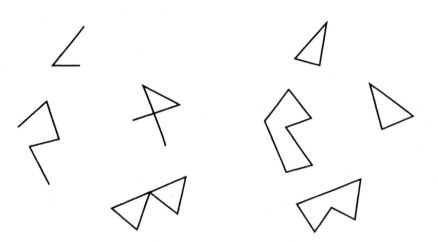

Figure 19.1: Some contours. The contours on the right are polygons.

x and y coordinates, so they can have different ranges. For example, to model a video display whose origin is the upper left corner of the screen, x might range over $0 .. 1280$ and y might range over $0 .. -1024$. For now we'll let x and y range over all the integers.

$$X == \mathbb{Z}$$

$$Y == \mathbb{Z}$$

$$POINT == X \times Y$$

$$CONTOUR == \text{seq } POINT$$

A polygon is a special kind of contour. The defining characteristic of a polygon is that it divides the plane into two regions, an inside and an outside. We have to express this formally, using only the data included in a contour. A polygon is a closed contour, and a contour is closed when its first and last points coincide. A polygon must enclose some area, so the simplest polygon we can have is a triangle, which contains four points, counting the duplicated point at the end. A polygon has just a single interior region; we don't allow shapes that cross over themselves like the figure eight. In other words, there are no duplicated points except the last point, and no segment in the contour intersects any others. The *Polygon* schema expresses these constraints:

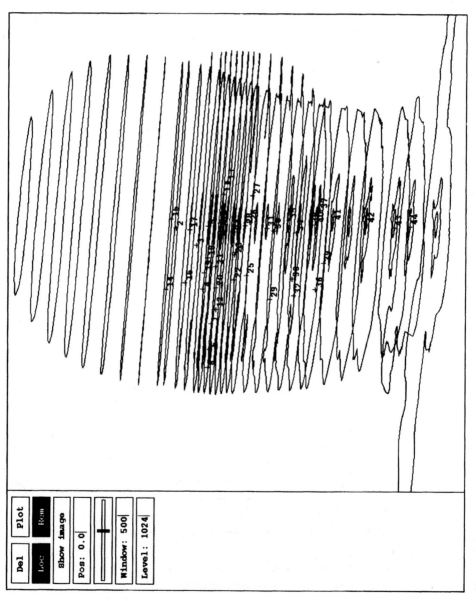

Figure 19.2: Polygons represent human anatomy in a radiation therapy treatment plan.

```
┌─ Polygon ──────────────────────────────────────────
│  c : CONTOUR
│ ───────────────────────────────────────────────────
│  #c ≥ 4
│  head c = last c
│  front c ∈ iseq POINT
│  ∀ s₁, s₂ : segments c | s₁ ≠ s₂ • ¬ (s₁ intersects s₂)
└────────────────────────────────────────────────────
```

The first line in the predicate says that the contour c has at least four points. The second line says that the first point is duplicated at the end; the *head* and *last* functions return the first and last elements of a sequence, respectively. The third line says that there are no duplicated points except the last point; the *front* function returns a sequence with the last element removed, and an injective sequence iseq has no duplicate elements. The last line says that no segment intersects any others. The *segments* function returns all the segments in a contour, and the predicate s_1 *intersects* s_2 is *true* when the two segments s_1 and s_2 cross over each other (however s_1 *intersects* s_2 is *false* when the two segments merely touch at their endpoints).

The functions *head, last,* and *front* and the abbreviation iseq are already defined in the Z mathematical tool-kit. We have to define the *segments* function and the *intersects* relation ourselves.

A segment is a pair of points. The *segments* function returns all the consecutive pairs of points in a contour. So if a, b, and c are points that form the triangular contour $\langle a, b, c, a \rangle$ then

$$segments \langle a, b, c, a \rangle = \{(a, b), (b, c), (c, a)\}$$

The formal definition uses the segment relation in from the mathematical tool-kit; s in t is *true* when sequence s forms a contiguous part of sequence t.

$$segments == (\lambda c : CONTOUR • \{ a, b : POINT | \langle a, b \rangle \text{ in } c \})$$

Now let's work on *intersects*. It helps to look at a picture. In Figure 19.3 contour $\langle a, b, c, d, e, f, g, h, i, e, k, l, a \rangle$ is closed because its first point a is duplicated at the end, but it is not a polygon because an interior point e is also duplicated and several of the segments intersect.

Two segments *intersect* each other if they actually *cross*, as segments (a, b) and (k, l) do in the figure. We require that a polygon has a single interior region, not two or more, so we say that two segments intersect even if they only *touch* each other, as segments (e, f) and (g, h) do in the figure. We will define two relations *crosses* and *touches* to express this.

A relation is *symmetric* if it means the same thing when its arguments are exchanged: $x \underline{R} y \Leftrightarrow y \underline{R} x$. Our *crosses* and *touches* relations are not symmetric;

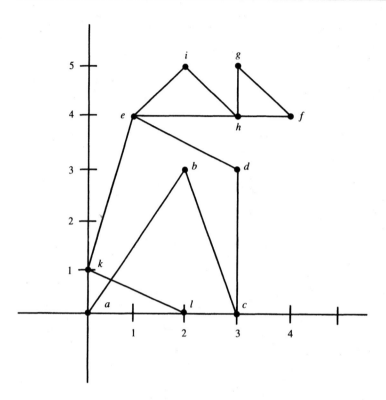

In contour $\langle a, b, c, d, e, f, g, h, i, e, k, l, a \rangle$, (a, b) _intersects_ (k, l) because
(a, b) _crosses_ (k, l). However (g, h) _intersects_ (e, f) because (g, h) _touches_ (e, f).

Figure 19.3: Contour intersections, crossings, and touchings.

they are *asymmetric*. We say (d, e) _crosses_ (a, b) because its two ends d and e lie on
opposite sides of the line through (a, b), however (a, b) does not cross (d, e) because
its two ends a and b both lie on the same side of (d, e). Also, (g, h) _touches_ (e, f)
because point h lies between e and f, but (e, f) does not touch (g, h) because
neither e nor f lies between g and h.

Two segments intersect if they both cross each other. In the figure
(a, b) _intersects_ (k, l) because (a, b) _crosses_ (k, l) and also (k, l) _crosses_ (a, b).
However (a, b) does not intersect (d, e) even though (d, e) crosses (a, b), because
(a, b) does not cross (d, e). Two segments intersect if either touches the other;
(e, f) _intersects_ (g, h) because (g, h) _touches_ (e, f) even though (e, f) does not
touch (g, h).

Now we can define *intersects* in terms of *crosses* and *touches*:

$SEGMENT == POINT \times POINT$

$intersects, crosses, touches : SEGMENT \leftrightarrow SEGMENT$

$\forall s_1, s_2 : SEGMENT \bullet$
$\qquad s_1 \; \underline{intersects} \; s_2 \Leftrightarrow$
$\qquad\qquad (s_1 \; \underline{crosses} \; s_2 \wedge s_2 \; \underline{crosses} \; s_1) \vee s_1 \; \underline{touches} \; s_2 \vee s_2 \; \underline{touches} \; s_1$

Exercise 19.1   Is the *intersects* relation symmetric?

To define *crosses* and *touches* we use some results from computational geometry. It turns out that we do not have to calculate the point of intersection to tell whether segments cross or touch. That is fortunate, because it usually isn't possible: The point of intersection cannot be represented in integer arithmetic at all. As you can see in the figure, the point of intersection between segments (a, b) and (k, l) does not lie on one of the integer grid points. Even when we can use floating point arithmetic, we should avoid calculating the intersection because the calculations have limited accuracy and might yield the wrong answer if the two segments are very short and nearly parallel.

There is another way to check for intersections, using a formula for calculating the area of a triangle from the coordinates of its vertices. According to this formula, the area is positive when the peak of the triangle lies on one side of the base and negative when it lies on the other side. We can use this formula to determine whether one segment crosses another.

The area formula uses the synonyms x and y for the predefined projection functions *first* and *second*: $x\,a$ and $y\,a$ are the x and y coordinates of point a, respectively[2].

$x == first; \;\; y == second$

$area2 == (\lambda\, a, b, c : POINT \bullet (x\,a) * (y\,b) - (y\,a) * (x\,b)$
$\qquad\qquad\qquad\qquad\qquad +(y\,a) * (x\,c) - (x\,a) * (y\,c)$
$\qquad\qquad\qquad\qquad\qquad +(x\,b) * (y\,c) - (x\,c) * (y\,b))$

The function is called *area2* because it actually calculates twice the area of the triangle. Twice the area is always an integer, but the area itself might not be. Consider the triangle (a, b, k) in the figure. We have $a = (0, 0)$, $b = (2, 3)$, and $k = (0, 1)$ so $area2(a, b, k) = 2$. Also $l = (2, 0)$ so $area2(a, b, l) = -6$. The two areas have opposite signs, so k and l lie on opposite sides of (a, b).

Now we can define *crosses*: $(c, d) \; \underline{crosses} \; (a, b)$ is *true* when $area2(a, b, c)$ and $area2(a, b, d)$ have opposite signs. When this condition is true, the product of the

---

[2] To be strictly correct, the definitions should actually be written $x == first[X, Y]$, etc., because *first* is a *generic* function. See Chapter 14.

two areas will be negative. In the following discussion, s_1 and s_2 are the segments (a, b) and (c, d), respectively. We package their definitions in a schema so we don't have to write them over and over.

```
┌─ Segments ──────────────────────────────────────
│  s₁, s₂ : SEGMENT
│  a, b, c, d : POINT
├──────────────────────────────────────────────────
│  s₁ = (a, b) ∧ s₂ = (c, d)
└──────────────────────────────────────────────────
```

Finally, here is the formal definition of *crosses*.

$$\forall \, Segments \; \bullet$$
$$s_2 \; \underline{crosses} \; s_1 \Leftrightarrow area2(a, b, c) * area2(a, b, d) < 0$$

We do not have to declare *crosses* here because we already declared it in the same paragraph where we defined *intersects*. This ability to declare objects before completing their definitions makes it possible to use a top-down definition style in Z.

The formal definition of *touches* uses the new relation *on*. The point a is *on* segment s if a is collinear with (lies on the same line as) s, and a lies between the two points of s. In the figure we have $h \; \underline{on} \; (e, f)$. We use *area2* for the collinearity test: The area is zero when the three points lie on the same line.

$$(collinear\_) == \{ \, a, b, c : POINT \mid area2(a, b, c) = 0 \, \}$$

It is not enough just to test for collinearity; h is also collinear with (c, d) but it does not lie on (c, d) because h is not between c and d. We can check whether one of three collinear points lies between two others by checking just the x or y coordinates. A number j lies between i and k if i, j, and k form an ascending or descending sequence.

$$(between\_) == \{ \, i, j, k : \mathbb{Z} \mid i < j < k \lor i > j > k \, \}$$

Our definition of *between* uses strict inequality ($<$ not $\leq$), so *between* is *false* if the point coincides with either end of the segment. We say that segments which coincide only at their endpoints do not touch (otherwise we would have to say that every segment in a polygon intersects its two neighbors, which is not what we want to express).

Now we can define *on*. We have to be careful about using *between* in the special cases where the line is vertical or horizontal.

Computational Geometry

$X == \mathbb{Z};\ Y == \mathbb{Z}$

$POINT == X \times Y$

$CONTOUR == \text{seq } POINT$

$SEGMENT == POINT \times POINT$

$x == first[X, Y];\ y == second[X, Y]$

$area2 == (\lambda a, b, c : POINT \bullet (x\ a) * (y\ b) - (y\ a) * (x\ b)$
$$+ (y\ a) * (x\ c) - (x\ a) * (y\ c)$$
$$+ (x\ b) * (y\ c) - (x\ c) * (y\ b))$$

$segments == (\lambda c : CONTOUR \bullet \{\, a, b : POINT \mid \langle a, b \rangle \text{ in } c \,\})$

$(between\_) == \{\, i, j, k : \mathbb{Z} \mid i < j < k \lor i > j > k \,\}$

$(collinear\_) == \{\, a, b, c : POINT \mid area2(a, b, c) = 0 \,\}$

$on : POINT \leftrightarrow SEGMENT$
$touches, crosses, intersects : SEGMENT \leftrightarrow SEGMENT$

$\forall s_1, s_2 : SEGMENT;\ a, b, c, d : POINT \mid s_1 = (a, b) \land s_2 = (c, d) \bullet$

$\quad (a \underline{\ on\ } s_2 \Leftrightarrow collinear(c, a, d) \land$
$$((x\ c \neq x\ d \land between(x\ c, x\ a, x\ d))$$
$$\lor (y\ c \neq y\ d \land between(y\ c, y\ a, y\ d))) \land$$

$\quad (s_1 \underline{\ touches\ } s_2 \Leftrightarrow a \underline{\ on\ } s_2 \lor b \underline{\ on\ } s_2) \land$

$\quad (s_2 \underline{\ crosses\ } s_1 \Leftrightarrow area2(a, b, c) * area2(a, b, d) < 0) \land$

$\quad (s_1 \underline{\ intersects\ } s_2 \Leftrightarrow$
$$(s_1 \underline{\ crosses\ } s_2 \land s_2 \underline{\ crosses\ } s_1) \lor s_1 \underline{\ touches\ } s_2 \lor s_2 \underline{\ touches\ } s_1)$$

Figure 19.4: Computational geometry definitions used by *Polygon*.

$on : POINT \leftrightarrow SEGMENT$

$\forall\, Segments \bullet$
$\qquad a \underline{\;on\;} s_2 \Leftrightarrow collinear(c, a, d) \wedge$
$\qquad\qquad\qquad ((x\, c \neq x\, d \wedge between(x\, c, x\, a, x\, d))$
$\qquad\qquad\qquad \vee (y\, c \neq y\, d \wedge between(y\, c, y\, a, y\, d)))$

Finally we can write the formal definition of *touches*.

$\forall\, Segments \bullet$
$\qquad s_1 \underline{\;touches\;} s_2 \Leftrightarrow a \underline{\;on\;} s_2 \vee b \underline{\;on\;} s_2$

This completes the development. We have described a data type: Every polygon is a binding of our *Polygon* schema. It is helpful to collect the definitions together in bottom-up (definition before use) order (Figure 19.4).

We have not specified any executable code, but our definitions suggest how to write code that checks whether a contour is a polygon. Such code is included in the utilities that prepare data for the planning program illustrated in Figure 19.2.

20 Rule-based programming

Some problems present us with a large collection of facts and rules, but no underlying theory that we can use to design a compact algorithm for calculating a solution. Examples of such problems include medical diagnosis and treatment planning, scheduling jobs in a machine shop, diagnosis and repair of malfunctioning machinery, and determining customers' eligibility for financial credit. In these areas there are no simple first principles from which everything follows; instead, there are a lot of empirical observations and rules gleaned from hard experience or laid down by fiat. Sometimes you can find an acceptable solution by searching for relevant facts and applying the pertinent rules. *Rule-based programming* mechanizes this style of problem solving.

Rule-based programs are sometimes called *expert systems* and are said to display *artificial intelligence*, but they are just computer programs that employ some specialized techniques that have been found useful for certain kinds of problems. If such a program is intended for a serious purpose, it must meet the same standards of quality and correctness required of other programs. How can we tell if a rule-based program has computed the right answer?

Rule-based programs are often evaluated by submitting some sample results to a panel of human experts. This kind of validation can be helpful but it does not provide sufficient coverage to detect every incorrect result nor does it provide any guidance for design and implementation. We need a way to check any program output against an independent standard of accuracy. A formal specification can provide that standard.

In this chapter we develop a formal specification for a rule-based program that can be used to predict the answer to any query, or check any output. It also shows how the program works and suggests a strategy for implementing it.

20.1   Elements of rule-based programming

A rule-based program has two major components, and the correctness of each component is an independent problem. The first component is a database of rules, which is sometimes grandly called a *knowledge base*. The second is a *rule interpreter* that can deduce new facts from known facts and the rule database. The rule interpreter is sometimes called the *inference engine*.

The facts and rules should make sense. They must model the real world accurately. There is no way to check this formally; review by real experts is indispensable. But the rules should not include any contradictions; this we can check formally.

The rule interpreter is just a program; making it work correctly is a programming problem that need not require participation by experts in the subject matter of the application. Most programs contain errors, and we can easily imagine an incorrect rule interpreter that fails to reach the conclusions it should, or reaches the wrong conclusions. A correct rule interpreter infers all of the pertinent conclusions entailed by its facts and rules, and does not infer any conclusions that are not justified by them. Our formal specification expresses this precisely.

20.2   Facts and rules

Our case study in this chapter solves a toy problem: It deduces an animal's species. For example, from "the animal has stripes," "the animal has fur," and "the animal is a carnivore," it concludes "the animal is a tiger." This toy problem demonstrates techniques that can be used to solve real problems, such as diagnosing an illness from clinical findings and laboratory results.

We declare a basic type to represent facts; particular facts are elements of this type:

[*FACT*]

$$\mid \textit{stripes}, \textit{fur}, \textit{zebra}, \textit{sharp\_teeth}, \textit{carnivore}, \textit{herbivore}, \textit{mammal}, \textit{tiger} : FACT$$

Of course there are many more facts besides these.

Rules associate a set of facts called *premises* with a fact called the *conclusion*. If the premises are all true, we can infer that the conclusion is true as well. For example, "If an animal has stripes, is a mammal, and is a carnivore, then it is a tiger." In our Z model this rule is written

$$\{\textit{stripes}, \textit{mammal}, \textit{carnivore}\} \mapsto \textit{tiger}$$

Rules that have this *if . . . then . . .* form are called *production rules*, and rule-based programs are sometimes called *production rule systems.*

In our Z model we represent the rule database as a global constant: a relation from sets of facts to facts.

$$rules : \mathbb{P}\,FACT \leftrightarrow FACT$$

$$rules = \{$$

$$\vdots$$

$$\{fur\} \mapsto mammal,$$
$$\{sharp\_teeth\} \mapsto carnivore,$$
$$\{stripes, mammal, carnivore\} \mapsto tiger,$$
$$\{stripes, mammal, herbivore\} \mapsto zebra,$$

$$\vdots$$

$$\}$$

In this excerpt we show only four rules: the one about the tiger and three others: "if an animal has fur, it is a mammal," "if an animal has sharp teeth, it is a carnivore," and "if an animal has stripes, is a mammal, and is a herbivore, it is a zebra." Real rule-based programs have dozens, hundreds, even thousands of rules.

20.3   Deducing new facts

The program is initially loaded with a set of facts that are known to be true. The rule interpreter searches for a rule whose premises are all found in this set of facts and adds the conclusion of that rule to the set. Now the set of facts is larger, so more rules might apply. Another applicable rule is selected, and another new fact is added. This continues until some interesting conclusion is reached or nothing more can be concluded. (This explanation emphasizes *forward chaining* from facts to conclusions; we will also discuss *backward chaining* from conclusions.)

Of course this simple explanation leaves out a lot. Usually it is possible to infer a great many facts, but most of them are irrelevant to what the user wants to know. In order to achieve acceptable performance it is necessary to limit the search; there has to be a control strategy for selecting which rules to try, and the rules and facts are usually organized in data structures that support efficient search. The quest for efficiency and good performance makes the program complicated, and complicated programs usually contain errors. That is why the correctness of the rule interpreter is a real issue distinct from whether the contents of the rules are valid.

However, since we are only interested in the correctness of the program, we can ignore the complications. For now, we don't have to worry about limiting the search.

Instead we ask, what is the set of *all* the facts that the program should be able to infer? Any correct result must belong to this set. We don't have to consider which rules to try; we can imagine trying them all.

Imagine generating facts in stages. In each stage, examine the entire set of facts, apply all the applicable rules, and add all the new facts to the set. Repeat the stages until no new facts appear. Every stage can be modelled as an application of *deduce*.

$$deduce == (\lambda\, facts : \mathbb{P}\, FACT \bullet facts \cup rules(\!|\,\mathbb{P}\, facts\,|\!))$$

Here *deduce* is a function from an initial set of facts to a (possibly larger) final set of facts. All of the initial set *facts* also appear in the final set: Once the program concludes that a fact is true, it never retracts that conclusion. This is called *monotonic reasoning*.

In addition, *deduce* may infer new facts. The expression *rules*$(\!|\,\mathbb{P}\, facts\,|\!)$ is the set of all the conclusions of all the rules whose premises match some combination of the initial set of facts. The expression $\mathbb{P}\, facts$ is the set of all possible combinations of the initial facts. This expression uses the *power set* operator $\mathbb{P}$ (Section 8.1.8). In Z we usually see this operator in declarations but we can use it anywhere. If S is a set, the power set of S, $\mathbb{P}\, S$, is the set of all subsets of S. So if *facts* is

$$facts = \{stripes, sharp\_teeth, fur\}$$

then the power set of *facts* is

$$\mathbb{P}\, facts = \{\ \{stripes, sharp\_teeth, fur\}, \{stripes, sharp\_teeth\}, \{stripes, fur\},$$
$$\{sharp\_teeth, fur\}, \{stripes\}, \{sharp\_teeth\}, \{fur\}, \emptyset\ \}$$

The expression *rules*$(\!|\,\mathbb{P}\, facts\,|\!)$ uses the *relational image* brackets $(\!|\ldots|\!)$ (Section 9.3.2). The value of this expression is a set, the second elements (the conclusions) of all the pairs (rules) in relation *rules* whose first elements (premises) appear in the set $\mathbb{P}\, facts$. Here $\{fur\}$ matches the premises of the rule $\{fur\} \mapsto mammal$ and $\{sharp\_teeth\}$ matches $\{sharp\_teeth\} \mapsto carnivore$. So *rules*$(\!|\,\mathbb{P}\, facts\,|\!)$ contains the new facts *mammal* and *carnivore*:

$$deduce\, facts = \{stripes, sharp\_teeth, fur, mammal, carnivore\}$$

Now if we apply *deduce* again, we find a match with the rule whose premises are $\{stripes, mammal, carnivore\}$. We conclude *tiger*. Now our set of facts is

$$deduce\,(deduce\, facts) = \{stripes, sharp\_teeth, fur, mammal, carnivore, tiger\}$$

If we apply *deduce* once more, we do not conclude anything new. We have concluded all we can from the initial set of facts. In a realistic example we would apply *deduce* many more times and conclude a great many new facts, but eventually we would reach the same situation: We would exhaust all the applicable rules, and further applications of *deduce* would generate no more new facts.

We wish to define the function *complete* which applies *deduce* until no more new facts can be inferred. This is a special case of a general problem: Beginning with a *child* relation, define the corresponding *descendant* relation. The descendant relation is called the *transitive closure* of the child relation. In Z the transitive closure operator is the superscript plus sign, $^+$. Our *complete* function is the transitive closure of *deduce*.

$$complete == deduce^+$$

Our example can be expressed as a single application of *complete*.

$$complete \{stripes, sharp\_teeth, fur\} = \\ \{stripes, sharp\_teeth, fur, mammal, carnivore, tiger\}$$

The *complete* function is the basis for our formal definition of a correct rule interpreter. But first we return to the database of rules.

20.4 Checking the rules

It is no use having a correct rule interpreter if the rules don't make sense. Human experts must review all the rules to make sure that their contents are valid. This is not sufficient, however, because rules that appear valid may contradict each other.

After discussion with an expert, a programmer might put the rule $\{stripes, mammal\} \mapsto tiger$ in the database. Some time later, another programmer might add $\{stripes, fur\} \mapsto zebra$. Each rule seems reasonable, but they contradict each other. From *stripes* and *fur* the rule interpreter could infer both *tiger* and *zebra*. Both cannot both be true. These two rules are *inconsistent*.

When a large rule database is built by several people over a period of time, there is a real danger that it will become inconsistent. We need a systematic way to search for inconsistencies, which means we need a precise definition of inconsistency.

We cannot just compare pairs of rules, because rules interact: The rules about tigers and zebras depend on the rule about mammals and fur. We have to consider all of the rules together: They are *consistent* if, starting from a consistent set of facts, there is no way to deduce inconsistent facts.

We begin by defining what it means for facts to be inconsistent. In our example we can just enumerate them: The set *inconsistent* contains sets of facts that we know are inconsistent. Mutually exclusive categories are inconsistent: An animal cannot have both *fur* and *feathers*; it cannot be both *mammal* and *bird*.

$$inconsistent == \{$$

$$\vdots$$

$$\{fur, feathers, scales, \ldots\},$$
$$\{mammal, bird, fish, \ldots\},$$
$$\{tiger, zebra, ostrich, goldfish, \ldots\}$$

$$\vdots$$

$$\}$$

A consistent set of facts contains no more than one element from each set of mutually exclusive alternatives:

$$consistent : \mathbb{P}(\mathbb{P}\, FACT)$$

$$\forall facts : consistent;\ mutually\_exclusive : inconsistent \bullet$$
$$\#(mutually\_exclusive \cap facts) \leq 1$$

In the predicate, *facts* ranges over all sets of *consistent* facts, and *mutually_exclusive* ranges over all sets of *inconsistent* facts.

Our rules are consistent if, starting from a consistent set of facts, we can only deduce more consistent facts. We express this formally using our *complete* function.

$$\forall facts : consistent \bullet complete\, facts \in consistent$$

Or, if you prefer prefix syntax[1].

$$\forall facts : \mathbb{P}\, FACT \bullet consistent\, facts \Rightarrow consistent\, (complete\, facts)$$

This predicate actually expresses a requirement on *rules*, which occurs here by way of the definition of *complete*.

20.5 Specifying rule-based programs

Now that we have formal definitions for deduction and for consistent facts and rules, we can specify rule-based programs.

The state of a rule-based program is the collection of facts that it takes to be true. Some of these facts may have been loaded into the system, and others may have been deduced, but we make no distinction between these two categories in the system state.

---

[1] To be strictly correct in using prefix syntax, we should redefine *consistent* with an underscore: *consistent_*. In the interests of brevity we skip it.

The central activity of a rule-based program is to consider some *data* and deduce some *conclusions* relevant to some *goal*. We model all this with the *Deduce* operation schema.

$$
\begin{array}{l}
\textit{\underline{Deduce}}\\[2pt]
\quad facts, facts' : \mathbb{P}\,FACT\\
\quad data, goals, conclusions! : \mathbb{P}\,FACT\\
\hline
\quad (\textbf{let } all == complete\,(facts \cup data) \bullet\\
\qquad facts \subseteq facts' \subseteq all \wedge\\
\qquad conclusions! = goals \cap all \subseteq facts')
\end{array}
$$

Here *facts* and *facts'* are the state of the system before and after the *Deduce* operation (in this example we don't bother to define a state schema; it is shorter to include the before and after variables in the operation schema explicitly). The *data* are new *facts* that are introduced in this operation, and the output *conclusions*! are the pertinent facts that this operation deduces.

20.5.1 Control

Rule interpreters traditionally incorporate two components: a *generative* part that deduces new facts and a *search control* part that directs the generative part. In our formal model these two parts are modelled by the function *complete* and the predicate *goals*, respectively. A practical program cannot just implement *complete*. A huge number of facts might be deduced, but usually we are only interested in a few of them. We need a way to control the generation of new facts; the *goals* provide that control.

The goals distinguish the facts we seek from all the rest. So *goals* must be a unary predicate on facts, that is, a set of facts. In our example, if we wish to know the species of the animal, *goals* is the set of all facts that name the animal's species: {*tiger, zebra, ostrich, goldfish, . . .*}. Alternatively, if we only want to know the kind of animal, *goals* would be {*mammal, bird, fish, . . .*}. In this latter case, our program might reach a conclusion more quickly.

Now we can understand the predicate of *Deduce*. The local variable *all* is the set of all valid facts that can be deduced from the initial set of facts and the new data, as described by *complete*. Here *facts* ⊆ *facts'* says that the program never retracts any conclusions; it mechanizes *monotonic* reasoning. Here *facts'* ⊆ *all* says that all the new facts are valid deductions; the program never deduces anything it shouldn't. Here *goals* ∩ *all* ⊆ *facts'* says that the program deduces all valid goals; its deductions are *complete* in the sense that it never fails to deduce what it should. The final predicate *conclusions*! = *goals* ∩ *all* says that the goals that could be deduced are the conclusions reported in the output.

Deduce suggests a naive implementation: First generate *all* valid facts by applying *complete* to the stored *facts* and new *data*. Then search *all* the facts for those that also occur in *goals* and report those as the *conclusions*!. This strategy is correct, but it is far too inefficient to be feasible because it wastefully generates too many irrelevant facts. Any practical rule-based program must incorporate a control strategy that attempts to reach the goals with the fewest possible deductions. Our formal definition can be much shorter than any program because it doesn't have to describe the control strategy, it only describes its effects.

Deduce does not require all the facts in *all* to be generated but it does not prohibit this either. In other words, *Deduce* does not require an optimally efficient solution. A good formal specification defers such issues to the later implementation stages.

20.5.2 Forward and backward chaining

Our *Deduce* operation models the essential core of rule-based programming. It can be specialized in various ways to model particular strategies. It supports both data-driven *forward chaining* and goal-driven *backward chaining*.

Forward chaining is *data-driven*. The inputs are data: You provide the program with some new observations and see what conclusions emerge.

```
_Forward_____
Deduce
observations? : P FACT
_____
data = observations?
```

Submitting *observations?* = {*stripes, sharp_teeth, fur*} and obtaining *conclusions!* = {*tiger*} are examples of forward chaining.

Backward chaining is *goal-driven*. The inputs are goals or *queries*. You load up the system with facts, then make queries. A query is a set of facts (you wish to know which of these facts are true). The conclusions are the facts in the query that could be deduced from the rules and facts already in hand.

```
_Backward_____
Deduce
queries? : P FACT
_____
goals = queries?
```

Submitting *queries?* = {*tiger, zebra*} and obtaining *conclusions!* = {*tiger*} are examples of backward chaining.

Rule-based programming

[*FACT*]

$rules : \mathbb{P}\,FACT \leftrightarrow FACT$

... rules omitted ...

$deduce == (\lambda\,facts : \mathbb{P}\,FACT \bullet facts \cup rules(\!|\mathbb{P}\,facts|\!))$

$complete == deduce^{+}$

$consistent, inconsistent : \mathbb{P}(\mathbb{P}\,FACT)$

$\forall\,facts : consistent;\; mutually\_exclusive : inconsistent \bullet$
$\quad \#(mutually\_exclusive \cap facts) \leq 1$

$\forall\,facts : consistent \bullet complete\,facts \in consistent$

Deduce _____

$facts, facts' : \mathbb{P}\,FACT$
$data, goals, conclusions! : \mathbb{P}\,FACT$

$(\textbf{let}\; all == complete\,(facts \cup data) \bullet$
$\quad facts \subseteq facts' \subseteq all \;\wedge$
$\quad conclusions! = goals \cap all \subseteq facts')$

$Backward \mathrel{\widehat{=}} [Deduce;\; queries? : \mathbb{P}\,FACT \mid goals = queries?]$

$Forward \mathrel{\widehat{=}} [Deduce;\; observations? : \mathbb{P}\,FACT \mid data = observations?]$

Figure 20.1: Rule-based programming.

Other variations are possible. For example, many backward-chaining systems prompt the user to enter more data if a query cannot be answered from facts already on hand.

20.6 Conclusion

The complete formal model is presented in Figure 20.1. It shows how to predict or check the answer to any query. The independent checking process suggested by our model is laborious, but it can serve as an *oracle* for generating the correct results expected for selected test cases, or comparing against suspect program output. It also suggests a strategy for designing and implementing the program.

21 Graphical user interface

This chapter presents a more realistic model for the graphical user interface we introduced in Chapter 6. It is based on the control console of a real medical device, but the same techniques can be applied to any system where the operator uses a pointing device such as a mouse to select items from on-screen windows and menus, and uses a keyboard to enter information into dialog boxes. Such facilities are provided by many software systems in wide use today, for example the X window system.

A graphical user interface is an example of a *state transition system* driven by *events*. This chapter explains how to model event-driven state transition systems in Z, and shows how to illustrate a Z text with a kind of *state transition diagram* called a *statechart*. This chapter also shows how to use Z to express designs that are partitioned into units or *modules* that are largely independent. In Z these units can include both data and the operations that act on it, so they can represent *classes* in object-oriented programming.

21.1 Events

A great advantage of a graphical user interface is that it allows the users to choose operations in whatever order makes the most sense to them, it does not force users through a fixed sequence determined by the designers. All operations are always potentially available, although some operations might have to be disabled at certain times.

This is a good match to Z, where we define operations that have preconditions that might not be satisfied in certain states. In fact, the lack of any built-in sequencing construct in Z is a positive advantage for modelling this kind of system. We will not be tempted to make unfounded assumptions about the ordering of operations because there is none. The order of operations cannot be predicted; it is completely determined by what the user wants to do. Systems that must respond to events from the outside world whose order of arrival cannot be predicted are said to be *event-driven*.

In our graphical user interface, the events of interest are mouse clicks and keystrokes. The core of every operation is to receive an event and handle it somehow. These events occur in a system called *Console* which we will describe in the next section.

[*EVENT*]

$$
\begin{array}{|l}
\hline
\_Event_____ \\
\Delta Console \\
e? : EVENT \\
\hline
\end{array}
$$

Many events are simply ignored (they do not change the *Console* state).

Ignore $\hat{=}$ *Event* $\wedge$ $\Xi Console$

21.2 Displays and dialogs

Now let's fill in the *Console* state. The console provides several different displays such as those shown in Figures 6.3 and 6.4. The display which is currently visible on the console is an important component of the state because it determines which items appear and which operations are available.

The rest of the state is concerned with the dialog that occurs when the user enters a new value for one of the settings that controls the machine. The user begins a dialog by positioning the cursor over a setting on a display such as shown in Figure 6.4 and clicking on the mouse button. Then a dialog box appears where the user may type a new value (Figure 21.1, compare to Figure 6.4) and click on buttons to accept or cancel the value. The characters that the user types into the dialog box are stored as a string of text in a buffer. Normally a user can select almost any operation at any time, but once the dialog begins it must be completed before any other operation can be selected. So the state includes a mode to indicate when a dialog is in progress.

[*DISPLAY, SETTING, VALUE, CHAR*]

TEXT == seq *CHAR*

MODE ::= *idle* | *dialog*

BUTTON ::= *accept* | *cancel*

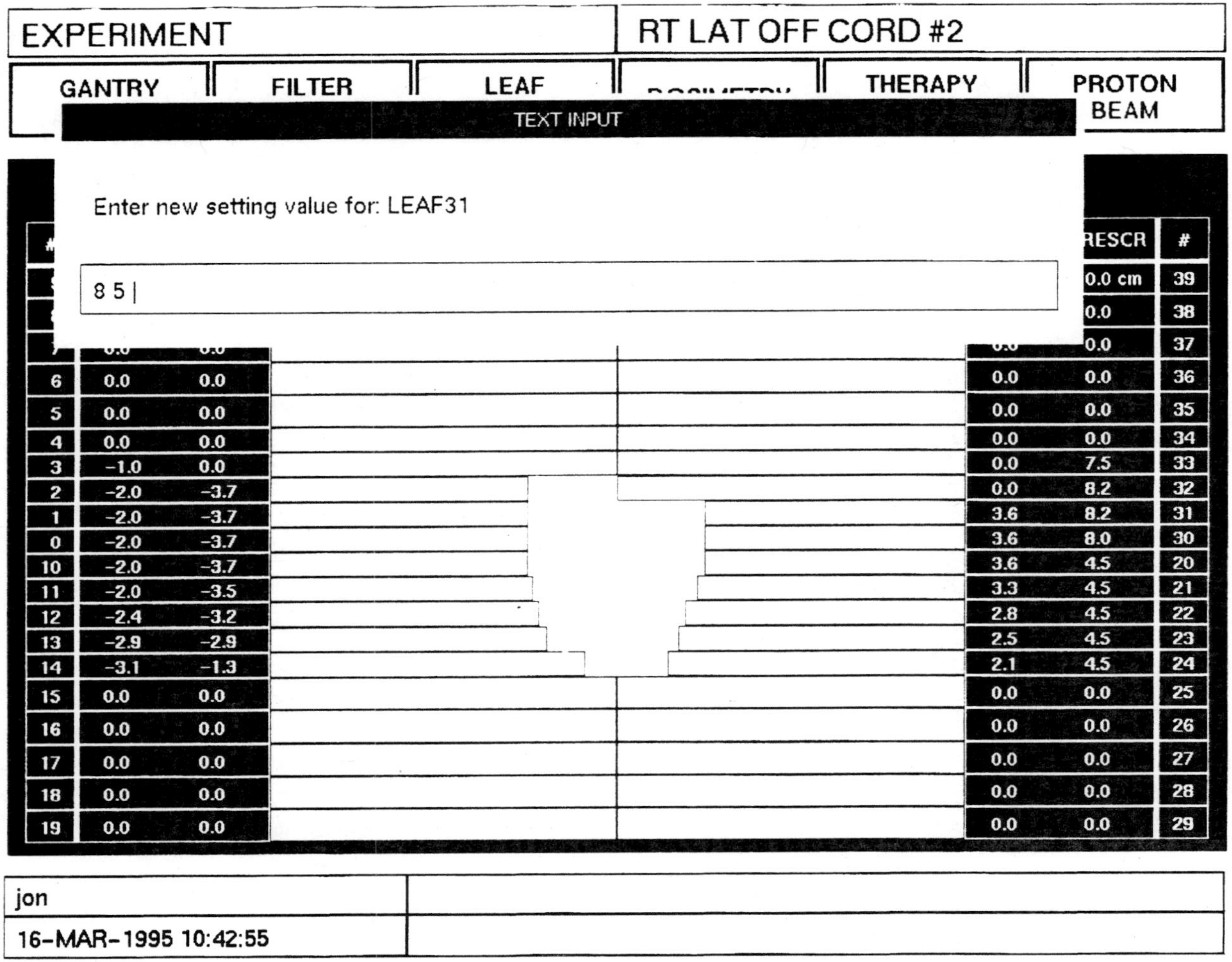

EXPERIMENT

RT LAT OFF CORD #2

GANTRY	FILTER	LEAF	THERAPY	PROTON BEAM

TEXT INPUT

Enter new setting value for: LEAF31

8 5 |

#					RESCR	#
	0.0		0.0		0.0 cm	39
	0.0				0.0	38
			0.0		0.0	37
6	0.0		0.0		0.0	36
5	0.0		0.0		0.0	35
4	0.0		0.0		0.0	34
3	-1.0		0.0		7.5	33
2	-2.0	-3.7	0.0		8.2	32
1	-2.0	-3.7	3.6		8.2	31
0	-2.0	-3.7	3.6		8.0	30
10	-2.0	-3.7	3.6		4.5	20
11	-2.0	-3.5	3.3		4.5	21
12	-2.4	-3.2	2.8		4.5	22
13	-2.9	-2.9	2.5		4.5	23
14	-3.1	-1.3	2.1		4.5	24
15	0.0	0.0	0.0		0.0	25
16	0.0	0.0	0.0		0.0	26
17	0.0	0.0	0.0		0.0	27
18	0.0	0.0	0.0		0.0	28
19	0.0	0.0	0.0		0.0	29

jon

16-MAR-1995 10:42:55

Figure 21.1: Graphical user interface: dialog box.

$\_Console_____$
$display : DISPLAY$
$mode : MODE$
$buffer : TEXT$
$setting : SETTING$

21.3 Selecting a display

The user selects a new display by pressing a function key on the console keyboard (there is a different key for each display). Each time a key is pressed, the *Event* operation occurs. The value of the input event *e*? tells us which function key was pressed, and that corresponds to the display that the user wants to see. An instance of *EVENT* is actually a data structure that includes an encoded representation of the key.

Here we don't have to provide a detailed description of the event data structure or give directions for decoding the event to determine the function key, and then translate from the function key to the intended display. We hide all of this in a partial function *disp* that examines the event and returns the display that the user wants to see. The function is partial; events in the domain of *disp* correspond to display selections.

In Z it is permitted to declare a function without providing its full definition. This supports a top-down specification style where details are deferred.

Here is the operation that selects a new display. This operation is only enabled when the console is not engaged in a dialog.

$\mid \quad disp : EVENT \nrightarrow DISPLAY$

$\_SelectDisplay_____$
$Event$
$_____$
$mode = idle$
$e? \in \mathrm{dom}\, disp$
$display' = disp\ e?$
$mode' = mode$

The predicate $e? \in \mathrm{dom}\, disp$ checks that this event came from one of the display selection keys, and the function application *disp e*? determines which display the user selected. The screen updates with the new display; this is modelled by $display' = disp\ e?$. In this definition it is necessary to say the mode does not change: $mode' = mode$ (or $mode' = idle$ would mean the same thing). We do not need to say anything about *buffer* and *setting* here because their values do not matter unless a dialog is in progress.

If a dialog is in progress, attempts to select a new display are ignored.

$\begin{array}{|l}\hline \textit{IgnoreDisplay} \\ \textit{Ignore} \\ \hline e? \in \mathrm{dom}\ disp \\ mode = dialog \\ \hline \end{array}$

We use schema disjunction to combine the two cases.

$$DisplayEvent \;\widehat{=}\; SelectDisplay \vee IgnoreDisplay$$

The total operation *DisplayEvent* describes everything that can happen when the user presses one of the display selection function keys.

21.4 Changing a setting value

Users can enter new prescribed settings at the console. To model this seemingly simple action in Z, we have to break it down into stages and write an operation schema for each stage. In *SelectSetting* the user selects a setting and the dialog begins. Then the user types in the new value; each keystroke invokes *GetChar*. Finally, the user may *Accept* the new value into the machine or *Cancel* the dialog to leave the machine state unchanged. If the user attempts to enter an invalid setting value, the system will not accept it but will *Reprompt*.

21.4.1 Starting the dialog

The *SelectSetting* operation occurs when the user clicks on a setting name displayed on the screen. Each such event lies in the domain of the *stg* function. The *setting* state variable records which setting has been selected, as determined by *stg*. A dialog box appears on the screen, and the dialog begins with an empty text buffer (Figure 21.1).

$$stg : EVENT \nrightarrow SETTING$$

SelectSetting
Event

$mode = idle$
$e? \in \text{dom } stg$
$setting' = stg\ e?$
$mode' = dialog$
$buffer' = \emptyset$
$display' = display$

If a dialog is already underway, this operation is disabled.

IgnoreSetting
Ignore

$e? \in \text{dom } stg$
$mode = dialog$

$$SettingEvent \mathrel{\widehat{=}} SelectSetting \lor IgnoreSetting$$

21.4.2 Typing the new value

Each time the user strikes one of the alphanumeric keys, an event occurs, and the *GetChar* operation handles the event. The *char* function extracts the new character from the event, and *edit* updates the buffer. Usually the new character is simply appended to the end, but there might be editing characters that have more complex effects.

$$char : EVENT \nrightarrow CHAR$$
$$edit : (TEXT \times CHAR) \rightarrow TEXT$$

GetChar
Event

$mode = dialog$
$e? \in \text{dom } char$
$buffer' = edit\,(buffer, char\ e?)$
$mode' = mode$
$setting' = setting$
$display' = display$

When the console is not engaged in a dialog, alphanumeric characters are ignored.

```
┌─ IgnoreChar ────────────────────────────────
│ Ignore
├───────────────────
│ e? ∈ dom char
│ mode = idle
└─────────────────────────────────────────────
```

$$CharEvent \;\widehat{=}\; GetChar \lor IgnoreChar$$

21.4.3 Finishing the dialog

When users are finished editing, they may click on an "accept" button in a dialog box (not shown in Fig. 21.1). The system converts the text in the buffer to a value. If the value lies within the range of valid values for the selected setting, it is used to update the prescribed machine settings.

```
│ button : EVENT ⇸ BUTTON
│ value : TEXT → VALUE
│ valid_ : SETTING ↔ VALUE
```

```
┌─ Accept ────────────────────────────────────
│ Event
├───────────────────
│ mode = dialog
│ e? ∈ dom button
│ button e? = accept
│ valid(setting, value buffer)
│ mode' = idle
│ display' = display
└─────────────────────────────────────────────
```

When the dialog ends, indicated by *mode'* = *idle*, the dialog box disappears. If the value derived from the buffer contents is not valid, the machine state remains unchanged and the dialog continues. The system may issue a message to reprompt the operator, but we do not model this formally.

```
┌─Reprompt─────────────────────────────────────────────
│ Event
│ ┌──────────────
│
│ mode = dialog
│ e? ∈ dom button
│ button e? = accept
│ ¬ valid(setting, value buffer)
│ buffer' = buffer
│ mode' = mode
│ display' = display
└──────────────────────────────────────────────────────
```

Alternatively, the user may cancel the dialog at any time, for example by clicking on a button in a dialog box (not shown in Fig. 21.1).

```
┌─Cancel───────────────────────────────────────────────
│ Event
│ ┌──────────────
│
│ mode = dialog
│ e? ∈ dom button
│ button e? = cancel
│ mode' = idle
│ display' = display
└──────────────────────────────────────────────────────
```

Dialog buttons are not available when the console is idle, so these three operations cover all possibilities.

$$ButtonEvent \mathrel{\widehat{=}} Accept \lor Cancel \lor Reprompt$$

21.5   Z and state transition systems

We have used Z to define a system with states and transitions between states: a *finite state machine*. Pictures can help us understand state machines. Figure 21.2 illustrates our system with a kind of *state transition diagram* called a *statechart* [Harel, 1987].

Each bubble in the statechart represents a set of states that satisfies some predicate. In this diagram the outermost bubble represents all *Console* states. The two large bubbles represent the states where *mode = idle* and *mode = dialog*. The two smaller bubbles represent the states in *mode = dialog* where the buffer contents represent a valid setting or not: *valid(setting, value buffer)* and ¬ *valid(setting, value buffer)*, respectively. This nesting of state bubbles is one of the innovations that distinguishes

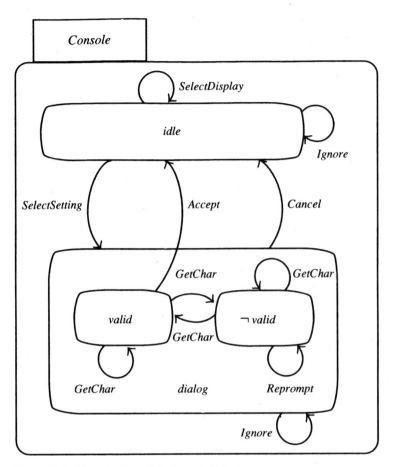

Figure 21.2: Graphical user interface: statechart.

a statechart from an ordinary state transition diagram, such as the one in Figure 6.6. More deeply nested state bubbles correspond to stronger state predicates.

The arrows represent transitions between states, which correspond to Z operation schemas. Each arrow is labelled with the Z operation name, and you can refer to the schemas to find the events that can trigger the transition.

The diagram shows how the operations work together and helps us check for completeness. It is easy to see that we have provided ways in and out of each state bubble and to check that we have dealt with all possible events in every state. However the Z texts contain some essential information that does not appear in the diagram. For example, the *valid* predicate depends on the values of *buffer* and *setting*.

A statechart (or any other diagram) is incomplete; it is always necessary to provide some additional text to explain the diagram. We can use Z to annotate a statechart.

Or, if you prefer to look at it in another way, a statechart can illustrate Z text. The diagram and the formal text complement each other.

21.6   Changing the machine state

By itself, a user interface is useless — it has to connect to something else. The purpose of this user interface is to enable the operator to control a machine. We have to model the machine, too.

A good design can be partitioned into units or *modules* that can be described independently. Not just the data, but also the operations can be separated. A unit composed of data and the operations that act on it are abstract data types (ADTs). An abstract data type can model a *class* in object-oriented programming. Our *Console* subsystem and its operations form such a unit. Next we will define the *Machine* subsystem.

The state of the machine is determined by the values of its settings. We don't have to name the settings individually; we can model all of them by a total function from settings to values. In fact there are two functions, one for the *prescribed* settings loaded from a prescription file and another for the *measured* settings read by sensors.

---
*Machine*_____

measured, prescribed : SETTING $\rightarrow$ VALUE

The *NewSetting* operation describes what happens in the *Machine* when a new value $v?$ is assigned to *prescribed* setting $s?$.

---
*NewSetting*_____

$\Delta Machine$
$s? : SETTING; \; v? : VALUE$

$prescribed' = prescribed \oplus \{s? \mapsto v?\}$
$actual' = actual$

We use the override operator $\oplus$ (Section 9.3.2) rather than the equation *prescribed' s?* $= v?$ to express that the values of all the other settings remain unchanged.

Now we can combine the user interface and the machine to make the whole system.

---
*Sys*_____

Console
Machine

ChangeSetting describes what happens to the whole system when the user edits a setting.

```
┌─ ChangeSetting ──────────────────────────────────────
│ ΔSys
│ Accept
│ NewSetting
├──────────────────────────────────────────────────────
│ s? = setting
│ v? = value buffer
└──────────────────────────────────────────────────────
```

This is typical Z style for building up operations on whole systems. We use schema inclusion to combine the *Accept* operation from the *Console* subsystem with the *NewSetting* operation from the *Machine* subsystem. The predicate provides the glue that couples the two operations together.

Here ΔSys is redundant because all the necessary before and after state variables are declared in *Accept* and *NewSetting*. We include ΔSys anyway to make it clear that *ChangeSetting* affects the combined system state.

In fact *ChangeSetting* is the only operation we have defined where the two subsystems interact. We can extend the other operations to make it clear that the machine state is unaffected by most activities at the user interface.

$$SysDisplayEvent \mathrel{\widehat{=}} DisplayEvent \land \Xi Machine$$

$$SysSettingEvent \mathrel{\widehat{=}} SettingEvent \land \Xi Machine$$

$$SysCharEvent \mathrel{\widehat{=}} CharEvent \land \Xi Machine$$

$$SysButtonEvent \mathrel{\widehat{=}} ChangeSetting \lor (Reprompt \land \Xi Machine)$$
$$\lor (Cancel \land \Xi Machine)$$

It works the same way in the other direction, too. There are many operations on the *Machine* state that do not involve the user interface. We make the design clean and easy to understand by separating the subsystems. Z nicely supports this modular approach to design.

21.7 Conclusions

A Z model like this one can serve as a bridge from requirements expressed in prose and diagrams to code in an executable programming language. The Z texts are more explicit than the informal requirements but they are free of the mass of low-level detail that you have to include to make a program run.

We did not model the appearance of the display or the internals of the event data structure. We did not show how to decode events, how setting values are represented as numbers, or how to test for a valid setting value. We did not describe how to couple *Console* and *Machine* in *ChangeSetting*; we just used schema inclusion (which is essentially logical conjunction) to combine the requirements. The conjunction could be implemented by shared variables or a procedure call with passed parameters. *Console* and *Machine* might even be two different computers communicating across a network. In Z we needn't commit to any of these.

In Z we can defer the details while we focus on essential design issues: partitioning the whole system into subsystems, determining which variables belong in each subsystem, separating required subsystem behaviors into discrete operations, and expressing precisely when each operation is enabled and how it changes the subsystem state.

Exercise 21.7.1   The console modelled in this chapter does not work quite like the one we described in Chapter 6. Our *SelectDisplay* operation here allows the user to select any display whenever the console is idle, but in Chapter 6 we described an *Enter* operation that selects one particular display after another in fixed sequence (see Figures 6.6 and 6.7). Define the *Enter* operation that selects the *fields* display when the *patients* display is visible, selects the *setup* display when the *fields* display is visible, and has no effect in other states.

22 Safety-critical protection system

In this chapter we pursue the safety issues introduced in the therapy machine study from Chapter 6. To ensure that patients are treated as directed by their prescriptions, many machine settings must be set properly. The radiation beam should only be allowed to turn on when the correct settings have been achieved. This chapter presents a formal specification for the control software that permits the beam to turn on. It is an example of a *safety-critical protection system* because it prevents some potentially hazardous action from occurring unless particular safety requirements are satisfied.

This study also illustrates how Z can express two important design strategies: partitioning a complex system into largely independent subsystems or modules and refining from an abstract model to a detailed design.

22.1 Partition

First we develop a more detailed model of the therapy machine system *Machine* that we introduced in Chapter 21. Much of the apparent complexity of the therapy machine arises from the interaction of several subsystems which, by themselves, are simpler. We partition the system into subsystems and describe simple operations on each. For each operation on the system as a whole, we define a separate operation on each affected subsystem. The complex behaviors of the whole system emerge when we compose these simpler operations together.

The advantages of this approach arise because many operations involve only a few of the subsystems, and many complex operations can emerge when simpler operations appear together in different combinations. As a result, the formal description of the partitioned design is shorter and clearer than would be possible with a monolithic design. These advantages carry over into the implementation as well.

We partition *Machine* into several subsystems, including the two we consider in this chapter: *Field* and *Intlk* (interlocks).

22.1.1 *Field* subsystem

The therapy machine has dozens of named settings that must be adjusted differently for each treatment run: gantry angle, dose, collimator leaf positions, and so forth. The machine state, or setup, is largely determined by the values of all the settings. We don't have to model each setting as a separate system state variable; we can model the entire setup as a function from setting names to values: A particular setup might have *value gantry* = 270 (degrees) and *value leaf*$_{19}$ = 174 (millimeters). This time we model the values as integers so we can do arithmetic on them (some settings might actually be implemented with floating point types). Prescribed setups are selected from a database of prescriptions where they have unique field names.

$$[FIELD, SETTING]$$

$$VALUE == \mathbb{Z}$$

$$SETUP == SETTING \rightarrow VALUE$$

$$\mid \quad prescription : FIELD \nrightarrow SETUP$$

The prescription database is modelled as a function from field names to setups. Retrieving a setup from the database is modelled as an application of the *prescription* function to a particular member of *FIELD*, returning that field's setup, which is itself a function. A function that returns another function, as *prescription* does here, is called a *higher-order function*.

The *Field* schema includes the state variables that represent settings for the currently selected field. Sensors report measured setting values. Prescribed setting values are read from the prescription database. The operator may override some settings to indicate that they need not be checked against their prescribed values. It is necessary to remember the value of each setting when it was overridden, so these are also part of the system state.

```
┌─Field──────────────────────────────────────
│ field : FIELD
│ measured, prescribed : SETUP
│ overridden : SETTING ↛ VALUE
├────────────────────────────────────────────
│ field ∈ dom prescription
│ prescribed = prescription field
└────────────────────────────────────────────
```

The invariant of *Field* says that the currently selected field and its prescribed settings occur in the prescription database. We will not model the operations that the therapist uses to select a field and override settings.

Exercise Why is *overridden* a partial function? What about *measured* and *prescribed*?

22.1.2 *Intlk* subsystem

The *Intlk* schema declares state variables that model interlocks and status flags. The *status* function indicates the readiness of each setting; settings might be *ready*, *not_ready*, or *overridden*. Interlocks prevent undesired or potentially hazardous situations. The function *intlk* indicates the status of each interlock; operations are inhibited when interlocks are *set* and are enabled when interlocks are *clear*. Most members of *INTERLOCK* are hardware sensors, for example the therapy room *door* sensor. When the door is open, *intlk door = set*, and the beam must not turn on. This requirement is enforced by a nonprogrammable hardware interlock, but our control program also monitors the door sensor.

The master therapy interlock *therapy_intlk* is an output of the control program that must be clear to allow the beam to turn on. It is a special software-controlled interlock that is not included with the sensors in *intlk*. Clearing this master therapy interlock is the central safety-critical act of the control program. When the master therapy interlock is clear, the operator can turn on the beam (using a nonprogrammable mechanism not described here).

$[INTERLOCK]$

$INTLK ::= clear \mid set$

$READY ::= ready \mid not\_ready \mid override$

Intlk
$therapy\_intlk : INTLK$
$intlk : INTERLOCK \rightarrow INTLK$
$status : SETTING \rightarrow READY$

The master therapy interlock indicates the combined effect of all the safety conditions that are checked by the control program[1]. In the following sections we formally describe the software that sets and clears this interlock.

[1] Many interlocks are also implemented directly in hardware, and the master therapy interlock output is implemented by redundant hardware interlocks.

22.2 Refinement

22.2.1 Abstract safety requirements

The central idea in the control system is this *safety requirement*: The beam can only turn on (or remain on) when the measured setup of the machine is physically safe, and matches a prescription that the operator has selected and approved. We can begin to express these requirements formally by declaring two relations, *safe* and *match*; we can provide their definitions later.

$$
\begin{array}{|l}
safe\_ : \mathbb{P}\ SETUP \\
match\_ : SETUP \leftrightarrow SETUP
\end{array}
$$

$$
\begin{array}{|l}
\_SafeTreatment \underline{\hspace{6cm}} \\
measured, prescribed : SETUP \\
\underline{\hspace{3cm}} \\
safe(measured) \\
match(measured, prescribed) \\
prescribed \in \text{ran}\ prescription
\end{array}
$$

The whole design follows from this simple model. The entire purpose of the control program is to establish and confirm the *SafeTreatment* condition. The *prescribed* setup must be selected; the *measured* setup must be achieved; and the *safe* and *match* conditions must be tested.

The condition *safe(measured)* ensures that the beam can only be on when the setup is physically safe. It expresses generic safety requirements that must be met by any treatment and do not depend on the prescription. It prevents the beam from turning on when the machine is in some inconsistent state, for example when it is in transition between setups. Failure to ensure this kind of condition in other machines has contributed to fatal accidents [Leveson and Turner, 1993; Leveson, 1995].

The other two conditions *prescribed* ∈ ran *prescriptions* and *match(measured, prescribed)* do concern the particular features of each prescribed setup. They express that the setup should be the particular one selected by the therapist. These conditions depend on setting values that are different for each setup, so they would be quite difficult to check with a nonprogrammable mechanism. Our control program is largely concerned with these conditions.

22.2.2 Concrete safety requirements

The readiness of each setting is computed from variables in the *Field* state. We distinguish two kinds of settings: *scales* are continuously variable over some range;

examples are gantry angle and every collimator leaf position. *Selections* can only take on certain discrete values; examples are wedge filter and flattening filter selection.

Each setting has a particular range of valid (physically reasonable) values. We declare a function named *valid* that checks sensor readings for faults; the value of *valid s* is the set of all valid values for setting *s*. Setting *s* is considered to be safe only if its measured value is in *valid s*. In this study we omit the more complicated conditions that involve combinations of settings.

Settings are *ready* when their *prescribed* and *measured* values match. *Selections* match when their prescribed and measured values are equal; *scales* match when their prescribed and measured values are within tolerance (each setting has its own tolerance range; to check this we use the absolute value function we defined in Chapter 11). A setting is *overridden* if the operator has overridden it and it remains at that overridden value. If the value of an overridden setting changes from when it was first overridden, it reverts to *not_ready*.

$$selection, scale : \mathbb{P}\,SETTING$$

$$tol : scale \to VALUE$$
$$valid : SETTING \to \mathbb{P}\,VALUE$$

$$Match\_ : \mathbb{P}(SETTING \times SETUP \times Field)$$
$$Safe\_, Overridden\_, Ready\_ : SETTING \leftrightarrow Field$$

$\forall s : SETTING;\ setup : SETUP;\ Field \bullet$

    $(Safe(s, \theta Field) \Leftrightarrow$
      $measured\ s \in valid\ s) \wedge$

    $(Match(s, setup, \theta Field) \Leftrightarrow$
      $(s \in selection \wedge measured\ s = setup\ s) \vee$
      $(s \in scale \wedge |measured\ s - setup\ s| \le tol\ s)) \wedge$

    $(Overridden(s, \theta Field) \Leftrightarrow$
      $s \in dom\ overridden \wedge$
      $Safe(s, \theta Field) \wedge Match(s, overridden, \theta Field)) \wedge$

    $(Ready(s, \theta Field) \Leftrightarrow$
      $Safe(s, \theta Field) \wedge Match(s, prescribed, \theta Field))$

In these definitions *measured*, *overridden*, and *prescribed* are declared by *Field* in the declaration part of the quantified predicate.

The *Safe* and *Match* predicates defined here resemble the *safe* and *match* relations introduced in Section 22.2.1[2]. We say that *Safe* and *Match* are *refinements* of *safe* and *match*, respectively, because they express the same ideas with more detail. This is an informal definition of refinement; a formal definition appears in Chapter 26.

Having partitioned our system and described the parts separately, we must compose the parts together again. We collect together all the field settings and all the interlock and status flag conditions in the *TreatmentStatus* schema. It shows how the status flags in *Intlk* depend on the prescribed and measured settings in *Field*, as determined by the functions and relations we just defined.

$$
\begin{array}{l}
\rule[0.5ex]{0pt}{0pt}\textit{TreatmentStatus} \\
\hline
\textit{Field} \\
\textit{Intlk} \\
\hline
status = \\
\quad (\lambda\, s : SETTING \bullet not\_ready) \oplus \\
\quad (\lambda\, s : SETTING \mid Overridden(s, \theta Field) \bullet override) \oplus \\
\quad (\lambda\, s : SETTING \mid Ready(s, \theta Field) \bullet ready)
\end{array}
$$

The predicate fixes the value of the *status* flags. The lambda expression $(\lambda\, s : SETTING \bullet not\_ready)$ is a function that associates every setting with the status value *not_ready*, while $(\lambda\, s : SETTING \mid Ready(s, \theta Field) \bullet ready)$ associates only those settings that satisfy the *Ready* predicate with the *status* value *ready*. We use the function overriding operator $\oplus$ (Section 9.3.2) to combine the lambda expressions; their order conveys that settings are *not_ready* unless they have been *Overridden* or have become *Ready*.

The *SafeTreatment* schema describes what it means for the system to be in a safe state. It occurs when, accounting for all of the conditions in *TreatmentStatus*, we find that all interlocks are clear and every setting is ready, or has been overridden by the operator.

$$
\begin{array}{l}
\rule[0.5ex]{0pt}{0pt}\textit{SafeTreatment} \\
\hline
\textit{TreatmentStatus} \\
\hline
\operatorname{ran} intlk = \{clear\} \\
\operatorname{ran} status \subseteq \{ready, override\}
\end{array}
$$

This can be considered a refinement of the original *SafeTreatment* schema in Section 22.2.1.

---

[2] We capitalize the names *Safe*, *Match*, etc., just to distinguish them from names we have already defined.

22.3 Enforcing the safety requirements

Finally we can define the operation that actually tests the safety conditions and sets the flags and the interlock. The control program invokes this operation periodically; we call this scanning the interlocks. The *ScanIntlk* schema describes the effect of a single scan.

$$
\begin{array}{|l}
\hline
\_\textit{ScanIntlk} \underline{} \\
\;\;\Xi \textit{Field} \\
\;\;\Delta \textit{Intlk} \\
\hline
\;\;\textit{TreatmentStatus}' \\
\;\;\textit{therapy\_intlk}' = \textbf{if } \textit{SafeTreatment}' \textbf{ then } \textit{clear} \textbf{ else } \textit{set} \\
\hline
\end{array}
$$

ScanIntlk sets or clears the master therapy interlock, depending on whether the *SafeTreatment'* predicate holds. This predicate must be tested in the after state. The *TreatmentStatus'* predicate is not an invariant; it can only be guaranteed in the after state (as indicated by the prime decoration). This is because the measured setting values may change at any time, and it requires computational effort to recompute the status flags and reestablish the *TreatmentStatus'* condition.

Here Ξ*Field* expresses that this operation only requires read access to variables in *Field*. This means that *ScanIntlk* can be scheduled independently of other operations that might change the contents of *Field*, without fear of interference (provided that *ScanIntlk* can only observe *Field* when *Field* itself is in some consistent state — that is, when its own invariant holds).

In Section 28.9, we'll derive code from this specification.

23 Modelling large systems

All of our examples so far have been small: They have only a few state variables. In this chapter we tackle a large system that has hundreds of state variables. Z provides several structuring techniques that make this feasible. The system is large but the Z description is concise. It is built up from components, subsystems, conditions, and modes that are developed separately, but also accounts for behaviors that emerge at the system level. The description illustrates several useful idioms of the Z notation, including one called *promotion*.

The case study in this chapter is the control system for a cyclotron, a type of particle accelerator. A radiation therapy machine includes an accelerator that produces a radiation beam and therapy equipment that uses the beam. In Chapters 6, 21, and 22 we described some of the controls for the therapy equipment. Now we turn to the controls for the accelerator.

Our system is built up from many components, and most of its size derives from repetition of similar components. We can make our specification much shorter and easier to grasp by identifying the components, describing them separately, and then combining them. We will define a schema type for each kind of component. The system contains multiple copies of most kinds of components, so the system model contains multiple bindings of those schema types. Many features are common to several kinds of components, and these can be concisely represented by schemas that are included elsewhere. Each kind of component can be considered an abstract data type and could be implemented by a class in object-oriented programming.

23.1 A single subsystem

Most of our requirements can be expressed by a quite simple framework: A system is a collection of *state variables* that must obey certain *control laws* and *safety assertions*. This can be modeled by a Z state schema.

23.1.1 State

The state variables are named in the schema declaration and can be discrete indicators or numeric quantities. The *control laws* and *safety assertions* are system invariants which appear as schema predicates. Control laws are formulas that relate state variables in a way that produces the intended system behaviors. In classical control theory, control laws are usually differential equations that relate continuous variables, but our control laws also include discrete variables and logical connectives. Safety assertions are formulae that place additional constraints on the state variables, as required by considerations of human safety and equipment protection.

Here are some definitions and a (much simplified) state schema for our cyclotron. The schema shows a few of the state variables and laws concerned with the radio frequency (RF) amplifiers that accelerate the particles, the main magnet that confines them, and the sensor switch on the shielding door that protects staff and visitors from scattered radiation.

$STATUS ::= disabled \mid off \mid on \mid error$

$SWITCH ::= open \mid closed$

$CURRENT == -100 .. 900$

Many more definitions . . .

$\mid \quad \epsilon : CURRENT$

Cyclotron _____

$rf, mainfld : STATUS$
$mainfld\_setpoint, mainfld\_preset, mainfld\_current : CURRENT$
$door : SWITCH$

Many other state variables . . .

$mainfld \in \{disabled, off\} \Rightarrow mainfld\_setpoint = 0.00$
$mainfld \in \{on, error\} \Rightarrow mainfld\_setpoint = mainfld\_preset$
$mainfld = on \Rightarrow |mainfld\_setpoint - mainfld\_current| \leq \epsilon$

Many other control laws . . .

$rf = on \Rightarrow door = closed$
$rf = on \Rightarrow mainfld = on$

Many other safety assertions . . .

The particle beam is considered to be on whenever the RF drive amplifiers are on. When the main magnet field is off, its current is zero; when it is on, its current is held at a nominal preset value (this magnet also has a disabled state from which it cannot be turned on, and an error state where it has been turned on but is not running correctly). The safety assertions say that the beam can only be on when the vault door is closed and the main field is running within its nominal range (this last assertion uses the absolute value function we defined in Chapter 11.4.3).

An important part of the documentation for a real system is a *glossary* that ties the formal model to the real world. The glossary explains each formal state variable such as rf, *mainfld_setpoint*, and so forth in the vocabulary of the informal documentation.

23.1.2 Operations

The control system provides a repertoire of operations that can change the values of some state variables. These are modeled by Z operation schemas.

For example, this operation turns on the main field power supply, unless it has been disabled:

```
┌─ TurnOnMainfld ─────────────────────────────────────────
│  ΔCyclotron
├──────────────────────────────────────────────────────────
│  mainfld ≠ disabled
│  mainfld_setpoint' = mainfld_preset
└──────────────────────────────────────────────────────────
```

Changing *mainfld_setpoint* usually causes *mainfld_current* to follow (the control law for this is rather complicated and is not shown). The control laws require that *mainfld* must change as well; it either becomes *on* or *error*, depending on whether *mainfld_current* approaches *mainfld_setpoint*.

This illustrates a common technique for writing concise operation definitions: The variables explicitly changed in the operation schema drive other variables, as dictated by the control laws. Therefore, operation definitions usually do not include predicates that fix the values of variables that are not explicitly changed.

23.1.3 Interlocks

A distinguishing feature of safety-critical control systems is that many operations are interlocked; they are not allowed to proceed if certain potentially hazardous conditions exist. When an interlock is *set* or *active*, the operation must not proceed; otherwise the interlock is *clear*.

In Chapters 10 and 22 we modelled interlocks with binary variables but this is not strictly necessary. Any condition can be used as an interlock. In our present framework, interlocks are modelled by predicates that act as preconditions in operation schemas. Consider the operation invoked by pressing the BEAM ON button. Here the condition $rf \neq disabled$ acts as an interlock that prevents the beam from turning on when the RF system is disabled.

$$
\begin{array}{|l}
\hline
\_\mathit{TurnOnBeam} _____ \\
\quad \Delta \mathit{Cyclotron} \\
\hline
\quad rf \neq disabled \\
\quad rf' \in \{on, error\} \\
\hline
\end{array}
$$

This schema says that pressing the BEAM ON button when the RF system has not been disabled will attempt to turn on the RF drive amplifiers (it cannot be guaranteed that they will turn on; they may indicate an error).

23.2 Many subsystems

The following sections describe some components that occur in this application. Each kind of component is specified as a different schema type with its own state, operations, and interlocks, using the basic framework presented in Section 23.1. Subsequent sections show how the component specifications are combined into a system specification.

23.2.1 Analog control parameters

The three state variables *mainfld_setpoint*, *mainfld_preset*, and *mainfld_current* that appeared in the *Cyclotron* schema in Section 23.1 reveal a pattern that appears in many other components. We define a schema for this recurring pattern, which we call a *control parameter* or simply a *parameter* (in this paper we use the word "parameter" in this sense, not the programming language's sense). The value of a parameter is a *signal*, a quantity that varies with time. We need to do arithmetic on signals so we model them as integers[1].

$$SIGNAL == \mathbb{Z}$$

$$
\begin{array}{|l}
\hline
\_\mathit{Param} _____ \\
\quad preset, setpoint, value : SIGNAL \\
\hline
\end{array}
$$

---

[1] Integers are the only numeric type built into Z. In fact some signals are implemented as floating-point numbers.

It is useful to define a schema for the situation where the parameter's value is nearly equal to the setpoint.

$$\epsilon : SIGNAL$$

```
┌─ ParamValid ─────────────────────────────
│ Param
├──────────────────────
│ |setpoint − value| ≤ ε
```

23.2.2 Power supplies and servomotors

Many of the state variables in our system are devoted to about forty power supplies that provide current to the magnets that confine, focus, and steer the beam. The main field supply discussed in Section 23.1 is just one of these. Here is a slightly more realistic generalization; this model also includes the contactor that connects the supply to its power source and represents the various faults that induce the *disabled* and *error* states. The control law says that current cannot flow when the contactor is open. The safety assertions say that we must not try to drive current when faults exist or the contactor is open.

$$FAULT ::= overload \mid line\_voltage \mid overtemp \mid ground\_short$$

```
┌─ PS ─────────────────────────────────────
│ Param
│ contactor : SWITCH
│ faults : ℙ FAULT
├──────────────────────
│ contactor = open ⇒ value ≤ ε
│ faults ≠ ∅ ⇒ setpoint = 0
│ contactor = open ⇒ setpoint = 0
```

Explicitly modelling the contactor and faults reveals that the status values of Section 23.1 (*disabled*, *off* etc.) actually indicate different power supply states, so we no longer need an explicit *status* variable. The supply is *Off* when the contactor is open and there are no faults:

```
┌─ Off ────────────────────────────────────
│ PS
├──────────────────────
│ contactor = open
│ faults = ∅
```

The supply is *On* when the contactor is closed, there are no faults, and *setpoint* and *value* (nearly) equal *preset*. Note that power supplies can use any properties defined for parameters, such as *ParamValid*.

```
┌─ On ─────────────────────────────────────────────
│  PS
│ ─────────────
│  ParamValid
│  contactor = closed
│  setpoint = preset
│  faults = ∅
└───────────────────────────────────────────────
```

There are several other states, including an *Error* state. It is easy to define operations in terms of these states. Here is the operation to turn on a power supply.

$$TurnOn \mathrel{\widehat{=}} Off \wedge (On' \vee Error')$$

Off is the initial state, and the primed schemas *On'* and *Error'* are the possible final states.

Several other kinds of components besides power supplies include control parameters. For example, in servomotors the signals represent position, not current.

$$MODE ::= enabled \mid disabled$$

```
┌─ Servo ──────────────────────────────────────────
│  Param
│  enable : MODE
│ ─────────────
│  Other state variables specific to servomotors . . .
└───────────────────────────────────────────────
```

23.2.3 Discrete indicators

It is convenient if every state variable in the system is handled in a uniform way, as part of an instance of some class of components. Those few system-level state variables that do not belong to any obvious component can be handled by defining simple components with only one state variable.

```
┌─ Indicator ──────────────────────────────────────
│  status : SWITCH
└───────────────────────────────────────────────
```

23.2.4 Combining the components

With several kinds of components now in hand, we return to the system level. Every component has a name. For each class of component, there is a set that names all the components of that class. Each class of components in the system is modelled as a function from names to bindings (instances of the state schema for that class). The roster of components in the system is fixed, so each of these functions is total (their domains are constant), and each maplet (such as $rf \mapsto \theta PS$ in the function *supply*) represents the name and state of a persistent object (in this case the radio frequency power supply).

This simplified example shows only three classes of components: power supplies, servos, and indicators, whose names form the sets ps, s, and i, respectively. Here rf and *mainfld* are the names of power supplies, the main probe *mainprb* is a servo, and the *door* is an indicator. In a real specification, these constant definitions would be fully filled in: This inventory of components and their classification into categories are important parts of the system documentation.

$[NAME]$

$$
\begin{aligned}
&ps, s, i : \mathbb{P}\,NAME \\
&rf, mainfld, mainprb, door : NAME \\
\hline
&door \in i \\
&mainprb \in s \\
&rf \in ps \;\wedge\; mainfld \in ps
\end{aligned}
$$

$$
\begin{aligned}
&\underline{\;Cyclotron\;} \\
&supply : ps \to PS \\
&servo : s \to Servo \\
&indicator : i \to Indicator \\
\hline
&supply\,rf \in On \Rightarrow supply\,mainfld \in On \\
&supply\,rf \in On \Rightarrow (indicator\,door).status = closed \\
&\text{Other system level laws} \ldots
\end{aligned}
$$

All of the state variables and most of the predicates from the basic framework are now inside the various components, so the system state schema can be much shorter. Laws that relate state variables in different components can only be expressed at the system level. These include the two safety assertions discussed in section 23.1. Here the value of the function application *supply rf* is the binding of *PS* that represents the state of the radio frequency power supply, and *indicator door* is the binding of *Indicator* that tells whether the door is open.

23.3 Some useful idioms

Specifying the operations of a system described this way requires several constructions in the Z notation that are not obvious. I call them *idioms*. These idioms are not described in the reference manual nor taught in many introductory textbooks; they must be gleaned from case studies, technical reports, or more advanced textbooks. Here are two useful ones.

23.3.1 Promotion

Much useful behavior can be modelled at the component level. However, methods defined at the component level are not, by themselves, meaningful at the system level. For example, at the system level it makes no sense to merely turn on a power supply. It is necessary to say *which* supply and to explain what happens to the whole system when a particular supply turns on. Component-level operations that must be made available at the system level can be adapted by applying a Z idiom called *promotion*.

First, for each type of component we have to define a *framing schema*, where the identifier of the component of interest is an input parameter. For power supplies, the framing schema is $Cyclo\Phi PS$, pronounced *cyclo frame p.s.* The symbol Φ is the Greek letter *phi*; it is not an operator, but is merely another naming convention like Δ (*delta*) and Ξ (*xi*).

$$
\begin{array}{|l}
\hline
\_Cyclo\Phi PS _____ \\
\Delta Cyclotron \\
\Delta PS \\
ps? : ps \\
\hline
\{ps?\} \lhd supply' = \{ps?\} \lhd supply \\
\theta PS = supply\ ps?\ \wedge\ \theta PS' = supply'\ ps? \\
\hline
\end{array}
$$

This framing schema says that the cyclotron changes and some power supply named in *ps?* changes. It also uses the *domain anti-restriction operator* $\lhd$ (Section 9.3.2) to say that all the other power supplies besides *ps?* remain unchanged. However it does not say *which* power supply changes, nor *how* the power supply changes. That comes next. Here is the operation that turns on the main field magnet in the cyclotron:

```
┌─ TurnOnMainfld ─────────────────────────────────
│ CycloΦPS
│ TurnOn
├─────────────────────────
│ ps? = mainfld
```

This schema completes the description by saying that the *TurnOn* operation occurs, and the *mainfld* power supply is the one that turns on. Other power supply operations can be promoted in the same way.

Sometimes, additional predicates must be added to promoted operations to account for requirements that emerge at the system level. In order to turn on the RF amplifiers, the door must be closed and the main field must be on.

```
┌─ TurnOnBeam ────────────────────────────────────
│ CycloΦPS
│ TurnOn
├─────────────────────────
│ ps? = rf
│ (indicator door).status = closed
│ supply mainfld ∈ On
```

23.3.2 Operations on multiple components

Other system level operations are obtained by performing the same method on multiple components. For example, a common operation is to turn on all the power supplies in some subsystem, say Beam Line A. This is provided at a single button to save the operator the trouble of switching each supply on individually. It can be expressed by another Z idiom.

```
│ blaps : ℙ ps
```

```
┌─ TurnOnBLA ─────────────────────────────────────
│ ΔCyclotron
├─────────────────────────
│ ∀ p : blaps • ∃ TurnOn •
│     θPS = supply p ∧ θPS′ = supply′ p
```

Here *blaps* holds the names of all the power supplies in Beam Line A, the bound variable p ranges over them all, and the *TurnOn* operation applies to each.

23.4 Subsystems, conditions, and modes

In addition to components, we use a few other ideas to organize the specification. Other authors have noted the usefulness of conditions and modes. Subsystems are also helpful.

23.4.1 Subsystems

The various subsystems include the RF system, the cyclotron proper[2], the three beamlines A, B, and C, the isocentric treatment room, the fixed beam treatment room, and so forth. Each is simply a collection of components, identified by their names.

$$rfsys, cyclo, bla, blb, blc, iso, fix : \mathbb{P}\, NAME$$

Note that these collections contain elements of different types. For example the cyclotron subsystem *cyclo* includes the main field power supply *mainfld*, the main probe servo *mainprb*, and so on. The objects themselves have different types, but they all have the same type of name. This makes it possible to define collections of dissimilar objects by defining sets of names.

In the interest of brevity we do not list the components in each subsystem here, but this inventory is an important part of the system documentation.

23.4.2 Conditions

It is useful to define state schemas to abbreviate conditions that appear frequently in the specification. Some conditions are quite simple. When the radio frequency power supplies are on, the beam is considered to be on:

$$
\begin{array}{|l}
\hline
\_\,BeamOn\,\rule[0.5ex]{14cm}{0.4pt} \\
Cyclotron \\
\hline
supply\, rf \in On \\
\hline
\end{array}
$$

Others are more complex; subsystems often appear in these definitions. For example, the cyclotron is ready when the vault door is closed and all of its power supplies are on.

---

[2] Somewhat confusingly, we use the term *cyclotron* both for the whole system and for a particular subsystem within it consisting mostly of magnet power supplies but not the radio frequency subsystem nor the beam lines, etc. Formally, these are the *Cyclotron* state schema and the *cyclo* subsystem, respectively.

```
┌─ CycloReady ─────────────────────────────────────────────
│ Cyclotron
│ ─────────────────────
│ (indicator door).status = closed
│ supply(|cyclo ∩ ps|) ⊆ On
└───────────────────────────────────────────────────────────
```

Here $cyclo \cap ps$ is the set of names of all the power supplies in the cyclotron subsystem, and the relational image $supply(|cyclo \cap ps|)$ returns the set of all their states.

This is a precondition for many operations. Here is a more realistic specification for turning on the beam[3].

```
┌─ TurnOnBeam ─────────────────────────────────────────────
│ CycloΦPS
│ TurnOn
│ ─────────────────────
│ ps? = rf
│ CycloReady
│ BeamOn'
└───────────────────────────────────────────────────────────
```

23.4.3 Modes

Our cyclotron can be operated in different *modes*. Each mode is characterized by the destination and purpose of the beam. The beam can be delivered to two treatment rooms or an isotope production station. It can be used to treat patients or for experiments and testing.

Modes, like conditions, are modelled by state schemas. For example

```
┌─ IsoTest ─────────────────────────────────────────────────
│ Cyclotron
│ ─────────────────────
│ Isocentric treatment room, test mode ...
└───────────────────────────────────────────────────────────
```

Modes are important because the control laws and safety assertions depend on which mode is selected. In order to turn on the beam in a room, the beam line to that room must be ready. *BLAReady* is the state schema that expresses this condition for Beam Line A. Moreover, different safety interlocks must be cleared, depending on whether

---

[3] Recall that rf is not one of the power supplies in the *cyclo* subsystem; $rfsys$ is a separate subsystem.

we are preparing to treat a patient or, alternatively, run an experiment with no people in the room. This is expressed by using modes and other conditions to write the control laws and safety assertions. *IsoReady* describes the states where it is safe to run the beam in the isocentric treatment room in test mode, and *IsoSafe* describes the states where it is safe to run the beam in the isocentric room with a patient present.

```
┌─ SafeCyclotron ──────────────────────────────────
│ Cyclotron
│──────────────────────────────────────────────────
│ IsoTest ∧ BeamOn ⇒ CycloReady ∧ BLAReady ∧ IsoReady
│ IsoTreat ∧ BeamOn ⇒ CycloReady ∧ BLAReady ∧ IsoSafe
│
│ Laws for other modes ...
└──────────────────────────────────────────────────
```

These predicates concisely express many important properties. For example, if any of the conditions included in *IsoSafe* become false while the beam is on in *IsoTreat* mode, the beam must turn off.

Modes and conditions also appear in the operation schemas:

```
┌─ SafeTurnOnBeam ─────────────────────────────────
│ TurnOnBeam
│──────────────────────────────────────────────────
│ IsoTest ⇒ CycloReady ∧ BLAReady ∧ IsoReady
│ IsoTreat ⇒ CycloReady ∧ BLAReady ∧ IsoSafe
│
│ Preconditions for other modes ...
└──────────────────────────────────────────────────
```

When users attempt operations that are interlocked, the system state does not change. Pressing the BEAM ON button turns on the RF drive if all the interlocks relevant to the selected mode are clear; otherwise, nothing happens. Therefore, the full specification for this and every other operation must be *total*; they must cover both possibilities. This is expressed:

$$T\_TurnOnBeam \mathrel{\widehat{=}} SafeTurnOnBeam \lor (Interlocked \land \Xi Cyclotron)$$

The active interlocks, conditions, and modes are displayed at the control console so operators can see which operations are enabled.

Exercise 23.4.3.1 Define *Interlocked* at the same level of detail as *SafeTurnOnBeam*.

Exercise 23.4.3.2 Define *TurnOnBLA* without using quantifiers.

23.5 Conclusion

Much of the effort in developing large applications like this one is devoted to identifying the system state variables and describing the operations that must be provided, taking care that nothing is omitted and no inconsistencies are introduced. The Z notation can help us organize this work.

Z is particularly effective for systems whose size derives from repetition of components which are not identical but share many features in common. The Z schema calculus permits recurring features to be factored out and described with texts that apply to all, supplemented with brief texts that address the differences.

24 Object-oriented programming

Object-oriented programming is a method for creating programs that use a particular kind of model. Object-oriented programming languages such as Smalltalk and C++ can implement these models, but a simpler notation that is independent of any programming language is more useful when you are creating and analyzing the models. Z can serve as that notation. You can do object-oriented design in ordinary Z, and there are several Z dialects that are intended to provide better support for object-oriented programming.

24.1 The object-oriented model and Z

The data in an object-oriented program are encapsulated in record-like data structures called *objects*. Objects belong to types called *classes*. You change or examine the data in an object, called its *attributes* or *instance variables*, by invoking one of the *methods* defined for the object's class.

Z is a good match to this object-oriented model. A Z state schema together with the operation schemas on that state define a class. The state variables in the state schema are the attributes or instance variables of that class; the operation schemas are the methods. Bindings, which are instances of the state schema type, are objects, which are instances of the class.

The cyclotron control sytem model in Chapter 23 can be considered an object-oriented design in this sense. All the data are encapsulated in objects, and the only way to read or change any data is by invoking a method.

24.2 Inheritance and schema inclusion

In object-oriented programming it is possible to define new classes that *inherit* all the attributes and methods of a previously defined one, and include new ones as well. Schema inclusion in Z is similar to inheritance. Recall the control parameter schema we defined in Chapter 23, which encapsulates a preset value, a set point, and a measured value.

```
┌─ Param ────────────────────────────────────────────────
│ preset, setpoint, value : SIGNAL
└────────────────────────────────────────────────────────
```

We can consider this state schema to be part of the definition of a class called *Param* (the Δ*Param* operation schemas that define the methods for this class are not shown).

We defined a new state schema to model power supplies. The power supply state schema *P S includes* the *Param* state schema and adds some additional state variables as well.

```
┌─ PS ───────────────────────────────────────────────────
│ Param
│ contactor : SWITCH
│ faults : ℙ FAULT
├────────────────────────────────────────────────────────
│ . . .
└────────────────────────────────────────────────────────
```

We can say that *P S inherits Param*. In the nomenclature of object-oriented programming, *Param* is the *base class* and *P S* is the *subclass* or *derived class*. A derived class has all of the attributes of its base class, and Z schema inclusion provides this as well. *Param* and *P S* both have state variables named *setpoint* (etc.).

This definition declares two objects, *panel* and *mainfld*, which are instances of *Param* and *P S*, respectively, and constrains the main field *setpoint* to track the setpoint on the control panel.

```
│ panel : Param;  mainfld : P S
├──────────────────
│ panel.setpoint = mainfld.setpoint
```

However schema inclusion in Z is not quite the same as inheritance in object-oriented programming. In most object-oriented languages, instances of a derived class are also considered to belong to the base class: *mainfld* is not just a *P S*, it would also be a *Param*, and any method defined for *Param* also applies to a *P S*. In Z, however, each variable can only have a single type: *mainfld* is a *P S*; it is not a *Param* even though it includes *Param*. Operations defined for *Param* cannot be applied directly to a *P S*.

Here is how it works out in practice. Let's define a method for *Param* that reports the difference between the setpoint and the value; we call this the *offset*. This method merely reads a *Param* object's attributes and returns a single number; it does not change the object's state, so we model the method by a function.

$offset == (\lambda\, Param \bullet value - setpoint)$

Now we can form expressions by applying the *offset* function to *Param* objects. To model "invoking the *panel* object's *offset* method" or even "sending the *offset* message to the *panel* object," we just write

offset panel

However we cannot apply our *offset* function to the *mainfld* object. This would be a type error in Z, because the domain of *error* is *Param*, but *mainfld* is a *PS*.

offset mainfld   [TYPE ERROR! Here *mainfld* is a *PS*, not a *Param*.]

With just a little extra work we can express what we want in Z. Every *PS* includes a *Param*, so can use the projection function $(\lambda\, PS \bullet \theta Param)$ to extract the *Param* part of any *PS*.

$offset\, ((\lambda\, PS \bullet \theta Param)\, mainfld)$

This expression is correct and expresses the intended meaning. The lambda expression extracts the *Param* from *mainfld* so *offset* can be applied.

24.3 Object-oriented Z dialects

Several formal notations based on Z are intended to provide better support for object-oriented programming. They are designed to allow text in the notation to more closely resemble code in an object-oriented programming language. Object-Z, MooZ, OOZE, and Z++ are examples of such dialects.

25 Concurrency and real time

Z has no built-in facilities for modelling concurrency and real time, but we can do it anyway. In fact, Z is well suited for expressing many of the classic issues in concurrent and real-time systems. We need to be able to do this in order to understand what happens when (for example) the user interface from Chapter 21 and the protection system from Chapter 22 are both executing in the same system.

In this chapter we'll model a multi-tasking system and confront the problems that arise when several tasks try to share resources. We'll represent real-time deadlines and model timeouts.

25.1 Concurrency

A *process* is a single task or thread of control. We'll model a simple multi-tasking system where several processes run concurrently. Each process owns some *virtual memory* in which it can store its own data. Processes also exchange data in shared *resources* that might include regions of memory, blocks of disk storage, and communication channels.

The basic types *PROCESS* and *RESOURCE* model the fixed complement of processes and resources in this simple system. *DATA* models the contents of a resource or virtual memory. For each process p in *PROCESS*, the value of $vm\ p$ is the contents that processes' virtual memory. Likewise, $data\ r$ is the contents of resource r.

[*PROCESS, RESOURCE, DATA*]

___ *Sys* _____
| $vm : PROCESS \rightarrow DATA$
| $data : RESOURCE \rightarrow DATA$
|_____

The state *Sys* is shared by all the processes. Anything that any process can do is modelled by a Z operation on this state. The execution of each process is a sequence of Z operations. We still view the execution of the whole system as a sequence of discrete, nearly instantaneous operations, but now the operations might be invoked by several different processes, not just one. Operations invoked by different processes might alternate or *interleave*. This is called the *interleaving model of concurrency*.

Any process might attempt to invoke any operation at any time. If the preconditions of the operation are satisfied, the operation is *enabled*. An operation that is enabled will eventually occur: The system is *fair*. If several operations invoked by different processes are all enabled at the same time, then any one of them might be next to occur; we cannot predict which: The system is *nondeterministic*. We have to assume that there is a scheduler that selects and executes enabled operations, but we do not model this in Z.

A process can invoke the *Write* operation to store the contents of its virtual memory in a resource. The process and the resource are the inputs $p?$ and $r?$ to the *Write* operation.

__*Write*__
ΔSys
$p? : PROCESS;\ r? : RESOURCE$

$data' = data \oplus \{r? \mapsto vm\ p?\}$
$vm' = vm$

Here we use the override operator $\oplus$ (Section 9.3.2) rather than the equation $data'\ r? = vm\ p?$ to indicate that all the other resources remain unchanged. A process can invoke *Read* to load its virtual memory with contents from a resource.

__*Read*__
ΔSys
$p? : PROCESS;\ r? : RESOURCE$

$vm' = vm \oplus \{p? \mapsto data\ r?\}$
$data' = data$

There is a problem with *Write* and *Read*. There is no way for a process to ensure that anything it writes can ever be read again, because some other process might destroy it by writing something else on the same resource. For example, process p_1 might write the data x on resource r_1, intending to read it back later, but in the meantime process p_2 writes y on r_1. Later, when p_1 reads r assuming it will find x, it gets y instead, and disaster ensues. This scenario demonstrates the problem common to most difficulties involving concurrency, such as race conditions. To prevent such difficulties, a process must be able to gain exclusive control of a resource and prevent other processes from writing on it.

The classic solution to this problem is to provide a new kind of object called a *mutex* (for *mutual exclusion*). A mutex is sometimes called a *binary semaphore*. Each resource is protected by a mutex. To write on the resource, a process must possess the mutex. The mutex can only belong to one process at a time; this can be modelled by a partial function from mutexes to processes.

[*MUTEX*]

$$\mid mutex : RESOURCE \rightarrowtail MUTEX$$

```
┌─ ProtectedSys ──────────────────────────────
│ Sys
│ owner : MUTEX ⇸ PROCESS
│
└─────────────────────────────────────────────
```

The *owner* function is partial because sometimes no process owns a particular mutex; in that case we say the mutex is *free*. If the mutex is free, a process may seize it.

```
┌─ Seize ─────────────────────────────────────
│ ΔProtectedSys
│ p? : PROCESS; m? : MUTEX
├─────────────
│ m? ∉ dom owner
│ owner' = owner ⊕ {m? ↦ p?}
│ data' = data
└─────────────────────────────────────────────
```

Seize must be implemented as an *atomic* operation: Once it begins, it must be allowed to complete without interference or interruption. When a process executes *Seize* it first tests the precondition. If this condition is *true*, the process must be able to establish the *owner' = owner ⊕ {m? ↦ p?}* postcondition before another process can test the *m? ∉ dom owner* condition. Otherwise, the second process might also conclude that the mutex is free and attempt to use the same resource.

When a process owns the mutex, it may write on its resource.

```
┌─ ProtectedWrite ────────────────────────────
│ ΔProtectedSys
│ Write
├─────────────
│ p? = owner(mutex r?)
│ owner' = owner
└─────────────────────────────────────────────
```

When a process is finished using a resource, it should release the mutex.

```
┌─ Release ──────────────────────────────────────────────
│ ΔProtectedSys
│ p? : PROCESS;  m? : MUTEX
├────────────────────────────────────────────────────────
│ p? = owner m?
│ owner' = {m?} ⩤ owner
│ data' = data
└────────────────────────────────────────────────────────
```

This definition uses the *domain antirestriction* operator ⩤ (Section 9.3.2). It has the effect of removing the pair $m? \mapsto p?$ from *owner*.

25.2 Events

A system that interacts with the outside world must respond to *events* whose time and order of arrival cannot be predicted. Such systems are said to be *event-driven* or *interrupt-driven*. Processes in these systems wait for events and handle each one. For example, an event might indicate that a resource has new data ready, and then the handler reads the data from the resource and perhaps does some computation on it.

We define a new data type to model events. We augment our system state with a set of events that have occurred but have not yet been handled, and a relation that associates processes with the events they await.

[EVENT]

```
┌─ EventSys ─────────────────────────────────────────────
│ Sys
│ events : ℙ EVENT
│ waiting : PROCESS ↔ EVENT
└────────────────────────────────────────────────────────
```

A process can wait for several events, and an event might have several processes waiting for it. When (p, e) is a member of *waiting*, process p is waiting for event e. A waiting process performs no operations. We can ensure this by including the precondition $p \notin \text{dom } waiting$ in every operation. Dividing tasks among processes in a multi-tasking system allows work to be done by some processes while others are waiting.

Process $p?$ can invoke the *Wait* operation to begin waiting for the next occurrence of any of the events in set $es?$:

```
┌─ Wait ─────────────────────────────────────────────────────
│ ΔEventSys
│ p? : PROCESS;  es? : ℙ EVENT
├───────────────────────────────────────────────────────────
│ waiting′ = waiting ∪ { e? : es? • p? ↦ e? }
│ events′ = events
└───────────────────────────────────────────────────────────
```

The *Signal* operation signals the occurrence of event *e?* by placing it in the set of unhandled events. *Signal* might be invoked by a running process to awaken a waiting process, or it might be invoked by hardware to signal an occurence in the outside world. An event signalled by hardware is called an *interrupt*.

```
┌─ Signal ───────────────────────────────────────────────────
│ ΔEventSys
│ e? : EVENT
├───────────────────────────────────────────────────────────
│ events′ = events ∪ {e?}
│ waiting′ = waiting
└───────────────────────────────────────────────────────────
```

A process responds to an event by invoking a *handler*. The handler becomes enabled when an unhandled event appears. The handler *clears* the event by removing it from the set of unhandled events and also removes all of its entries from *waiting*. This allows processes that were waiting for the event to proceed.

```
┌─ Handler ──────────────────────────────────────────────────
│ ΔEventSys
│ p? : PROCESS;  e? : EVENT
├───────────────────────────────────────────────────────────
│ e? ∈ events ∧ (p?, e?) ∈ waiting
│ events′ = events \ {e?}
│ waiting′ = waiting ⊳ {e?}
│
│ ... handle event e? ...
└───────────────────────────────────────────────────────────
```

This definition uses the *range antirestriction* operator ⊳ (Section 9.3.2) to remove all the pairs that refer to *e?* from *waiting*. The handler can also perform computations specific to the event. If the event indicates that new data are ready, the handler could read the data into its processes' virtual memory.

25.3 Real time

We can model real time as an ordinary Z state variable. We augment our event driven system with a real-time clock. The value of the current time stored in the variable *clock* is just a number; perhaps it indicates the number of milliseconds that has elapsed since system startup. We assume that the value of our clock variable grows larger as each successive operation is invoked. Each process has a timer that it can use to measure elapsed time.

$$TIME == \mathbb{N}$$

```
┌─ RealTimeSys ─────────────────────────────────
│ EventSys
│ clock : TIME
│ timer : PROCESS → TIME
│
└───────────────────────────────────────────────
```

If a process wishes to limit the time it will wait, it uses the *TimedWait* operation to request a timeout. A *timeout* is an event that is signalled after a deadline expires. Each process has its own timeout event, so we declare the *timeout* function with the *injection* arrow ↣ (Section 9.4.3). The *TimedWait* operation sets up the timeout by registering for the timeout event and recording the current time in its processes' timer.

```
│ deadline : TIME
│ timeout : PROCESS ↣ EVENT
```

```
┌─ TimedWait ───────────────────────────────────
│ ΔRealTimeSys
│ Wait
├───────────────
│ timeout p? ∈ es?
│ timer' = timer ⊕ {p? ↦ clock}
└───────────────────────────────────────────────
```

If the process is still waiting when the deadline expires, the timeout is signalled.

Timeout

$\Delta RealTimeSys$
$Signal$

$e? \in \mathrm{ran}\ waiting$
$e? \in \mathrm{ran}\ timeout$
$(\textbf{let}\ p == timeout^{\sim}\ e? \bullet clock - timer\ p > deadline)$

Here p is the process associated with the timeout event $e?$, obtained by inverting the _timeout_ function. The system determines that a timeout has occurred by comparing the current _clock_ value to the start time recorded in _timer p_.

Further reading

A real document control system (Chapter 16) is described in Tichy's paper [1982] on the RCS.

The text filling problem (Chapter 17) has been discussed in many books and papers. Some of the published solutions don't quite work. Bertrand Meyer [1985] reviews this literature, traces some of the errors to difficulties with informal definitions, and proposes a formal one. I believe Meyer's paper also reveals some disadvantages of using ordinary mathematics as a specification notation and motivates the kinds of conventions we use in Z.

Richard Bird [1986] demonstrates several different text-filling strategies and develops a program from his formal definition. Carroll Morgan [1990] presents another version in his book.

My *words* function owes much to the word count study and the blue pencil problem in the book by Rosalind Barden, Susan Stepney, and David Cooper [1994].

Smith [1990] observed that a solution to the eight queen's problem (Chapter 18) is a bijection.

The development in Chapter 19 is based on the computational geometry book by O'Rourke [1994], which also includes a derivation of the *area*2 formula.

Definitions for fundamental objects such as polygons can be built up further to define more complex objects, such as anatomical structures, that are useful in particular applications. A collection of such definitions serves as the foundation for a suite of software tools for radiation therapy planning [Jacky *et al.*, 1994]. In order to make them widely accessible, the definitions in that project were expressed in a semiformal style using formulas and formatted text. The presentation style was influenced by my experience with Z.

Radiation therapy treatment planning is discussed in the textbooks by Johns and Cunningham [1983] and Khan [1984]. Fig. 19.2 was created with the Prism treatment planning system [Kalet, 1996].

Marshall [1990] uses the VDM notation to describe several approaches to a related problem: Given the integer coordinates of two points, calculate the integer coordinates of all the points which best approximate a continuous real line between the two. This problem must be solved to draw line graphics on raster display devices.

Patrick Henry Winston's textbook *Artificial Intelligence* [1977] provides a good introduction to rule-based programming and is the source of the animal example in Chapter 20.

The example in Chapter 20 has many limitations. Most obviously, it has no variables. Many useful rule-based programs do have variables, and facts can be predicates such as *carnivore*(x), *herbivore*(y), and *eats*(x, y). The results of deductions can be assignments of values to variables, such as $x = lion$, $y = zebra$. Deduction with variable assignments is called *unification*. John S. Fitzgerald [1990] and Sunil Vadera [1990] have both described unification in the VDM notation. Craig [1991] uses Z to model larger artificial intelligence programs in his book.

Large programs built with mostly conventional techniques can incorporate rule-based components to solve particular subproblems. An example from radiation therapy planning is described by Mary Austin-Seymour *et al.* [1995].

Transitive closure is explained in almost any book on discrete mathematics. In Z, Jim Woodcock and Martin Loomes employ transitive closure in the configuration manager model in their textbook [1990], and Bernard Sufrin [1989] uses it in his model of the Unix *make* utility. The book by Barden *et al.* [1994] includes several more examples.

The case study in Chapter 21 is based on an X window application. Jonathan Unger and I describe our implementation in [Jacky and Unger, 1995] The X window system is described in the paper by Scheifler and Gettys [1986]. The book by Nye [1988] is a standard reference on X window programming. Jonathan Bowen [1992] modelled some display aspects of the X window system in Z.

David Harel [1987] describes statecharts.

Matt Jaffe, Nancy Leveson, Mats Heimdahl and Bonnie Melhart [1991] showed how to analyze state transition systems for completeness and other properties relevant to safety. Nancy Leveson's book [1995] is devoted to safety issues. I discuss safety in a textbook chapter [Jacky, 1991; Jacky, 1996].

The protection system in Chapter 22 has some similarities to the reactor protection system modelled in VDM by Bloomfield and Froome [1986] and Fields and Elvang-Gøransson [1992].

The cyclotron case study in Chapter 23 is based on the Clinical Neutron Therapy System at the University of Washington, Seattle [Risler *et al.*, 1984; Jacky *et al.*, 1990; Jacky *et al.*, 1992]. The chapter is based on a conference paper [Jacky, 1993b] and a journal article [Jacky, 1995]. Other work on formalizing this system appears in [Jacky, 1990; Jacky, 1993a].

Carroll Morgan and Bernard Sufrin [1984] introduced promotion in their Z model of the Unix file system. Promotion is also discussed in the technical report by Ruaridh

Macdonald [1991] and the Z textbook by John Wordsworth [1992]. Several more examples appear in the book by Barden *et al.* [1994].

The paper by Heninger [1980] shows how conditions and modes were used to simplify the formal specification of an avionics program.

The paper by Stepney, Barden, and Cooper [1992b] surveys object-oriented style in ordinary Z as well as several object-oriented Z dialects. Their book [Stepney *et al.*, 1992b] includes several papers that demonstrate these techniques and notations. Several chapters in the book by Lano and Haughton [1993] use object-oriented Z dialects.

Andy S. Evans observed that Z can model interleaved concurrency, and showed how to prove safety and progress or *liveness* properties [Evans, 1994a; Evans, 1994b].

Part V

Programming with Z

26 Refinement

Development often proceeds from an abstract specification to a detailed design. This process is called *refinement*[1]. Both the specification and the design are models, but the specification is closer to the users' view, while the design is closer to an executable program. If we express both models in mathematics, we can use formal reasoning to check that the design faithfully expresses the intent of the specification. We can prove that the specification and the design are really two views of the same thing. This ability to check the correctness of design steps is one of the distinguishing features of a formal method.

26.1 What is refinement?

An abstract model has some of the properties of the thing it models, but not all of them. A design is more concrete than a specification. A design is correct if it has all the properties of the specification; it usually has some additional properties as well. This relation is expressed precisely by logical implication: The predicate that describes the design must imply the predicate that describes the specification.

Here is a trivial example. Our specification requires that we increase the value of x:

$$x' > x$$

We propose to achieve this by adding one to x. Our design is this stronger predicate:

$$x' = x + 1$$

The design should imply the specification:

---

[1] Some authors call it *reification*.

$$x' = x + 1 \Rightarrow x' > x$$

This implication is clearly *true*, so the refinement is correct. We can say that $x' = x+1$ refines $x' > x$.

Exercise 26.1.1   Write a truth table for the implication $p \Rightarrow q$ where p is $x' = x+1$, and q is $x' > x$. Add two more columns to the table for x and x' and fill in each row with integer values that cause p and q to take on the truth values called for in that row.

26.2 A refinement example

Z provides a rich collection of types; some are abstract, but others are similar to the data types we find in programming languages. For example, sets are central in Z but are not provided in most programming languages. On the other hand, Z sequences resemble the arrays and lists provided in many languages. In this section we will refine a specification with sets to a design with sequences.

26.2.1 From sets to sequences

Our abstract state is a set s of elements of type X.

$[X]$

```
_Abstract_____
 s : ℙ X

```

We define an abstract operation that stores an element in the set, using the set union operator.

```
_AStore_____
 ΔAbstract
 x? : X
_____
 s' = s ∪ {x?}

```

We plan to implement this system in a programming language that has no built-in set data type, but does have arrays and lists. We decide to refine our abstract specification to a detailed design based on sequences because we expect this will be easier to map into the target programming language.

Our concrete state is not a set but a sequence ss of elements of type X.

```
┌─ Concrete ──────────────────────────────────
│ ss : seq X
│
└──────────────────────────────────────────────
```

Here is the concrete operation that stores an element in the sequence, using the concatenation operator.

```
┌─ CStore ────────────────────────────────────
│ ΔConcrete
│ x? : X
├──────────────────────────────────────────────
│ ss′ = ss ⌢ ⟨x?⟩
│
└──────────────────────────────────────────────
```

Already we have added some detail. A sequence has more structure than a set; to add an element to a sequence, we have to say where to put it in the sequence order. To keep things simple we just put the new element at the end. This is an implementation decision that should not affect the programmers who use the store operation. Putting the new element at the front or inserting it somewhere in the middle would be equally acceptable from the point of view of the abstract specification.

26.2.2 Checking the refinement

This example is a bit more complicated than the $x' > x$ example from Section 26.1 because the specification and the design use different data structures. To show that the design correctly refines the specification, we must say how the two data structures are related. The sequence should always hold the same elements as the set. A sequence is a function from natural numbers to elements, so the elements stored in the sequence are the range of this function. The range of the sequence must be the same as the set.

$$s = \operatorname{ran} ss \wedge s' = \operatorname{ran} ss'$$

This must be true before and after any operation, so equations appear for unprimed and primed variables.

Now we can form the implication that expresses the refinement. The predicate of the abstract operation *AStore* appears on the right of the implication arrow, and the predicate of concrete operation *CStore* is on the left, along with the equations relating s and ss.

$$ss' = ss \frown \langle x? \rangle \wedge s = \operatorname{ran} ss \wedge s' = \operatorname{ran} ss' \Rightarrow s' = s \cup \{x?\}$$

The refinement is correct if this predicate is true. Figure 26.1 illustrates the argument: The initial and final states are related by the store operations, and the abstract and concrete states are related by the range function.

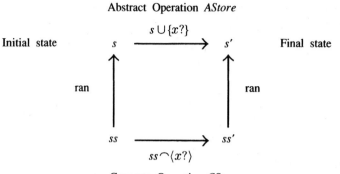

Abstract Operation *AStore*

Concrete Operation *CStore*

Figure 26.1: Refinement of *AStore* by *CStore*.

This refinement is easy to prove. We use two laws about sequences. The range of a sequence is the union of the ranges of its constituents: $ran(s \frown t) = (ran\ s) \cup (ran\ t)$. The range of a singleton sequence is just the element itself: $ran\langle x \rangle = \{x\}$. We also apply a classic technique for proving implications. To prove $p \Rightarrow q$, *assume the antecedent*: Treat the antecedent p as if it were a law. If it is possible to prove the consequent q using p in this way, then the entire implication is true. In our proof format it looks like this:

$$p \Rightarrow q \hspace{6cm} \text{[To prove]}$$

$$\Leftrightarrow q \hspace{6cm} \text{[Assume antecedent.]}$$

$$\vdots$$

$$\Leftrightarrow true \hspace{5cm} \text{[Justified by antecedent } p]$$

Here is the proof of the refinement:

$$ss' = ss \frown \langle x? \rangle \wedge s = ran\ ss \wedge s' = ran\ ss' \Rightarrow s' = s \cup \{x?\} \hspace{1cm} \text{[Given]}$$

$$\Leftrightarrow s' = s \cup \{x?\} \hspace{4cm} \text{[Assume antecedent.]}$$

$$\Leftrightarrow ran\ ss' = s \cup \{x?\} \hspace{3.5cm} \text{[Antecedent } s' = ran\ ss'.]$$

$$\Leftrightarrow ran(ss \frown \langle x? \rangle) = s \cup \{x?\} \hspace{2.5cm} \text{[Antecedent } ss' = ss \frown \langle x? \rangle.]$$

$$\Leftrightarrow ran\ ss \cup ran\langle x? \rangle = s \cup \{x?\} \hspace{2cm} \text{[Law about } ran(s \frown t).]$$

$$\Leftrightarrow ran\ ss \cup \{x?\} = s \cup \{x?\} \hspace{2.5cm} \text{[Law about } ran\langle x? \rangle.]$$

$$\Leftrightarrow s \cup \{x?\} = s \cup \{x?\} \hspace{3cm} \text{[Antecedent } s = ran\ ss.]$$

$$\Leftrightarrow true \hspace{5.5cm} [e = e \Leftrightarrow true.]$$

This concludes the proof of correctness for this refinement.

26.3 Generalizing refinement

The preceding example was very simple. We can generalize the technique to larger systems by writing an *abstraction schema* that includes the abstract state, the concrete state, and the predicate that relates them. Here is the abstraction schema for our little example.

```
┌─ Abs ──────────────────────────────────────────────
│ Abstract
│ Concrete
│ ────────────────────────────────────────────
│ s = ran ss
└────────────────────────────────────────────────────
```

Here the predicate is simply $s = \text{ran } ss$; s is declared in *Abstract*, and ss is declared in *Concrete*. An abstraction schema can relate many different state variables, and the predicate need not be an equation.

In general, the correctness condition is a schema expression, not just an equation. In this example it is

$$\forall \Delta Abstract;\ \Delta Concrete;\ x? : X \bullet$$
$$\text{pre } AOp \wedge COp \wedge \Delta Abs \Rightarrow AOp$$

where AOp and COp are the abstract and concrete operations. In this example they are *AStore* and *CStore*, and pre AOp is the precondition of *AStore*, which is *true*. Expanding this schema expression for our example we obtain

$$\forall \Delta Abstract;\ \Delta Concrete;\ x? : X \bullet$$
$$true \wedge ss' = ss \frown \langle x? \rangle \wedge s = \text{ran } ss \wedge s' = \text{ran } ss' \Rightarrow s' = s \cup \{x?\}$$

This is equivalent to the condition presented earlier. Figure 26.2 illustrates the method. The abstraction schema *Abs* relates the concrete and abstract states in the same way that the range function did in Fig. 26.1.

Exercise 26.3.1 In our example, our concrete operation *CStore* interprets the sequence ss to be a list and implements the abstract operation *AStore* by appending the new element to the end of the list. Define an alternate concrete operation *CStore*1 that interprets the sequence ss to be an array and implements *AStore* by updating the element at the end of the array. You may not use the Z concatentation operator $\frown$. Prove that your refinement is correct.

Exercise 26.3.2 There are other ways to refine *AStore*. Instead of storing the new element at the end of the sequence, we might use a *hash function* to compute the

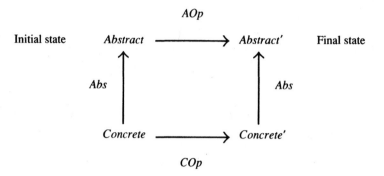

Figure 26.2: Refinement using an abstraction schema *Abs*.

index where the new element should be stored. Propose a declaration for the hash function and define the concrete operation *CStore2* that uses it. What must be true of the hash function to make the refinement correct?

26.4 Refinement strategies

In refinement we wish to make a model that is sufficiently concrete so that translating it to a programming language is a simple exercise. You might have to apply several different refinement strategies to reach that goal. The preceding example illustrated one of them: Replace an abstract data structure with a more concrete one.

Another refinement strategy replaces nonconstructive definitions that describe items by their properties to definitions that show how to construct the items. This example from elementary algebra provides a nonconstructive definition of x:

$$ax^2 + bx + c = 0$$

This predicate does not resemble a statement in an executable programming language because x, the item whose value we wish to know, appears embedded in an expression. We obtain this equivalent constructive definition by using the quadratic formula:

$$x = -b \pm \sqrt{b^2 - 4ac} \, / \, 2a$$

This predicate more closely resembles an assigment statement because x appears by itself on one side of an equation[2].

---

[2] In this example only, x might denote a real or complex number.

Another strategy replaces *nondeterministic* definitions with *deterministic* ones. Nondeterministic definitions admit more than one solution. Nondeterminism is often a good thing to have in a specification because it permits designers to choose among alternative solutions. Subsequent design steps remove the nondeterminism by selecting a particular solution. In the preceding solution to the quadratic equation, we could make the solution deterministic by replacing $\pm$ with $+$ or $-$. A larger example occurs in Chapter 17 where we developed the *words* function that takes a stream of text and returns a sequence of words. Its definition includes the equation

$$words(l \frown s \frown r) = (words\ l) \frown (words\ r)$$

This says that wherever the text contains a space s, you can discard the space and break the text in two. This is nondeterministic because any space will do. It can be replaced by the deterministic equation

$$words(w \frown s \frown r) = \langle w \rangle \frown (words\ r)$$

which always breaks off the initial word in the text. This latter equation is closer to a program that scans the text from beginning to end.

27 Program derivation and formal verification

At last we reach code. This chapter shows how to derive code from formulas taken from a Z specification and demonstrate that the code does what the formulas require. *Program derivation* is the systematic derivation of code from a formal specification. A *proof of correctness* demonstrates agreement between code and its specification. Such a proof is a by-product of every program derivation. It is also possible to attempt a *formal verification* to prove the correctness of an already completed block of code.

Almost all code in use today was produced by traditional informal methods, which are based on adapting code from previously solved problems and making modifications guided by programmers' intuitions about what happens when a computer executes a program. Thinking about what happens in the computer is called *operational* reasoning (in contrast to *formal* reasoning, which only considers the program text). Operational reasoning is fallible because it requires programmers to imagine how the values of variables evolve through time as execution takes one path or another through the code. For any but the smallest programs, there are far too many variables, values, and paths to consider, so programmers often resort to running their code to see if it behaves as they intend. This is a trial-and-error process, so it can take a great deal of effort to produce an acceptable product.

Formal program derivation proposes a radical alternative: A program is a formula. It can be derived from a specification, and its properties can be checked by calculation. There is no need to try to imagine what happens in the computer, and you shouldn't need to rely on tests to find out what your program means. In this view testing is primarily intended to detect misunderstandings in the specification and check assumptions about the operating environment, including the compiler, the operating system, and the hardware.

Program derivation requires creativity and judgment; there is nothing mechanical or automatic about it. At each step you must invent the next fragment of code, but the formal specification can help show you the way, and you can check each fragment as soon as you write it. Moreover, your calculations check correctness for all cases, not just a single test case. This ability to detect errors immediately, without having to finish the code and run tests, is one of the biggest advantages of formal program derivation over traditional methods. Moreover, a formal development can be documented as a sequence of steps that you or anyone else can review. This is essential when you must convince yourself or others that your program meets requirements for safety, accuracy, security, or any other critical property.

Program derivation need not replace traditional coding methods. Many programming problems are routine; experienced programmers can adapt a correct solution from their files or their heads more quickly than they can derive one. You can hold formal derivation in reserve for those difficult problems where intuition doesn't work very well. It is rarely useful to attempt a formal derivation or verification of an entire program. Formal methods work at any scale, in the sense that they can be applied to critical pieces extracted from large programs, so you can concentrate on deriving or verifying the difficult parts.

Chapter 28 teaches a practical method of programming that supplements experience and intuition with formal derivation. This chapter is only a very brief introduction to program derivation and verification intended to show you that code (not just specifications and designs) can be treated formally. The few examples in this chapter were deliberately chosen to be very simple so you can follow them easily and use your own intuition to confirm the results of the formal calculations. Deeper examples are cited in the further readings.

Program derivation makes the connection between two formal notations: a mathematical notation such as Z and an executable programming language. There are two popular styles of program derivation. The original *axiomatic* approach is closer to first principles. The more recent *refinement calculus* approach can be more convenient.

27.1 Axiomatic program derivation and verification

When we write code, we should include comments to help explain how the code works. Some of the most helpful comments are predicates that describe the state of the computation when execution reaches a particular point. Here is our integer square root function from Chapter 5 commented in this style:

```
int iroot(int arg)
/* Integer square root, using 1 + 3 + 5 + ... + 2*i-1 = i*i */
{
    int i,term,sum;

    /* 0 =< arg */
    term=1; sum=1;
    for (i = 0; sum <= arg; i++) {
        term=term+2;    /* term = 2*i-1 */
        sum=sum+term;   /* sum  = 1 + 3 + 5 + ... + 2*i - 1 */
    }
    return i; /* 0 <= i*i <= arg < (i+1)*(i+1) */
}
```

The comments show why the function works. What had seemed mysterious is now obvious. But how was this code invented? And how can we make sure that the code agrees with the comments? The axiomatic method shows how.

The product of an axiomatic derivation (or verification) is code with predicates (or *assertions*) interleaved. The assertion before the beginning of the code describes the precondition and subsequent assertions are stronger until the final assertion after the end of the code describes the postcondition or goal. Each statement in the program should make progress toward the goal by establishing a stronger predicate.

The axiomatic method considers the program state: the program variables and their values. Executing a statement in an imperative programming language usually causes the state of the program to change, for example a new value might be assigned to some variable. We can characterize any program fragment by describing how it changes the program state, using notation called the *Hoare triple*.

$$\{ P \} S \{ Q \}$$

P and Q are predicates in mathematical notation (the braces are merely delimiters), and S is a block of code in our chosen programming language; it might be a single statement or an entire program. If the program is in a state that satisfies predicate P, executing the code S will result in a new state that satisfies predicate Q. This triple defines the meaning or *semantics* of a block of code in the mathematical language of predicates. P and Q are very much like the "before" and "after" states of a Z operation schema; P is the precondition, and Q is the postcondition.

If S is a single programming language statement, a Hoare triple can be used as a formal definition of that statement. You can define every kind of statement in a programming language this way; the whole collection of definitions comprises an *axiomatic semantics* of the language. Most popular programming languages do not have a full axiomatic definition, but that is no obstacle, because we do have definitions of the three basic constructs that are present in every imperative language: assignment (= in C), branching (if in C), and loops (while in C). These are sufficient to express any algorithm; the other constructs are just conveniences that can be expressed in terms of these three. You can do formal development in popular programming languages such as C by first deriving code in the basic constructs that have axiomatic definitions, and then using *source language transformations* to reach more complex constructs. For example, in C you can transform the while loop s; while (p) { u; t; } into the for loop for (s; p; t) u[1]. Many of the distinctive idioms that distinguish one programming language from another (making C appear different from Pascal or Ada for example) can be expressed by source language transformations.

---

[1] This transformation is only valid when the code fragment u does not contain the C continue statement. Irregularities like this one make programs hard to verify.

27.1.1 Assignment

Here is an axiomatic definition of the assignment statement that assigns the value of expression e to variable x.

$$\{\, e \text{ is defined} \,\} \; x \; = \; e \; \{\, x' = e \,\}$$

This can be read, "starting in a state where expression e is defined, executing the statement x $=$ e results in a state where the predicate $x' = e$ holds."

The precondition here is a disclaimer against expressions that cause division by zero, arithmetic overflow, and other actions that can crash the program or cause undefined behavior. Expressing this predicate formally can be quite difficult because it requires detailed knowledge of the programming language and its run-time system, the number representation, and so forth. We often just assume it is true. It is also necessary that evaluating expression e does not have any *side effects* that change the values of program variables (C permits the expression on the right side of the assignment to be another assignment or a function call with side effects, but in those cases our definition may not be valid). The assignment statement itself is written here in the syntax of C which uses the equal sign, nevertheless assigment is different from equality. The second predicate uses the same convention as Z to indicate that the primed variable x' is the value of the program variable x in the state after the assignment.

There is a more useful axiomatic definition of assignment. We usually write code with some goal in mind. This triple relates the goal (the postcondition Q) to the state before the assignment

$$\{\, Q[e/x'] \,\} \; x \; = \; e \; \{\, Q \,\}$$

Substitution in predicates corresponds to assignment in code; $Q[e/x']$ means predicate Q with expression e substituted for x' (from now on we assume that e is defined). $Q[e/x']$ is called the *weakest precondition* of Q with respect to the statement x $=$ e; it is the necessary and sufficient precondition for the execution of x $=$ e to end in postcondition Q. This definition makes it possible to derive assignment statements from goals. Let's say our goal is to increase the value of x: Q is the predicate $x' > x$ so $Q[e/x']$ is $e > x$. The single program variable x is modelled by two mathematical variables x and x' for the before and after states, respectively. Substituting these into the definition we obtain

$$\{\, e > x \,\} \; x \; = \; e \; \{\, x' > x \,\}$$

To achieve our goal, we can choose any expression e that makes the first predicate true. Many choices would work; we choose $e = x + 1$ and obtain

$$\{\, x + 1 > x \,\} \; x \; = \; \text{x+1} \; \{\, x' > x \,\}$$

This triple is a formal proof of correctness that the program x = x+1 satisfies its specification $x' > x$. We say it is formal because it does not depend on our intuition about how assignment works. It can be verified by merely comparing formulas: Our triple matches the axiomatic definition, and its postcondition matches our goal, therefore it is correct.

27.1.2 Control structure

What happens when we introduce control structure and multiple statements? Let's try a slightly more complicated example: Compute the truth value of the conjunction $p \wedge q$ using *short-circuit evaluation*: Do not evaluate q when p is *false*.

In C we can implement the predicates p and q with integer-valued expressions where zero means *false*; any nonzero value means *true*. C provides a built-in *and* operator && that is supposed to provide short-circuit evaluation so we could easily implement $p \wedge q$ with p && q. For the purposes of this example we posit that our compiler does not provide &&, or that it violates the language standard and always evaluates both arguments to && (some programming languages, such as Pascal, do evaluate both arguments to *and*).

We wish to evaluate $p \wedge q$ as cheaply as possible. We happen to know that it is cheap to evaluate p but quite expensive to evaluate q. It seems there should be two cases (p could be *true* or *false*) so we try an if statement. We find this axiomatic definition:

$$\{ U \}$$
$$\text{if } (p) \{ U \wedge p \} S1; \{ V \} \text{ else } \{ U \wedge \neg p \} S2 \{ W \}$$
$$\{ V \vee W \}$$

The final predicates V and W depend on $S1$ and $S2$, which might be whole blocks of code. We can treat this definition as a template and fill it in to match our problem statement (here again, evaluating predicate p must not have side effects). We want the same result from both branches so both V and W are $p \wedge q$. We will return the truth value of the conjunction in a variable so the final predicate becomes $x' \Leftrightarrow p \wedge q$. Here x' is a Z predicate (not a variable) but it is implemented as the C integer variable x. We guess that $S1$ and $S2$ will be assignment statements, but we don't know yet what the assignments will be. Filling in the definition $\{ V[e/x'] \} $ x = $e \{ V \}$ for each assignment, we obtain:

$$\{ p \text{ and } q \text{ are defined} \}$$
$$\text{if } (p) \{ p \} \{ e_1 \Leftrightarrow p \wedge q \} \text{ x } = e_1; \{ x' \Leftrightarrow p \wedge q \}$$
$$\quad \text{ else} \{ \neg p \} \{ e_2 \Leftrightarrow p \wedge q \} \text{ x } = e_2 \{ x' \Leftrightarrow p \wedge q \}$$
$$\{ x' \Leftrightarrow p \wedge q \}$$

Next we choose predicates e_1 and e_2 that make the two bracketed preconditions true. In the if branch p is true so $\{ e_1 \Leftrightarrow p \wedge q \}$ is $\{ e_1 \Leftrightarrow true \wedge q \}$; in the else branch we have $\{ e_2 \Leftrightarrow false \wedge q \}$. We use two laws about *and*, *true* $\wedge q \Leftrightarrow q$ and *false* $\wedge q \Leftrightarrow false$, so e_1 is q, and e_2 is *false*, which is zero in C. We have:

$\{p$ and q are defined$\}$
if $(p) \{ p \}\{ q \Leftrightarrow p \wedge q \}$ x $= q; \{ x' \Leftrightarrow p \wedge q \}$
    else $\{ \neg p \}\{ false \Leftrightarrow p \wedge q \}$ x $= 0 \{ x' \Leftrightarrow p \wedge q \}$
$\{ x' \Leftrightarrow p \wedge q \}$

There is one last detail. In the then branch we have two adjacent bracketed predicates: $\{ p \}\{ q \Leftrightarrow p \wedge q \}$. The first predicate p comes from the definition of if, and the second predicate $q \Leftrightarrow p \wedge q$ comes from the definition of assignment. We have two adjacent predicates in the else branch as well, and adjacent predicates like these occur frequently in axiomatic program development. The program is correct when the first predicate in each adjacent pair implies the second. These are *verification conditions*: predicates that arise during formal verfication, that must be proved to show correctness. We have two verification conditions, $p \Rightarrow (q \Leftrightarrow p \wedge q)$ and $\neg p \Rightarrow (false \Leftrightarrow p \wedge q)$. These are clearly true, so our development is complete. Removing the embedded predicates to make the code clear, we get

$\{ p$ and q are defined $\}$
if (p) x $= q;$ else x $= 0$
$\{ x' \Leftrightarrow p \wedge q \}$

We have derived the code if (p) x $= q;$ else x $= 0$ and proved that it satifies its specification $x' \Leftrightarrow p \wedge q$. Many C programmers would apply a source transformation to this result to take advantage of the C conditional expression, obtaining x $=$ p ? q : 0.

Perhaps you find this derivation excessively long-winded for such a simple result. Section 27.2 demonstrates a more streamlined version. But first, we must show how the axiomatic method deals with loops.

Exercise 27.1.2.1 Prove the two verification conditions.

27.1.3 Loops

We'll use the integer square root example from Chapter 5. Here is a Z definition for the *iroot* function that takes an integer argument a and returns its integer square root r (in this version we've written out the predicates that say a and r must not be negative).

$iroot : \mathbb{N} \to \mathbb{N}$

$\forall a : \mathbb{N} \bullet (\textbf{let } r == iroot(a) \bullet$
$\quad 0 \le a \wedge$
$\quad 0 \le r * r \le a < (r + 1) * (r + 1))$

We can extract the predicates from this definition to write the Hoare triple:

$$\{\, 0 \le a \,\} \, R \, \{\, 0 \le r * r \le a < (r + 1) * (r + 1) \,\}$$

We have to solve for the code R that computes the root r. The postcondition of the triple can be seen as an acceptance test for r. It suggests an inefficient but effective algorithm: Count up through the integers, testing each one until the root is found. Counting suggests a loop, so we look up this axiomatic definition for the `while` statement:

$\{\, I \,\}$
`while` $(p) \, \{\, p \wedge I \,\} \, S \, \{\, I' \wedge v' < v \,\}$
$\{\, \neg \, p \wedge I \,\}$

Here p is a predicate called the *guard*, v is an integer expression called the *variant* or *bounding function*, and S is the code in the body of the loop. If the guard is true, the body is executed. Executing the body must cause the variant to decrease. When the guard is false the program exits in the loop. I is a predicate called the *loop invariant*. It must be true before and after the loop, so it must remain true after executing the body of the loop.

Once again we treat the axiomatic definition as a template to fill in. We begin by bracketing the definition with the pre- and postconditions from our Hoare triple. Our algorithm counts up through the natural numbers so we initialize the loop with `r = 0`; the body of the loop is simply `r = r + 1`.

$\{\, 0 \le a \,\}$
`r = 0;`
$\{\, I \,\}$
`while` $(p) \, \{\, p \wedge I \,\}$ `r = r + 1;` $\{\, I' \wedge v' < v \,\}$
$\{\, \neg \, p \wedge I \,\}$
$\{\, 0 \le r * r \le a < (r + 1) * (r + 1) \,\}$

Next we must choose the guard p and identify the invariant I, again by deriving them from the specification. The conjunction $\neg \, p \wedge I$ at the exit from the loop must imply our goal, the conjunction $0 \le r * r \le a \wedge a < (r + 1) * (r + 1)$. We choose the first conjunct $0 \le r * r \le a$ to be the invariant I, so the guard p must be the *negation* of the second conjunct $a \geq (r + 1) * (r + 1)$:

```
{ 0 ≤ a }
r = 0;
{ 0 ≤ r * r ≤ a }
while (a >= (r+1)*(r+1)) r = r + 1; { v′ < v }
{ a < (r + 1) * (r + 1) ∧ 0 ≤ r * r ≤ a }
{ 0 ≤ r * r ≤ a < (r + 1) * (r + 1) }
```

The last two adjacent predicates say the same thing, so the verification condition is obviously true. This example illustrates a useful heuristic for designing loops: Choose the invariant by deleting a conjunct from the goal. Then, to derive the guard, simply negate the deleted conjunct. There is no need to wonder whether the guard should say > or >=, r, or r+1. Algorithm design often turns on choosing the right loop invariant. The invariant can be seen as a weakened version of the goal; each pass through the loop makes progress toward the goal by conjoining a stronger predicate to the invariant.

To confirm that execution of the loop terminates we must identify the variant. The obvious answer is suggested by the guard: Let the variant v be the error or difference that remains between the argument a and the square of $r+1$, so $v = a - (r+1)*(r+1)$. Each repetition of the loop will make this difference smaller until the guard becomes false and execution terminates.

In general, a loop is correct if the five conditions in this checklist are all true:

1. Initialization (the invariant I is *true* before entering the loop).
2. Invariance (the body of the loop preserves the invariant): $\{ p \wedge I \} S \{ I' \}$.
3. Progress (the body of the loop decreases the variant): $\{ p \wedge I \} S \{ v' < v \}$.
4. Boundedness (when the variant falls below some constant k, the guard becomes *false*): $I \wedge v < k \Rightarrow \neg p$.
5. Exit (the invariant and the negation of the guard imply the goal or postcondition Q): $\neg p \wedge I \Rightarrow Q$.

In our example all five conditions can easily be confirmed by inspection; more difficult examples can give rise to verification conditions that are not so obvious and must be proved.

The axiomatic method works best when the predicates and code are developed together; the proof of correctness is a byproduct of the program derivation. When the development is finished it is useful to retain the assertions as comments. Some systems even provide a facility for checking such assertions at run time. Attempting to verify an already written program is more difficult because the verifier has to figure out which predicates to add. This can involve much guesswork and can result in verification conditions that are difficult to prove. Nevertheless, attempting a formal verification can be quite effective at detecting errors.

Exercise 27.1.3.1 In our loop example, what is the value of the bound k?

Exercise 27.1.3.2 In our loop example, why did we not choose the other conjunct $a < (r+1) * (r+1)$ to be the loop invariant?

Exercise 27.1.3.3 Prove invariance for our loop example.

Exercise 27.1.3.4 Apply source language transformations to produce a shorter version from the code derived in our loop example.

Exercise 27.1.3.5 Which condition(s) in the checklist become false if the body of the loop in our example is changed to r = r+2? If we substitute > for ≥ in the guard, or r for $r+1$?

Exercise 27.1.3.6 The version of *iroot* in Chapter 5 (repeated in here in Section 27.1) avoids multiplication by using the equation $1+3+5+\cdots+(2i-1) = i^2$. Annotate that code with predicates and write the verification conditions.

27.2 Refinement calculus

A *refinement calculus* provides another way to document a formal development. It can be more convenient than the axiomatic approach. Instead of axioms that define programming language statements in terms of predicates, it uses *refinement laws* that show how predicates can be replaced by programming language statements. The left side of a refinement law is a mathematical formula, and the right side is a code fragment, joined by the refinement symbol $\sqsubseteq$.[2] The refinement symbol can be pronounced "is implemented by" or "translates to." For example the refinement law named *Conditional predicate* shows how disjunction can be translated to a C conditional expression.

$$(p \wedge q) \vee (\neg p \wedge r) \sqsubseteq p\,?q:r \qquad\qquad \text{[Conditional predicate]}$$

On the left, the place-holders p,q, and r stand for predicates that are used as tests and

---

[2] The refinement symbol $\sqsubseteq$ is from Morgan [1994]. Unfortunately this symbol also has another meaning in Z. It is the *sub-bag relation* symbol, which is defined in the *Reference Manual* but is not used in this book.

do not specify a change of state. Such predicates can be implemented in C as integer expressions, where zero indicates false, and any nonzero value indicates true. The C fragment $p\,?q\,:r$ is an expression whose value is q when p is nonzero and r when p is zero. The place holders on the right side of the refinement law indicate that additional refinement steps will be needed to translate each of these place holders to code. For example this law says that *false* translates to 0 in C

$$false \sqsubseteq 0 \qquad\qquad\qquad\qquad\qquad\qquad\qquad [C\ false]$$

A development in refinement calculus resembles an ordinary proof in the style of Chapter 15, except some steps replace formulas with code. Here is a development of our short-circuit evaluation code from Section 27.1.2 in this style.

$$
\begin{array}{ll}
p \wedge q & \text{[Given]} \\[4pt]
\Leftrightarrow (p \wedge q) \vee false & [p \vee false \Leftrightarrow p] \\[4pt]
\Leftrightarrow (p \wedge q) \vee (\neg\, p \wedge false) & [p \wedge false \Leftrightarrow false] \\[4pt]
\sqsubseteq\ p\,?q : false & \text{[Conditional predicate]} \\[4pt]
\sqsubseteq\ p\,?q : 0 & \text{[C false]}
\end{array}
$$

This development can be read from top to bottom as a program derivation, or from bottom to top as a proof of correctness. It follows a common pattern for refinement calculus developments: First use ordinary laws to transform the formula until it matches the left side of a refinement law, then use refinement laws to replace formulas with code. This can be more compact and easier to follow than an axiomatic development because the presentation is linear and there are no separate verification conditions to prove; transformation from one mathematical formula to another appears in the same chain of reasoning as the translation to code.

In refinement calculus developments, the refinement symbol $\sqsubseteq$ plays much the same role that equivalence does in ordinary proofs. However the refinement symbol is not a logical connective like equivalence because it does not join two predicates, it joins a predicate and a code fragment. What does this refinement symbol really mean? How can we check whether a refinement law is valid?

We can define our refinement symbol formally. Every refinement law can be written $P \wedge Q \sqsubseteq S$, where P is a precondition, Q is a postcondition, and S is a programming language fragment (often the precondition P is implicitly *true*). This refinement law is an assertion that the Hoare triple { P } S { Q } can be proved by the axiomatic method. For example, here is a refinement law named *Swap* that shows how to implement the operation where two variables exchange values.

$$x' = y \wedge y' = x \sqsubseteq \mathtt{t = x;\ x = y;\ y = t} \qquad\qquad\qquad [Swap]$$

This refinement law is an assertion that we can prove the Hoare triple

$$\{\,true\,\}\;\mathtt{t}\;=\;\mathtt{x};\;\;\mathtt{x}\;=\;\mathtt{y};\;\;\mathtt{y}\;=\;\mathtt{t};\;\{\,x' = y \wedge y' = x\,\}$$

Now that we have defined refinement in terms of axiomatic semantics, we know how to check any refinement law to confirm it is valid. We can derive any number of refinement laws from just a few axiomatic statement definitions.

Refinement laws provide a way of summarizing the results of axiomatic derivations so they can be reused easily. Refinement calculus developments are reusable because the result of each development is a new refinement law that can contain place holders. For example the results of our short-circuit development can be summarized

$$p \wedge q \;\sqsubseteq\; p\,?q:0 \qquad\qquad\qquad\qquad \text{[Short circuit \textit{and}]}$$

Now we can reuse this result in other developments, just citing it by name. Likewise, our *Swap* law is actually a special case of a more general law called *Sequential assignment* that contains place holders:

$$x' = e_1(x, y) \wedge y' = e_2(x, y) \;\sqsubseteq\; \mathtt{t}\;=\;\mathtt{x};\;\;\mathtt{x}\;=\;e_1(x, y);\;\;\mathtt{y}\;=\;e_2(t, y)$$

$$\text{[Seq. =]}$$

When $e_1(x, y) = y$ and $e_2(x, y) = x$, this reduces to *Swap*.

Many programs are largely built up from a few basic patterns that reappear again and again. It is possible to create refinement laws that are matched to these patterns. A collection of such customized refinement laws serves as a formalization of a particular programming style and can help make formal program development practical. In Chapter 28 we will present more refinement laws for translating Z to C and demonstrate the method in action.

Exercise 27.2.1 Prove the Hoare triple for *Swap*: $\{\,true\,\}\;\mathtt{t}\;=\;\mathtt{x};\;\;\mathtt{x}\;=\;\mathtt{y};\;\;\mathtt{y}\;=\;\mathtt{t};\;\{\,x' = y \wedge y' = x\,\}$.

Exercise 27.2.2 Prove that the code $\mathtt{t}\;=\;\mathtt{x};\;\;\mathtt{y}\;=\;\mathtt{t};\;\;\mathtt{x}\;=\;\mathtt{y}$ does not correctly implement the swap operation.

28 From Z to code

This chapter teaches a practical method for writing code from Z specifications that supplements intuition and experience with formal derivation.

The preceding Chapters 26 and 27 on refinement and program derivation show how to get from Z to code by purely formal methods, where each development step is a formula manipulation. As you must have realized, it is rarely necessary to develop an entire system in this completely formal way. The programming problems that arise within a single project usually present a range of difficulty. Large parts of the project may be so routine that there is no need for any formal description other than the code itself. Only a portion requires specification in Z. In this portion, you might refine only a fraction to a detailed design in Z. And in this fraction you might derive and verify only a page or two of code. The rest is so obvious that it can be translated to code by intuition and then verified by inspection.

Nevertheless, you can choose a strategy for implementing Z that you could justify formally by the methods of Chapters 26 and 27 if you were challenged to do so. This chapter presents such a strategy. When you have a formal specification, you can check designs and code rigorously if doubts remain after informal inspection.

The examples in this chapter are in C. They could easily be adapted to other programming languages.

28.1 Data structures

In Z we use just a few kinds of mathematical structures to model all of the complex data structures we have to deal with in code. Z specifications can be much shorter and clearer than code because they can leave out detailed data representations and ignore efficiency considerations, but when you come to detailed design and coding you must confront these issues. There are many different ways to implement each mathematical structure; your choice of data structures will depend on the amount of data they must hold, the resources available in your target computer system, and the performance required of your application.

Z basic type declarations, free type declarations, and certain abbreviation definitions are usually implemented by data type declarations in the program. Some Z axiomatic definitions and abbreviation definitions can be implemented as data structures whose contents rarely change, such as program constants and data files. State schemas are usually implemented as program variables that hold *mutable* data structures whose contents can change frequently.

28.1.1 Sets

Free types in Z are a good match to the enumerated types provided in many programming languages. Small sets can be implemented by arrays of boolean flags, where there is an array index for each element in the type, and the flag tells whether the element is present in the set. In Section 23.2.2 we declared a free type to model power supply faults:

FAULT ::= *overload* | *line_voltage* | *overtemp* | *ground_short*

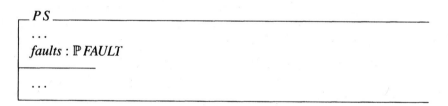

In C this can be implemented by

```
typdef enum { OVERLOAD = 0, LINE_VOLTAGE,
                OVERTEMP, GROUND_SHORT } fault;

#define  N_FAULTS  GROUND_SHORT + 1

int faults[N_FAULTS];
```

C array indices start at zero so this code defines OVERLOAD to be the index of the first array element. Subsequent values in the enumeration index successive elements in the array. The array declaration reserves one element for each enumeration value. In C the size of the array is one greater than the index of the last element.

Larger sets are modelled by other data structures. For example the set of all the subscribers to some service

[*NAME*]

$\mid$ *subscriber* : $\mathbb{P}$ *NAME*

could be implemented by a data file. In addition to the actual text of the subscriber's name, each entry might include additional identifying information, so each element of *NAME* would be implemented by a C structure (this is called a record in many other languages). If the number of subscribers is large, the file should be organized in some way that enables it to be searched quickly, so the name records might include keys as well.

```
/* NAME */
typedef struct
{
    char name_string[name_length];
    int  id;
    int  name_key;
} Name;

/* Subscriber set, a file of Name */
FILE *subscriber;
```

28.1.2 Relations

Z relations often represent data structures, such as this telephone directory:

$$phone : NAME \leftrightarrow \mathbb{N}$$
$$\mathrm{dom}\,phone = subscribers$$

This relation is a set of pairs of type *NAME* $\times \mathbb{N}$. The pair can be implemented by a C structure and the relation could be a file or an in-memory data structure organized to permit rapid search and retrieval.

```
/* Phone record */
typdef struct
{
    Name name;
    int  phone_num;
} phone_rec;

/* Phone relation, a file of phone_rec */
FILE *phone;
```

28.1.3 Functions

Z functions often represent data. A function is a binary relation where the first element of each pair is unique, so functions can be implemented by files or data structures where each item has a unique key. The keys correspond to the domain of the function, and the items stored in the structure correspond to the range. The simplest example is the array: The array indices are the domain, and the array elements are the range. For example these two Z functions

$$\left|\ \ u, v : \mathbb{Z} \rightarrow \mathbb{Z}\right.$$

can be implemented by two C arrays

```
int u[n], v[n];
```

28.2 State schemas

State schemas are usually implemented by *mutable* data structures whose contents can change frequently. If the system will contain just a single instance (binding) of a schema type, then the state schema can be implemented by ordinary program variables, and the binding is just the values which those variables hold. For example the trivial state schema S with two integer state variables x and y

$$S \cong [x, y : \mathbb{Z}]$$

becomes this declaration for two program variables

```
int x,y; /* state schema S */
```

Alternatively, a state schema can be implemented by the declaration of a C structure (a record in other languages). The members of the structure (fields of the record) are the state variables in the schema. Bindings of the schema type are implemented by variables which are instances of the structure (record) type, so it is possible to have many bindings of a single type. Implemented in this style, schema S becomes

```
/* Schema type S */
typedef struct
{
    int x,y;
} S;
```

Now we can declare several variables which are instances of this schema type, so the Z declaration

$$| \quad sa, sb, sc : S$$

becomes

```
S sa, sb, sc; /* instances of schema type S */
```

The power supply schema from Section 23.2.2 provides a more realistic example.

_PS_ _____

$contactor : SWITCH$
$preset, setpoint, output : SIGNAL$
$faults : \mathbb{P}\, FAULT$

$faults \neq \emptyset \Rightarrow setpoint = 0$
$contactor = open \Rightarrow setpoint = 0$
$contactor = open \Rightarrow output \leq \epsilon$

This can be implemented as follows. The `typedef` directive makes it possible to use similar type names in Z and C code.

```
typedef int signal;
typedef enum { OPEN, CLOSED } switch;

/* PS state */
typedef struct power_supply
{
    switch contactor;
    signal preset, setpoint, output;
    int    faults[N_FAULTS]
} PS;
```

The predicate of a state schema is an invariant which places restrictions on the values that its variables can take on. Invariants do not correspond directly to any construct in a programming language. Instead, we must write the executable code to ensure that the invariant is always true.

In large systems there are often many instances (bindings) of the same schema type, and the records that implement bindings are built into larger structures. In the accelerator, power supplies are collected into subsystems. For example, the Beam Line subsystem includes the supplies for Quadrupole Magnet 1, X Steering Magnet 1, and several others. This is modelled in Z by a set of power supply names and a function from power supply names to bindings.

$$blps == \{q1, x0, x1, y1, swm, bend, q2a, q3a, xwob, ywob\}$$

Cyclotron
```
. . .
beam_line : blps → PS
. . .
```

This can be implemented by an array of records indexed by name.

```
typedef enum { Q1=0, X0, X1, Y1, SWM, BEND, Q2A,
                  Q3A, XWOB, YWOB } blps;

#define   N_BLPS = YWOB + 1

PS beam_line[N_BLPS];
```

28.3   Refinement from Z to code

This section describes a development method based on refinement laws as described in Section 27.2. In this method much program derivation can be reduced to systematic substitution: You just replace formulas with fragments of code. Wherever a formula from your specification matches the left side of a refinement law, you can replace it with the code on the right side of the law. Much verification can be reduced to inspection: Compare each piece of specification to the corresponding code, confirming that they match a law. Of course, most specifications have sections that are too intricate to match the predefined laws, and these require additional work. Nevertheless the laws can often get you to a mostly complete program with a few difficult parts left to fill in later. As we shall see, there are formal ways to attack the difficult parts as well.

I do not attempt to provide a universally applicable set of refinement laws. Instead, I advocate creating a collection of refinement laws for each application, customized for its own data structures and programming style. The laws presented here are just examples to help you get started.

As explained in Section 27.2, any valid refinement law can be proved correct by axiomatic methods, but I present these laws without proof. In your own work, you are free to justify your refinement laws in any way you choose; a simple appeal to intuition may be sufficient. Writing down the refinement laws you use is valuable even when you provide no proof because the laws summarize the assumptions upon which the correctness of the code depends. If doubts arise about the validity of a refinement law, you can resort to a more formal justification.

28.3.1 Naming conventions

The method depends on matching formulas from your specification and fragments from your code with place-holders in the refinement laws, so the naming conventions used for the place holders are quite important.

The most important convention arises because predicates are used in Z in two quite different ways. Used in the first way, predicates are *descriptive*: They describe situations where specifications are applicable, and they might be true or false. In operation schemas, preconditions that only contain unprimed state variables and input variables are examples of these descriptive predicates. In our refinement laws, descriptive predicates are indicated by the place holders p, q, and r; $p(x)$ and so forth indicate a descriptive predicate that contains the (free) variable x. Descriptive predicates are implemented by code that merely evaluates or tests the predicate to determine its truth value but has no side effects that change the values of any state variables. In C these tests become integer-valued expressions or functions that contain no assignments to global variables.

Used in the second way, predicates are *prescriptive*: Such predicates are always true; they assert that the variables in the predicate must have values that make the predicate true. In operation schemas, postconditions that contain primed state variables and output variables are examples of prescriptive predicates. In our refinement laws, prescriptive predicates are indicated by the place holders s, t, and u. Prescriptive predicates are implemented by code that can assign new values to global variables.

Another important convention is that expressions (including function applications) are indicated in our refinement laws by e or e_1, e_2, and so forth for arbitrary expressions that might contain any variables, and $e(x)$ and so on for expressions that might (but need not) contain the (free) variable x and so forth. Our refinement rules require that evaluating an expression in the C implementation returns a value but has no side effects that change the values of any state variables. This prohibits certain idioms favored by some C programmers, such as expressions that include assignments and other C operators, such as ++ that can change variable values.

28.3.2 Expressions

Implementing expressions is easy. We merely use the obvious substitutions for our programming language. In C the arithmetic operators +, *, div, and mod become +, *, /, and %. Moreover, Z descriptive predicates are implemented in C as integer-valued expressions where equality ($=$) becomes ($==$), inequality ($\neq$) becomes ($!=$), the logical connectives $\wedge$ and $\vee$ become && and $||$, and so on, relational operators $<$ and $\leq$ become < and <= and so forth, and the two truth values *false* and *true* become zero and any nonzero integer, respectively. We justify refinement steps that use these substitutions by appealing to a single law called *C operators*, for example:

$$x \bmod 2 \neq 0 \qquad \text{[Given]}$$

$$\sqsubseteq \; \texttt{x\%2 != 0} \qquad \text{[C operators]}$$

28.3.3 Set membership

Each set membership test depends on how the set is implemented, and there are lots of possiblities. When the set is implemented by a data structure, the membership test is implemented by searching for the element in the structure. Without knowing more about the data structure, we have to express the right side of the refinement law informally:

$$x \in s \;\sqsubseteq\; \textit{Search for } \texttt{x} \textit{ in data structure } \texttt{s} \qquad \text{[Membership (data structure)]}$$

For example, when the set is implemented by a file, as in the subscriber database of Section 28.1.1, the membership predicate

$$\textit{name?} \in \textit{subscriber}$$

would be implemented by code that searches the file for a particular record (and possibly stores it in a cache of recently accessed records).

With more information about the data structure, we can formalize the right side of the law. When the set is implemented by an array of (integer) boolean flags indexed by the element names as recommended in Section 28.1.1, the membership test is simply the value of the array element at the index, where a nonzero value indicates that the element is a member of the set.

$$x \in s \;\sqsubseteq\; \texttt{s[x]} \qquad \text{[Membership (Boolean array)]}$$

For example in the power supply example of Section 28.1.1, we can have the Z membership predicate

$$\textit{overtemp} \in \textit{faults}$$

In C this is simply the value of the array element

```
faults[OVERTEMP]
```

where a nonzero value indicates that the fault has occurred. Other set implementations require different refinement laws.

Some sets are not implemented by data structures because they are too large. In those cases we determine set membership by testing the predicate that defines the set. This can be formalized by appealing to an ordinary law about set comprehension

$$x \in \{x : X \mid p(x)\} \Leftrightarrow p(x) \qquad \text{[Comprehension]}$$

We apply this law to implement predicates which are disguised membership tests. For example $odd(x)$ is true when x is a member of the set of odd integers. We can derive the C code x%2 this way:

$odd(x)$ [Given]

       $\Leftrightarrow x \in (odd\_)$ [Prefix relation syntax]

       $\Leftrightarrow x \in \{ x : \mathbb{Z} \mid x \bmod 2 \neq 0 \}$ [Definition]

       $\Leftrightarrow x \bmod 2 \neq 0$ [Comprehension]

       $\sqsubseteq$ x%2 != 0   [C operators]

       $\equiv$ x%2   [C true]

In this simple example we could easily derive the code by inspection, but we write out the formal derivation in great detail here because it illustrates a strategy that can be applied to more difficult problems: Express the Z formula in standard syntax, replace identifiers by their definitions, simplify using ordinary laws, then translate to code and simplify the code. The last step here is to replaces the C expression x%2 != 0 with the simpler equivalent x%2. This step can be justified by the source language transformation

$$e \; != \; 0 \equiv e \qquad \text{[C true]}$$

This law follows from the C convention that logical *true* is represented by any nonzero integer, so the truth value of $e \; != \; 0$ (e is not equal to zero) is the same as the truth value of the expression e itself. This example also shows that source language transformations can be represented in a similar form to refinement laws, but we introduce yet another symbol for them: The source transformation symbol ($\equiv$) signifies that two programming language fragments mean the same thing (This symbol is not part of Z itself).

28.3.4 Function application

Functions might be implemented by data structures or executable code, so the informal refinement laws are

$$u(x) \sqsubseteq \textit{Find item in } \mathrm{u} \textit{ with key } x \qquad \text{[Function application (data structure)]}$$

$$f(x) \sqsubseteq \textit{Evaluate } \mathrm{f} \textit{ with argument } x \quad \text{[Function application (executable code)]}$$

In the cases where data structure u and function f are implemented by an array and a C function, respectively, these become

$$u(x) \sqsubseteq \mathtt{u[x]} \qquad\qquad \text{[Function application (array)]}$$

$$f(x) \sqsubseteq \mathtt{f(x)} \qquad\qquad \text{[Function application (C function)]}$$

28.3.5 Assignment

The simplest refinement law for prescriptive predicates occurs where the primed after variable has the same value as the unprimed before variable. These predicates require no code at all!

$$x' = x \sqsubseteq \textit{(empty statement)} \qquad\qquad \text{[Skip]}$$

The next simplest law is *Assignment*. In a context where only one variable can change value, equality can be implemented by assignment:

$$x' = e \wedge y' = y \wedge z' = z \wedge \ldots \sqsubseteq \mathtt{x = e} \qquad\qquad \text{[Assignment]}$$

This law only applies in contexts where just one variable changes value. When there are several variables, we cannot simply replace equations with assignments because the assignments might interact: For example, we cannot implement the swap operation $x' = y \wedge y' = x$ with the naive solution $\mathtt{x = y; y = x}$. Equations can appear in any order, but we must do a *data flow analysis* to determine the order in which the assignments must be performed.

Let's do the data flow analysis for a pattern that is pervasive in state transition systems: At each transition, new values are assigned to each state variable, based only on the previous values of one or more variables. In Z it looks like this:

$$
\begin{array}{|l}
\hline
\textit{Op} \\\hline
\Delta S \\\hline
x' = e_1(x, y) \\
y' = e_2(x, y) \\\hline
\end{array}
$$

Most of the operation schemas in this book include instances of this pattern. The analysis is easy because this definition is constructive: The after (primed) variables appear by themselves on one side of an equation; furthermore, the other sides of the equations only contain the before (unprimed) variables. We can use new variables to store initial values, and order the assigments so no variable is used on the right side of an assigment after it has appeared on the left of another assignment after initialization. The *Sequential Assignment* law we quoted in Section 27.2 records the solution for two variables.

$$x' = e_1(x, y) \land y' = e_2(x, y) \land z' = z \dots \sqsubseteq$$
$$\text{t = x; x = } e_1(x, y); \text{ y = } e_2(t, y)$$

Here $z' = z$ is needed to prevent the left side from matching predicates with more than two variables. Similar laws can easily be derived for three or more variables. In the special case where the variables do not interact, we don't need the temporary variable. We can express this in the law *Independent Assignment*

$$x' = e_1(x) \land y' = e_2(y) \sqsubseteq \text{ x = } e_1(x); \text{ y = } e_2(y) \qquad \text{[Independent =]}$$

Sequential assignment often appears slightly disguised as a sequence of function calls; the assignments are in the function bodies.

Not all prescriptive equations can be directly implemented by assigments, because the Z variable that appears in the equation might denote a program variable which cannot be the target of an assignment. This occurs when the program variable is a complex data structure. For example the set union operator indicates that more elements should be added to a data structure, but without knowing more implementation details we can only express this informally:

$$S' = S \cup \{x\} \sqsubseteq \text{ \textit{Put} x \textit{ in data structure} s} \qquad \text{[Union]}$$

When the set is implemented by an array of Boolean flags, we add an element by setting its flag to any nonzero (true) value. This can be formalized

$$S' = S \cup \{x\} \sqsubseteq \text{ s[x] = TRUE} \qquad \text{[Union (Boolean array)]}$$

In the power supply example from Section 28.1.1 we use set union to express that a fault has occurred

$$faults' = faults \cup \{overtemp\}$$

In C this becomes assigment to an array element

```
faults[OVERTEMP] = TRUE;
```

where TRUE is any nonzero integer. Other set implementations require different refinement laws.

28.3.6 Guarded command

A common pattern specifies that a change of state should occur when a precondition is satisfied. This can be implemented by an if statement, as described by the *Guarded Command* law.

$$p \wedge s \sqsubseteq \texttt{if} \ (p) \ s \qquad\qquad \text{[Guarded command]}$$

The descriptive predicate p and the prescriptive predicate s appear on the right side of the law, so it takes a few more refinement steps to reach code. For example here is the development of $x = e_1 \wedge x' = e_2$:

$$
\begin{aligned}
x = e_1 \wedge x' = e_2 & \qquad\qquad \text{[Given]}\\
\sqsubseteq \texttt{if} \ (x = e_1) \ x' = e_2 & \qquad\qquad \text{[Guarded command]}\\
\sqsubseteq \texttt{if} \ (\texttt{x} \ \texttt{==} \ e_1) \ x' = e_2 & \qquad\qquad \text{[C operator]}\\
\sqsubseteq \texttt{if} \ (\texttt{x} \ \texttt{==} \ e_1) \ \texttt{x} \ \texttt{=} \ e_2 & \qquad\qquad \text{[Assignment]}
\end{aligned}
$$

The first equation becomes a test, and the second equation becomes an assignment.

28.3.7 Disjunction

Disjunction is implemented by conditional branching, as expressed in the *Case Analysis* law.

$$(p \wedge s) \vee (q \wedge t) \sqsubseteq \texttt{if} \ (p) \ s; \ \texttt{else if} \ (q) \ t \qquad \text{[Case analysis]}$$

This only makes sense when p and q describe distinct (nonoverlapping) situations, so only one of the predicates can be true. Here t itself might be another disjunction, so we can apply the law repeatedly to obtain the results

$$
\begin{aligned}
&(p \wedge s) \vee (q \wedge t) \vee (r \wedge u)\ldots \sqsubseteq \\
&\qquad \texttt{if} \ (p) \ s; \ \texttt{else if} \ (q) \ t; \texttt{else if} \ (r) \ u \ \ldots
\end{aligned}
$$

There are some useful special cases. Sometimes there are just two mutually exclusive alternatives

$$(p \wedge s) \vee (\neg \, p \wedge t) \sqsubseteq \texttt{if} \ (p) \ s; \ \texttt{else} \ t \qquad\qquad \text{[Branch]}$$

When s and t are equations that describe the same variable, we can take advantage of the conditional expression syntax of both Z and C. This ordinary law describes the Z conditional expression

$$(p \wedge x' = e_1) \vee (\neg \, p \wedge x' = e_2) \Leftrightarrow x' = \textbf{if} \ p \ \textbf{then} \ e_1 \ \textbf{else} \ e_2 \quad \text{[Z Cond. expr.]}$$

This refinement law shows how to implement the conditional expression

$$\textbf{if } p \textbf{ then } e_1 \textbf{ else } e_2 \sqsubseteq p?e_1:e_2 \qquad \text{[Conditional expression]}$$

The conditional assigment law follows from these two

$$(p \wedge x' = e_1) \vee (\neg p \wedge x' = e_2) \sqsubseteq x = p?e_1:e_2 \text{ [Conditional assignment]}$$

Descriptive predicates that express two mutually exclusive alternatives can also be implemented by a conditional expression, as we saw in Section 27.2.

$$(p \wedge q) \vee (\neg p \wedge r) \sqsubseteq p?q:r \qquad \text{[Conditional predicate]}$$

28.3.8 Conjunction

There is no direct way to implement conjunction in general. Our guarded command and sequential assignment laws show how to implement certain conjunctions, but these are special cases where the conjuncts hardly interact. When both conjuncts are prescriptive predicates that constrain the same variables, no generally applicable refinement law exists.

Here is a simple example that illustrates the difficulty. In Section 12.2.1 we defined integer division of a number n by divisor d, yielding quotient q' and remainder r'. We defined *Division* by conjoining *Quotient* and *Remainder*, where the predicate of *Quotient* is

$$d \neq 0 \wedge n = q' * d + r'$$

and the predicate of *Remainder* is

$$r' < d$$

These do not match any of our assignment laws because the results q' and r' are not defined constructively. They do not appear by themselves on one side of an equation; they appear together on the same side. Nevertheless we can easily see solutions to both predicates separately. *Quotient* is true when $q' = 0 \wedge r' = n$ so it can be implemented by q = 0; r = n; *Remainder* is true when $r' = 0$ so it can be implemented by r = 0. But there is no way to combine these two code fragments to produce an implementation of their conjunction, *Division*:

$$d \neq 0 \wedge n = q' * d + r' \wedge r' < d$$

The whole problem is to find values for q' and r' that satisfy both conjuncts at the same time. Here is a solution that finds the quotient by repeated subtraction:

```
for (q = 0, r = n; r >= d; q++) r = r - d
```

This kind of situation often arises from conjunction: A solution cannot be assembled from components; it is necessary to find or invent an algorithm that solves the whole problem at once. Usually no simple refinement laws apply. If a formal solution is desired, it is necessary to resort to axiomatic methods.

Exercise 23.8.1   Derive an implementation of *Division* using the axiomatic method for developing loops.

28.3.9 New variables

It is often necessary to add new program variables to the implementation that are not present as mathematical variables in the specification. For example, our sequential assignment law uses the new program variable t to store the value of the mathematical variable x, the initial value of the program variable x. Another reason for introducing new variables is to factor out repeated expressions which are too lengthy to write or too expensive to evaluate more than once.

New variables in programs correspond to local definitions in Z. The ordinary law *Local definition* says that we can factor out an expression e and replace all of its occurrences by a new variable x:

$$s \Leftrightarrow (\textbf{let } x == e \bullet s[x/e]) \qquad\qquad \text{[Local definition]}$$

where $s[x/e]$ means predicate s with all occurrences of expression e replaced by variable x. The *New Variable* refinement law shows how to implement predicates with local definitions.

$$(\textbf{let } x == e \bullet s(x)) \sqsubseteq \texttt{x = } e; \; s(x) \qquad\qquad \text{[New variable]}$$

Here we apply these laws to implement the guarded command $p(y') \wedge y' = f\, x$, where the primed variable y' appears in the guard.

$$
\begin{aligned}
&p(y') \wedge y' = f\, x && \text{[Given]}\\
&\Leftrightarrow p(f\, x) \wedge y' = f\, x && \text{[Expand first } y'\text{]}\\
&\Leftrightarrow (\textbf{let } t == f\, x \bullet p(t) \wedge y' = t) && \text{[Local definition]}\\
&\sqsubseteq \texttt{t = } f\ \texttt{x; } p(t) \wedge y' = t && \text{[New variable]}\\
&\sqsubseteq \texttt{t = } f\ \texttt{x; if } (p(t))\ y' = t && \text{[Guarded command]}\\
&\sqsubseteq \texttt{t = } f\ \texttt{x; if } (p(t))\ \texttt{y = t} && \text{[Assignment]}\\
&\sqsubseteq \texttt{t = f(x); if (p(t)) y = t} && \text{[C operators]}
\end{aligned}
$$

28.3.10 Quantifiers

Predicates involving sets and quantifiers are implemented by loops that iterate over the elements of the set. Descriptive predicates test the elements; the universal quantifier requires that every element pass the test, and the existential quantifier requires that at least one element passes. The implementations assign the truth value of the quantified predicate to the boolean flag b.

$\forall x : S \bullet p(x) \sqsubseteq$ b = 1; for $(x\ in\ S)$ if $(!p(x))$ b = 0

[Universal test]

$\exists x : S \bullet p(x) \sqsubseteq$ b = 0; for $(x\ in\ S)$ if $(p(x))$ b = 1

[Existential test]

The iterator for $(x\ in\ S)$ is expressed informally because it depends on how we implement the set S. This code works correctly when S is empty: Universal test returns *true* and the existential test returns *false*.

If the set S is implemented by the array s so each array element s[i] corresponds to one set element x_i, we can reach all the elements by iterating over the array index. For an array with n elements, the first law becomes

$\forall x : S \bullet p(x) \sqsubseteq$
b = 1; for (i = 0; i < n; i++) if $(!p(s[i]))$ b = 0

This law is now completely formal, but the place-holder predicate p still appears on both sides of the refinement law. We need an additional refinement step to replace $p(s[i])$ with code. For example if $p(x)$ is *odd*(x) we can use the result from Section 28.3.3 to replace $p(s[i])$ with s[i]%2. Development using a refinement calculus typically proceeds in this fashion, replacing mathematical formulas with fragments of code until only code remains.

Prescriptive predicates assign new values to elements, as described informally in these two laws. Universally quantified predicates assign to every element while existentially quantified predicates can nondeterministically assign to any or all elements. Existentially quantified predicates often contain additional restrictions that confine the assignment to one particular element.

$\forall x : S \bullet s(x) \sqsubseteq$ for $(x\ in\ S)\ s(x)$ [Universal assignment]

$\exists x : S \bullet s(x) \sqsubseteq$ *Choose any or all x in S*; $s(x)$ [Existential assignment]

28.4 Functions and relations

Our refinement laws show how to translate formulas to executable code fragments, but we need to incorporate these fragments into some larger structure in order to produce a program. Z specifications have structure: Formulas are collected into paragraphs such as axiomatic definitions and schemas. These Z paragraphs can be made to correspond to programming language units in the implementation such as functions, procedures, and methods.

Some axiomatic definitions can be implemented as *functions*: executable program units that can the read the program state and return results but have no side effects that change the program state by assigning new values to global variables.

Z relations that are used as predicates can often be implemented in C by functions that return integer values, with zero indicating false and any nonzero value indicating true. In Section 28.3.3 we showed that the Z predicate $odd(x)$ could be implemented by the C code fragment x%2. The Z relation ($odd\_$) can be implemented by a C function that performs the test. Here is the definition of the Z relation

$$odd\_ : \mathbb{P}\,\mathbb{Z}$$
$$\forall i : \mathbb{Z} \bullet odd(i) \Leftrightarrow i \bmod 2 \neq 0$$

Here is the definition of the corresponding C function

```
int odd(int i) { return i%2; }
```

Z functions that return values, such as our integer square root example from Chapter 5, can also be implemented by C functions. The argument of the function belongs to the domain, and the value returned by the function belongs to the range.

$$iroot : \mathbb{N} \rightarrow \mathbb{N}$$
$$\ldots$$

```
int root(int a) { ... }
```

Here the returned value is the integer square root, not just a boolean flag.

28.5 Operation schemas

In Z, operation schemas usually model changes of state. They can be implemented by procedures that can change the program state by assigning new values to global variables. A *procedure* is a programming language construct that can change global variables. In C, procedures are implemented by the same construct as functions, which happens to be called function. In my C examples, I distinguish procedures by declaring their type to be void to indicate that they do not accomplish their work by returning a value.

When there is just a single binding of a schema type and it is implemented by a program variable, there is no need to pass a parameter to the procedure that implements the operation schema. The procedure can simply update the global variable. In C this is indicated by using a void parameter list. For example the Z schemas

$$S \mathrel{\widehat{=}} [\, x, y : \mathbb{Z} \,]$$

$$Op \mathrel{\widehat{=}} [\, \Delta S \mid x' = x + y \,]$$

Can be implemented

```
int x, y; /* State S */

void op(void) { x = x + y; }
```

28.5.1 Bindings

In more complex systems the Z binding operator is often used. Here is a simple example to show how it works. The operation *SumOp* has the same effect as *Op* but all the work is done by applying the function *sum* to a binding of *S*.

$$
\begin{array}{|l}
\hline
sum : S \to \mathbb{Z} \\
\hline
\forall S \bullet sum(\theta S) = x + y \\
\end{array}
$$

$$SumOp \mathrel{\widehat{=}} [\, \Delta S \mid x' = sum(\theta S) \,]$$

When you see the Z binding operator *theta*, as in θS, all the identifiers declared in the schema *S* are in scope. In this example *x* and *y* are in scope in the function *sum*. When there is only a single instance of *S* implemented by a global variable, the implementations of *sum* and *SumOp* don't need any passed parameters. Access to the binding is implicit in references to global variables. They can be implemented this way:

```
int x, y; /* Single binding of schema type S */

int sum(void) { return x + y; }
                        /* theta S is global */

void sum_op(void) { x = sum(); }
                        /* apply sum to theta S */
```

When there are multiple instances of *S*, the binding must be made explicit in the code as passed parameters, as in this example:

```
/* Schema type S */
typedef struct
{
    int x,y;
} S;

S sa, sb, sc;
                /* multiple bindings of schema type S */

int sum(S *s) { return (*s).x + (*s).y; }
                            /* theta S is a param.   */

void sum_op(S *s) { (*s).x = sum(s); }
                    /* apply sum to theta S */
```

I use the syntax `(*s).x` here instead of the more usual `s->x` to emphasize the similarity to $(\theta S).x$ in Z; the definition of *sum* could be written $sum(\theta S) = (\theta S).x + (\theta S).y$.

A more realistic example of a large system with multiple bindings of a single schema type appears in our accelerator case study in Chapter 23. Some relevant declarations appear in Section 28.2. Operation schemas from this system can be implemented as procedures where the structure, which is the target of the operation, is a passed parameter. We need to update members in the target structure, so in C the parameter must be a pointer. For example here is a (simplified) version of the *TurnOn* operation that turns on a power supply.

```
┌─ TurnOnPS ─────────────────────────────────
│ ΔPS
│ ────────────
│ contactor′ = closed
│ setpoint′ = preset
└─────────────────────────────────────────────
```

This is implemented

```
void turn_on_ps(PS *ps)
{
    ps->contactor = CLOSED;
    ps->setpoint = ps->preset;
}
```

As explained in Section 28.3.10, quantifiers are often implemented by loops. This schema from Chapter 23 specifies the operation that turns on all the power supplies in a beam line.

TurnOnBL
$\Delta Cyclotron$

$\forall \, ps : blps \bullet \exists \, TurnOn \bullet$
$\quad \theta PS = beam\_line \; ps \land \theta PS' = beam\_line' \; ps$

This procedure can be implemented by `turn_on_bl`, which uses the `blps` enumeration and `N_BLPS` constant defined in Section 28.2. In this example there is only one beam line so there is no need to pass it as a parameter; the procedure can simply refer to the global variable. The body of the procedure is implemented according to our *Universal Assignment* law from Section 28.3.10. The outer bound variable *ps* is the loop index; it iterates over all the power supplies in the beam line. The inner existential quantifier merely associates the *TurnOn* operation with the proper supply, which is implemented by passing the pointer to that supply in the call to `turn_on_ps`.

```
void turn_on_bl(void)
{
    blps ps;

    for (ps = 0; ps < N_BLPS; ps++)
        turn_on_ps(&beam_line[ps]);
}
```

28.5.2 Partial operations

We must be careful about preconditions when we implement partial operations. If the precondition of a Z operation schema is not satisfied, the final state of the operation is undetermined. In Z we are careful to combine such partial operations in schema expressions so that the combined operation is total: Its final state is defined for all possible input states. However, in code we sometimes implement partial operations by separate procedures whose results are combined elsewhere. In that case, it is essential that each such procedure leaves the state unchanged if its precondition is not satisfied. For example, the predicate in *Partial* says that the assignment to *y* can be made only if the final value y' would satisfy predicate *q*:

```
 ┌─ Partial ─────────────────────────────────
 │ ΔS
 │ ──────────────────────
 │ p(y′) ∧ y′ = f x
 └────────────────────────────────────────────
```

The predicate p should be tested with the final value y', not the initial value y. The development in Section 28.3.9 derives a correct implementation that uses a temporary variable to store the result of evaluating $f\ x$.

```
void partial(void)
{
    int t;

    t = f(x);
    if (p(t)) y = t;
}
```

This has the intended effect of leaving the state unchanged if $p(y')$ would be false.

28.6 Schema expressions

Schema expressions contain multiple schema references joined by schema calculus operators. Section 28.5 recommends implementing operation schemas by procedures, but this does not mean you should separately implement each schema in a schema expression. It often works better to expand the schema expression to a single schema according to the laws of schema calculus. Then you can write a single procedure that implements the expanded schema. This has many advantages; for example it often removes the necessity for dealing with partial operations.

For example schema disjunction often expresses case analyses. In this example the final state of $Op12$ is $S1$ or $S2$, depending on predicate p

$$Op1 \mathrel{\hat{=}} [\Delta S \mid p \wedge S1']$$

$$Op2 \mathrel{\hat{=}} [\Delta S \mid \neg\, p \wedge S2']$$

$$Op12 \mathrel{\hat{=}} Op1 \vee Op2$$

This schema expression is useful for purposes of description because it makes the cases explicit, but expressing it as a single schema box shows the best way to an implementation:

This can be implemented by applying the *Case Analysis* refinement law:

```
void op_12(void) { if (p) S1; else S2; }
```

Sometimes we must expand schema expressions in order to do the data flow analysis, as in this example

$$OpX \mathrel{\widehat{=}} [\Delta S \mid p(x) \wedge x' = f\ y]$$

$$OpY \mathrel{\widehat{=}} [\Delta S \mid q(y) \wedge y' = g\ x]$$

$$OpXY \mathrel{\widehat{=}} OpX \wedge OpY$$

Expanding the schema expression reveals

_OpXY_____

ΔS

$p(x) \wedge q(y)$
$x' = f\ y \wedge y' = g\ x$

We must test both preconditions before doing any assignments, use a temporary variable, and order the assignments correctly:

```
void op_xy(void)
{
    int t;

    if (p(x) && q(y)) {
        t = x; x = f(y); y = g(t);
    }
}
```

28.7 Modules and programs

A collection of related Z paragraphs can be implemented by the larger programming language constructs variously named modules, packages, or classes. In languages such as C that do not provide such constructs, some large-scale structuring can be achieved by placing the declarations of related program units together in a single header file and defining them together in a single file of related variables, function definitions, and supporting code.

A Z state schema, along with the operation schemas that include it and the definitions they use, can be implemented by one module. When one Z state schema includes another, this can be implemented by a module dependency, or inheritance in an object-oriented programming language. In C it can often be implemented by including a header file.

The Z notation itself has no structuring construct for collecting together related Z paragraphs. It is up to you to choose a layout and use informal prose text to make the intended organization of your Z paragraphs clear.

Z has no built-in concept of a program or any explicit control structure, and Z users often do not write any formal definition of the "main program" or "top level" that invokes the appropriate operation schemas when they are needed. Nevertheless, we often have to implement the top level anyway. It is usually intended that any operation whose preconditions are satisfied will be executed promptly, so we have to code the machinery to make that happen. That machinery can be defined formally, and the formal definition can help show the way to the implementation.

A top level system definition in Z is often determined by a collection of operation schemas. We can tell which operation schemas are at the top level because they are not included in any others. If we call these top level schemas $Op1, Op2, \ldots, OpN$ then the formal definition of the main program is just the disjunction of these operations.

$$Main \mathrel{\widehat{=}} Op1 \vee Op2 \vee \ldots \vee OpN \vee Exception$$

This is just like any other schema disjunction and can be implemented by all the same techniques. The precondition of each top level operation should be different from all the others, and together all the preconditions should cover all possible cases. It is a good idea to include an *Exception* operation to handle any cases that might have been overlooked. The precondition for *Exception* is usually implicit in the program logic: Control reaches *Exception* when no other operations are invoked.

A simple but effective programming strategy applies the *Case Analysis* law, implementing each operation such as $Op1$ with two program units: a boolean function test_1 that tests its precondition and a procedure do_1 that performs the state change by executing assignments. The heart of the main program is a loop that repeatedly tests preconditions and executes any enabled operation until some exit condition is reached. This can be made into an event-driven system by adding a statement at the beginning of the body of the loop that waits for events.

```
#include ...

main(...)
{
    ...

    while (ok)
    {
        get_event();

        if (test_1()) do_1();
        else if (test_2()) do_2();
          .

          .

          .
        else if (test_n()) do_n();
        else exception();
    }
}
```

This program is an example of an event-driven state transition system. Each of the test functions can examine the most recent event to determine whether its do operation should be invoked. Executing each operation's do procedure can change the program state so a different operation becomes enabled (a different test function will succeed on the next pass through the body of the loop). Control reaches exception if none of the other preconditions are satisfied.

28.8 A larger example

A specification that appears quite complicated might turn out to have a simple implementation. This example shows how to untangle complicated definitions. It is based on several pages of axiomatic definitions and schemas from a real formal specification. Its authors closely followed the organization of the original prose requirements document, which described several different but similar cases.

In the original formal specification, the schemas and functions had long names and contained complex expressions. Mnemonic names help convey the intended meaning of a specification and are needed during reviews and validation, but they can distract you from seeing the mathematical structure and they make calculations cumbersome. The first step in the development was to extract the Z text from the surrounding prose and rewrite it, representing complicated expressions with functions and relations, and using simple identifiers in place of mnemonic names. This was the result:

$[A, X, Y, Z]$

$x_1 : X;\ y_2 : Y$
$p_- : \mathbb{P}\,A;\ q_- : X \leftrightarrow Y$
$g, h : Y \to Z;\ f : Z \times Z \to Z$

$S \mathrel{\widehat{=}} [a : A;\ x : X;\ y : Y;\ z : Z]$

$OpX \mathrel{\widehat{=}} [\Delta S \mid a' = a \wedge x' = x_1]$

$Op1 \mathrel{\widehat{=}} [OpX \mid p(a) \wedge y' = y \wedge z' = z]$

$OpY \mathrel{\widehat{=}} [OpX \mid \neg\, p(a) \wedge y' = y_2]$

$Op2 \mathrel{\widehat{=}} [OpY \mid q(x', y') \wedge z' = f(z, g(y'))]$

$Op3 \mathrel{\widehat{=}} [OpY \mid \neg\, q(x', y') \wedge z' = f(z, h(y'))]$

$Op \mathrel{\widehat{=}} Op1 \vee Op2 \vee Op3$

This shows that the specification concerns a single state schema S with four state variables, two global constants x_1 and y_2, two descriptive predicates p and q, and three functions f, g, and h. It defines an operation Op composed of three alternatives $Op1$, $Op2$ and $Op3$, which are defined in terms of two operations OpX and OpY.

The next step is to expand the final merged operation schema Op according to the rules of the schema calculus. We obtain

$$
\begin{array}{|l}
\hline
\textit{Op} \underline{\hspace{6cm}} \\
\Delta S \\
\hline
a' = a \\
x' = x_1 \\
((p(a) \wedge y' = y \wedge z' = z)\ \vee \\
(\neg\, p(a) \wedge y' = y_2\ \wedge \\
\qquad (q(x', y') \wedge z' = f(z, g(y')))\ \vee \\
\qquad (\neg\, q(x', y') \wedge z' = f(z, h(y'))))) \\
\hline
\end{array}
$$

Now let's work on the predicate. Eliding the complicated bit at the end for now, we have

$$a' = a \wedge x' = x_1 \wedge ((p(a) \wedge y' = y \wedge z' = z) \vee (\neg\, p(a) \wedge y' = y_2 \wedge s))$$

Let's pick up the pace a bit. There is no need to write out every step, we can easily see that this translates to

```
x = x1; if (!p(a)) { y = y2; s }
```

We only need to implement s

$$(q(x', y') \wedge z' = f(z, g(y'))) \vee (\neg\, q(x', y') \wedge z' = f(z, h(y')))$$

We observe that the pattern $z' = f(z, e)$ appears in both disjuncts. It can be factored out this way

$$z' = (\textbf{let } t == \textbf{if } q(x', y') \textbf{ then } g(y') \textbf{ else } h(y') \bullet f(z, t))$$

According to *Conditional Expression* and *New Variable* this becomes

```
t = q(x,y) ? g(y) : h(y); z = f(z,t)
```

Putting all the pieces back together, we obtain the following code. In the actual implementation, the symbolic identifers are replaced by the original mnemonic names. The state schema S is implemented by a collection of global variables, and the operation schema Op is implemented by a procedure that uses them. The predicates p and q are implemented by functions that return integers and the functions f, g, and h are implemented by C functions that return the appropriate types. For brevity here we say that types A, X, Y and Z are all integers, and we elide all the function bodies with dots.

```c
typedef int A, X, Y, Z;

A a; X x,x1; Y y,y2;   Z z;

int p(A a) { ... }
int q(X x, Y y) { ... }

Z g(Y y) { ... }
Z h(Y y) { ... }

Z f(Z z, Z t);

void op(void)
{
    Z t;

    x = x1;
    if (!p(a)) {
        y = y2;
        t = q(x,y) ? g(y) : h(y);
        z = f(z,t);
    }
}
```

Exercise   In this development we implicitly used a new law:

$$(p \wedge x' = f(z, e_1)) \vee (\neg\, p \wedge x' = f(z, e_2))$$
$$\Leftrightarrow x' = (\textbf{let } t == \textbf{if } p \textbf{ then } e_1 \textbf{ else } e_2 \bullet f(z, t))$$

Prove it.

28.9 A final example

In this example we allocate the implementations of Z paragraphs to functions and files, choose data structures to efficiently implement Z types, and derive code that implements operators from the Z tool-kit.

In this example we'll implement the interlock system described in Section 22.2.2. Figure 28.1 shows the Z specification and Figures 28.2 and 28.3 at the end of the section show the C implementation. A programmer familiar with both notations could write the code by inspection, but it is possible to explain the rationale and even justify many of the steps formally.

28.9.1 Program units

The specification is based on two state schemas, *Field* and *Intlk*. It is implemented in four C source files: `field.h`, `field.c`, `intlk.h`, and `intlk.c`. The two header files `field.h` and `intlk.h` contain declarations that are used elsewhere in the implementation. The two `.c` files contain definitions whose internals are not needed elsewhere in the implementation. This example concentrates on `intlk.c`; the contents of `field.c` are not needed to explain the example so `field.c` does not appear in Figure 28.3.

State variables in the *Field* and *Intlk* schemas are implemented by C program variables defined at file level in `field.c` and `intlk.c`, respectively. Operation schemas that include the *Field* state only are implemented as C functions defined in `field.c`, and operations that include the *Intlk* state are implemented as C functions defined in `inltk.c`. Some operations that include *Intlk* also include the *Field*, so `intlk.c` includes `field.h` for the declarations of the identifiers and functions needed to access the contents of `field.c`.

28.9.2 Data structures

The Z basic sets *SETTING* and *INTERLOCK* are implemented by C enumerations `setting` and `interlock` whose values are the setting and interlock names. The

[*SETTING*, *INTERLOCK*]

MODE ::= *experiment* | *therapy*

INTLK ::= *clear* | *set*

READY ::= *ready* | *not_ready* | *override*

Intlk

mode : *MODE*
therapy_intlk : *INTLK*
intlk : *INTERLOCK* → *INTLK*
status : *SETTING* → *READY*

| *preset* : $\mathbb{P}$ *SETTING*

TreatmentStatus
Field
Intlk
___

dom *status* = **if** *mode* = *therapy* **then** *SETTING* **else** *preset*

status =
  (λs : dom *status* • *not_ready*) ⊕
  (λs : dom *status* | *Overridden*(*s*, θ *Field*) • *override*) ⊕
  (λs : dom *status* | *Ready*(*s*, θ *Field*) • *ready*)

SafeTreatment
TreatmentStatus
___

ran *intlk* = {*clear*}
ran *status* ⊆ {*ready*, *override*}

ScanIntlk
Ξ *Field*
Δ *Intlk*
___

TreatmentStatus'
therapy_intlk' = **if** *SafeTreatment'* **then** *clear* **else** *set*

Figure 28.1: Safety interlock specification.

```
/* field.h  -  setting names, exported function declarations etc. */

typedef enum { LEAF0 = 0, ..., LEAF1, WEDGE_ROT,
               GANTRY, ..., TURNTABLE } setting;

#define N_PRESETS  WEDGE_ROT + 1
#define N_SETTINGS TURNTABLE + 1

int overridden(setting s);
int ready_setting(setting s);

/* intlk.h - interlock names, exported function declarations etc. */
typedef enum { KEY = 0, DOOR, DOSIMETRY }  interlock;

#define N_INTERLOCKS DOSIMETRY + 1

typedef enum { EXPERIMENT, THERAPY } mode_status;
typedef enum { CLEAR, SET } intlk_status;
typedef enum { READY, NOT_READY, OVERRIDE } ready_status;

void scan_intlk(void);
```

Figure 28.2: Safety interlock implementation (header files).

status and *intlk* state variables are implemented by the `status` and `intlk` arrays which are indexed by the setting names and interlock names, respectively.

The order of the setting names in the C enumeration is critical because *SETTING* has a subset named *preset* which is used in the *TreatmentStatus* schema[1]. The implementation code only works if the elements of *preset* are consecutive enumeration values. We achieve this by placing the elements of *preset* together at the beginning of the C `setting` enumeration.

28.9.3 Operations and predicates

The three operations *TreatmentStatus*, *SafeTreatment*, and *ScanIntlk* are implemented by C functions. *TreatmentStatus* is not an operation schema at all; it is a state. However it is used in *ScanIntlk* where it appears primed: It describes the after state, so it is implemented by the procedure `treatment_status` that can assign new values to the elements of the array that implements *status*. The predicate of *TreatmentStatus* is complicated so we'll defer discussing the body of `treatment_status` for now.

---

[1] This detail was omitted from Chapter 22.

```
/* intlk.c - interlock state variables and function definitions */
#include "field.h"
#include "intlk.h"

/* Intlk state variables */
mode_status  mode;
intlk_status therapy_intlk;
intlk_status intlk[N_INTERLOCKS];
ready_status status[N_SETTINGS];

/* Intlk predicates and operations */
void treatment_status(void)
{
    setting s, ns;

    ns = (mode == THERAPY) ? N_SETTINGS : N_PRESETS;
    for (s = 0; s < ns; s++) {
        if (ready_setting(s)) status[s] = READY;
        else if (overridden(s)) status[s] = OVERRIDE;
        else status[s] = NOT_READY;
    }
}

int safe_treatment(void)
{
    int safe;
    interlock i;
    setting s, ns;

    safe = 1;
    for (i = 0; i < N_INTERLOCKS; i++)
        if (intlk[i] != CLEAR) safe = 0;
    ns = (mode == THERAPY) ? N_SETTINGS : N_PRESETS;
    for (s = 0; s < ns; s++)
        if (status[s] == NOT_READY) safe = 0;
    return safe;
}

void scan_intlk(void)
{
    treatment_status();
    therapy_intlk = safe_treatment() ? CLEAR : SET;
}
```

Figure 28.3: Safety interlock implementation.

The predicate of *TreatmentStatus* uses the two predicates *Overridden(s, θField)* and *Ready(s, θField)* defined in Section 22.2.2. These are implemented by the functions `overridden` and `ready_setting` which are declared in `field.h` and defined in `field.c`. The bindings *θField* indicate that *Overridden* and *Ready* require access to state variables in *Field*. These variables do not have to be passed parameters because they are implemented as variables at file level in `field.c` and are global to `overridden` and `ready_setting`. The only passed parameter required by these two functions is the setting s.

SafeTreatment is another state schema. It appears in *ScanIntlk* where it is used as a predicate in a conditional expression. *SafeTreatment* is primed in *ScanIntlk*; it tests the *status* and *intlk* state variables in the after state when they have constrained by *TreatmentStatus*. It is implemented by the function `safe_treatment` that tests `status` and `intlk`.

ScanIntlk is an operation schema that sets the master therapy interlock according to the truth value of the predicate *SafeTreatment*. It is implemented by a procedure that invokes `safe_treatment`. *TreatmentStatus* appears primed in the definition of *ScanIntlk*, so we invoke the `treatment_status` procedure first to assign values to the elements of the `status` array before they are tested by `safe_treatment` (the `intlk` array is assigned by procedures in other files not described here). *ScanIntlk* includes Ξ*Field*, so `treatment_status` and `safe_treatment` must not cause new values to be assigned to the program state variables in `field.c`.

28.9.4 Tool-kit operators

The specification uses operators from the tool-kit for which we have not defined any refinement laws. We will derive their implementations now.

SafeTreatment says that every interlock must be clear:

$$\text{ran } intlk = \{clear\}$$

Predicates about sets can often be translated to quantified predicates where the bound variable ranges over the set elements. Here we can use the *Constant range* law:

$$\text{ran } f = \{y\} \Leftrightarrow (\forall x : \text{dom } f \bullet f\, x = y) \qquad \text{[Constant range]}$$

The right side of this equivalance matches our *Universal Test* law. We obtain code that loops over all the elements in the array that implements *intlk*.

```
safe = 1;
for (i = 0; i < N_INTERLOCKS; i++)
    if (intlk[i] != clear) safe = 0;
```

The predicate of *TreatmentStatus* is complicated:

dom *status* = **if** *mode* = *therapy* **then** *SETTING* **else** *preset*

status =
    (λs : dom *status* • *not_ready*) $\oplus$
    (λs : dom *status* | *Overridden*($s, \theta Field$) • *override*) $\oplus$
    (λs : dom *status* | *Ready*($s, \theta Field$) • *ready*)

The conditional expression says that all settings must be checked in therapy mode, but only a subset of the settings (called "presets") should be checked in experiment mode. We accomplish this by the method described previously: Put all the elements of this subset at the beginning of the enumeration, and adjust the upper limit of the iteration appropriately:

```
ns = (mode == therapy) ? N_SETTINGS : N_PRESETS;
```

The lambda expressions and the overriding operator $\oplus$ are supposed to convey that settings are not ready unless they have been overridden or have become ready. It seems we need to do some conditional branching but we're not sure how. When it isn't exactly clear what to do, look up the definitions. Turning to the tool-kit, we find this definition of the overriding operator:

$$Q \oplus R = ((\text{dom } R) \triangleleft Q) \cup R \qquad \text{[Definition of } \oplus\text{]}$$

Expanding the definition of the range anti-restriction operator $\triangleleft$ we obtain

$$(\text{dom } R) \triangleleft Q = \{ s : X, t : Y \mid s \notin \text{dom } R \wedge s \underline{Q} t \} \qquad \text{[Definition of } \triangleleft\text{]}$$

expressing R itself in similar form we get

$$R = \{ s : X, t : Y \mid s \in \text{dom } R \wedge s \underline{R} t \} \qquad \text{[Definition of } \underline{R}, etc.]$$

Next we apply the law that relates set union and disjunction

$$\{ S \mid p \} \cup \{ S \mid q \} = \{ S \mid p \vee q \} \qquad \text{[Disjunction and union]}$$

replacing $\{ S \mid p \}$ in this law with R, and $\{ S \mid q \}$ with $(\text{dom } R) \triangleleft Q$, we obtain

$$Q \oplus R = \{ s : X, t : Y \mid (s \in \text{dom } R \wedge s \underline{R} y) \vee (s \notin \text{dom } R \wedge s \underline{Q} y) \}$$

Now the predicate in the set comprehension has the form $(p \wedge r) \vee (\neg p \wedge q)$. According to our *Branch* refinement law, this can be implemented by if (p) r; else q: Q appears before the $\oplus$ operator, but it corresponds to q in the second disjunct. We've got the answer we were looking for. The result of applying the function $(\lambda\,S \bullet e_1) \oplus (\lambda\,S \mid p \bullet e_2)$ to the argument x can be computed by the code `if (p) x = e_2; else x = e_1`. The expression that appears before the $\oplus$ in the formula appears in the `else` clause in the code. We feel certain we could work this up into a proper proof if we had to, but for now we're eager to write the code:

```
for (s = 0; s < ns; s++) {
        if (ready_setting(s)) status[s] = READY;
        else if (overridden(s)) status[s] = OVERRIDE;
        else status[s] = NOT_READY;
}
```

The completed implementation appears in Figures 28.2 and 28.3.

28.9.5 Conclusion

The preceding example shows that we can take Z down to any level of detail we wish; A Z formula can model a single line of code. Typically we model systems at a more abstract level, so the Z specification is usually much shorter than the completed code.

Now that we have the code, let's step back and see what we have accomplished. Here is the problem that motivated us: "The purpose of this program is to help ensure that patients are treated correctly, as directed by their prescriptions" (chapter 6). Our code doesn't resemble this statement in any obvious way, but we can show a sequence of steps connecting the two. The product of our development is not just the code, it is the entire sequence of steps. What the program is expected to do and what it will demand of its environment have been made explicit so they can be examined and criticized. Each step can be reviewed, and some steps can even be checked by formal calculation. Every development contains errors at first, but our methods make it possible to discover and correct most errors before the program is run. If the inspection and correction are performed with diligence, we can be confident that testing will confirm that the new program meets its requirements.

Further reading

I could only provide the briefest introduction to program derivation here. The recent textbooks by Cohen [1990] and Kaldewaij [1990] are good introductions to the axiomatic method, and the books by Morgan [1994] and Hehner [1993] both teach a refinement calculus that is deeper and more versatile than mine. Hehner's paper [1991] compares the two approaches and is the source of the axiomatic definitions I use. Gries' pioneering textbook [1981] is the source of the checklist for reviewing loops and the heuristic for deriving invariants from postconditions.

Hoare and Wirth [1973] present an axiomatic definition for most of Pascal which could be adapted to other languages as well. The early textbook by Alagić and Arbib [1978] teaches from this definition. The Bohm-Jacopini theorem [1966] establishes that any program can be written using only a few Pascal-like control structures.

Hart [1995] applies axiomatic methods to detecting and correcting errors in C programs. Clutterbuck and Carré [1988] verify assembly language programs. The Cleanroom method has applied a pragmatic kind of formal verification in numerous projects with several program languages, see Linger [1993].

Program verification is not new; Herman Goldstine, John von Neumann, and Alan Turing proved programs correct before 1950. Jones' report [1992] tells the history; Gries' textbook [1981] also includes some historical notes.

I chose C for the examples in this book to show that Z can be implemented in a popular programming language, not to suggest that C is best for every application. The real interlock system that suggested the example in Section 28.9 is programmed in a Pascal dialect. Cullyer, Goodenough, and Wichmann [1991] discuss the suitability of several programming languages for implementing safety-critical systems. All programming languages have their difficulties. Koening's book [1988] warns of pitfalls in C; Welsh, Sneeringer, and Hoare [1977] even uncover ambiguities and insecurities in Pascal. Hatton [1995] argues that compiler quality and programming practices are more important than the choice of language.

The correctness condition for refinement in Chapter 26 is from the *Reference*

Manual, which describes additional conditions concerning preconditions and initialization. Other Z textbooks also discuss refinement using slightly different notation.

The development methods taught in Chapters 27 and 28 relate the mathematical notation to *imperative* programming languages that use assignment statements to change the program state. A radical alternative is to use a programming language which is itself a mathematical notation. This vision is achieved in *functional* programming languages that do not require the use of assignment statements, such as Lisp [Abelson and Sussman, 1984], Miranda [Turner, 1986; Bird and Wadler, 1988], Haskell [Fasel *et al.*, 1992], and ML [Paulson, 1991]. Paulson [1991] shows how to verify functional programs. Valentine [1995] has shown that a subset of Z itself could be used as a functional programming language.

I describe a larger example of refinement from a nonconstructive to a constructive specification in [Jacky, 1993a]. Jonathan Unger and I built an efficient table-driven dispatcher for invoking top-level operation schemas in the event-driven state transition system described in Chapter 21 [Jacky and Unger, 1995]. Our development from Z to a Pascal dialect includes some formal refinement and verification.

A Glossary of Z notation

This glossary is based on the one by Jonathan Bowen at the Z home page, http://www.comlab.ox.ac.uk/archive/z.html. It includes all the notation used in this book.

Names

a, b	identifiers
d, e	declarations (e.g., $a : A$; $b, \ldots : B \ldots$)
f, g	functions
m, n	numbers
p, q	predicates
s, t	sequences
x, y	expressions
A, B	sets
Q, R	relations
S, T	schemas
X	schema text (e.g., d, $d \mid p$, or S)

Definitions

$a == x$	Abbreviation definition
$a ::= b \mid \ldots$	Free type definition
$[a]$	Introduction of a basic type (or $[a, \ldots]$)
$a\_$	Prefix operator
$\_a$	Postfix operator
$\_a\_$	Infix operator

Logic

true	Logical true constant
false	Logical false constant
$\neg\, p$	Logical negation, *not*
$p \wedge q$	Logical conjunction, *and*
$p \vee q$	Logical disjunction, *or*
$p \Rightarrow q$	Logical implication
$p \Leftrightarrow q$	Logical equivalence
$\forall\, X \bullet q$	Universal quantification
$\exists\, X \bullet q$	Existential quantification
(**let** $a == x;\ \ldots \bullet p$)	Local definition

Sets and expressions

$x = y$	Equality
$x \neq y$	Inequality
$x \in A$	Set membership
$x \notin A$	Nonmembership
$\emptyset$	Empty set
$A \subseteq B$	Subset
$A \subset B$	Proper subset
$\{x, y, \ldots\}$	Set display
$\{\, X \bullet x \,\}$	Set comprehension
$(\lambda\, X \bullet x)$	Lambda expression
(**let** $a == x;\ \ldots \bullet y$)	Local definition
if p **then** x **else** y	Conditional expression
$(x, y, \ldots)$	Tuple
(x, y)	Pair
$A \times B \times \ldots$	Cartesian product
$\mathbb{P}A$	Power set
$A \cap B$	Set intersection
$A \cup B$	Set union
$A \setminus B$	Set difference
first x	First element of an ordered pair
second x	Second element of an ordered pair
$\#A$	Number of elements in a set

Relations

$A \leftrightarrow B$	Binary relation ($\mathbb{P}(A \times B)$)
$a \mapsto b$	Maplet ((a, b))
dom R	Domain of a relation
ran R	Range of a relation
$Q \mathbin{\S} R$	Forward relational composition
$Q \circ R$	Backward relational composition ($R \mathbin{\S} Q$)
$A \triangleleft R$	Domain restriction
$A \mathbin{\lhd\!\!\!-} R$	Domain antirestriction
$A \triangleright R$	Range restriction
$A \mathbin{-\!\!\!\rhd} R$	Range antirestriction
$R(\!(A)\!)$	Relational image
$R^{\sim}$	Inverse of relation
R^{+}	Transitive closure
$Q \oplus R$	Relational overriding
$a \underline{R} b$	Infix relation

Functions

$A \nrightarrow B$	Partial functions
$A \rightarrow B$	Total functions
$A \nrightarrowtail B$	Partial injections
$A \rightarrowtail B$	Total injections
$A \twoheadrightarrowtail B$	Bijections
$f\ x$	Function application (or $f(x)$)

Numbers

$\mathbb{Z}$	Set of integers
$\mathbb{N}$	Set of natural numbers $\{0, 1, 2, \ldots\}$
$\mathbb{N}_1$	Set of strictly positive numbers $\{1, 2, \ldots\}$
$m + n$	Addition
$m - n$	Subtraction
$m * n$	Multiplication
m div n	Division
m mod n	Remainder (modulus)
$m \leq n$	Less than or equal
$m < n$	Less than

$m \geq n$	Greater than or equal
$m > n$	Greater than
$m \mathrel{..} n$	Number range
$min \; A$	Minimum of a set of numbers
$max \; A$	Maximum of a set of numbers

Sequences

seq A	Set of finite sequences
$\text{seq}_1 A$	Set of nonempty finite sequences
iseq A	Set of finite injective sequences
$\langle \rangle$	Empty sequence
$\langle x, y, \ldots \rangle$	Sequence display
$s \frown t$	Sequence concatenation
head s	First element of a sequence
tail s	All but the head element of a sequence
last s	Last element of a sequence
front s	All but the last element of a sequence
s in *t*	Sequence segment relation

Schema

$$
\begin{array}{|l}
\underline{ S } \\
d \\
\hline
p \\
\end{array}
$$

Axiomatic definition

$$
\begin{array}{|l}
d \\
\hline
p \\
\end{array}
$$

Generic definition

$$
\begin{array}{|l}
\underline{[a, \ldots]} \\
d \\
\hline
p \\
\end{array}
$$

Schema calculus

$S \mathrel{\widehat=} [\, X \,]$	Horizontal schema
$[\, T; \ldots \mid \ldots \,]$	Schema inclusion
$z.a$	Component selection (given $z : S$)
θS	Binding
$\neg\, S$	Schema negation
$S \wedge T$	Schema conjunction
$S \vee T$	Schema disjunction
$S \mathbin{\mathrm{\,{}_9^o\,}} T$	Schema composition
$S \gg T$	Schema piping

Conventions

$a?$	Input to an operation
$a!$	Output from an operation
a	State component before an operation
a'	State component after an operation
S	State schema before an operation
S'	State schema after an operation
ΔS	Change of state
ΞS	No change of state

B Omitted features

These Z features are defined in the *Reference Manual* but are not discussed in this book.

- the unique existential quantifier $\exists_1$
- the definite description quantifier μ
- generalized union and intersection $\bigcup$ and $\bigcap$
- identity relation id
- relational iteration R^k
- reflexive transitive closure R^*
- partial surjections $\twoheadrightarrow$, total surjections $\twoheadrightarrow$, finite partial functions $\nrightarrow$, finite partial injections $\rightarrowtail$
- successor function *succ*
- sequence operators: distributed concatenation $^\frown/$, reverse *rev*, compaction *squash*, extraction $\upharpoonleft$, filtering $\upharpoonright$, prefix, suffix
- disjoint and partition
- the bag (multiset) datatype and all bag operators
- schema calculus operators: implication, equivalence, quantification, component renaming, and hiding.

C Operator precedence

Operators that join expressions into larger expressions bind more tightly than relational operators that join expressions into predicates.

$squares \lhd up \in SQUARE \rightarrowtail DIAGONAL$

means the same as

$(squares \lhd up) \in (SQUARE \rightarrowtail DIAGONAL)$

but the parentheses are not necessary because the domain restriction operator $\lhd$ and the injection arrow $\rightarrowtail$ form expressions, while the membership operator $\in$ forms a predicate.

Each infix function symbol has a priority from one to six which determines its binding power; higher numbers indicate tighter binding:

Priority 1: $\mapsto$

Priority 2: $..$

Priority 3: $+ - \cup \setminus \frown$

Priority 4: $* \operatorname{div} \operatorname{mod} \cap \,\mathbin{\fatsemi}\, \circ$

Priority 5: $\oplus$

Priority 6: $\lhd \rhd \mathbin{\vartriangleleft\mkern-10mu-} \mathbin{-\mkern-10mu\vartriangleright}$

For example, range restriction $\rhd$ binds more tightly than number range $(\_ .. \_)$ so the parentheses are necessary in

$phone \rhd (4000 .. 4999) = \{aki \mapsto 4019\}$

Domain restriction ◁ binds more tightly than relational overriding ⊕, and function application binds more tightly than any operator. Therefore we do not require parentheses in

$$variable' = variable \oplus vars? \lhd encode\ register'$$

although it is a good idea to include them anyway. This means the same but is much clearer:

$$variable' = variable \oplus (vars? \lhd (encode\ register'))$$

Operators with the same priority associate to the left, so

$$ODD \cup EVEN \setminus PRIME$$

is the same as

$$(ODD \cup EVEN) \setminus PRIME$$

The relation and function arrows associate to the right, so

$$FIELD \nrightarrow SETTING \rightarrow VALUE$$

is the same as

$$FIELD \nrightarrow (SETTING \rightarrow VALUE)$$

Function application associates to the left, so

$$prescribed\ lateral\ collimator$$

is the same as

$$(prescribed\ lateral)\ collimator$$

In decreasing order of binding power, the logical connectives are

$$\neg \quad \wedge \vee \Rightarrow \Leftrightarrow$$

Therefore, we don't have to parenthesize equivalences, and we usually don't have to parenthesize implications. This predicate

$$p \wedge q \vee r \Rightarrow s \Leftrightarrow t$$

is the same as

$$(((p \wedge q) \vee r) \Rightarrow s) \Leftrightarrow t$$

Implication associates to the right, so

$$p \Rightarrow q \Rightarrow r$$

is the same as

$$p \Rightarrow (q \Rightarrow r)$$

Implication is not associative, so $(p \Rightarrow q) \Rightarrow r$ means something else. The other binary logical connectives associate to the left but this is moot because they are all associative.

The scope of a quantifier extends as far as possible to the right, and quantifiers bind less tightly than any of the propositional connectives. Therefore parentheses are often required in quantified predicates, for example:

$$(\forall d \mid p \bullet q) \Leftrightarrow (\forall d \bullet p \Rightarrow q)$$

D The Z mathematical tool-kit

These selections from the tool-kit are based on the *Reference Manual*. They include all the operators used in this book and a few more that are needed to define them.

The definitions in the tool-kit require some Z constructs we have not used elsewhere. It uses generic definitions very heavily: X, Y, and Z stand for any type, S and T are sets of any type, and Q and R are binary relations between any two types. The tool-kit also makes extensive use of patterns in abbreviation definitions, for example it defines the binary relation symbol by $X \leftrightarrow Y == \mathbb{P}(X \times Y)$.

In a few places I've used English paraphrases for predicates, where the formal definition uses constructs or concepts not discussed in this book.

Sets

Glossary

$\emptyset$ — Empty set: a set that has no elements.

$x \notin S$ — Nonmembership: x is not an element of S.

$S \subseteq T$ — Subset: All elements of S belong to T.

$S \subset T$ — Proper subset: S is a subset of T, and S is not equal to T.

$S \cup T$ — Union: the set of elements in either S or T.

$S \cap T$ — Intersection: the set of elements in both S and T.

$S \setminus T$ — Set difference: the set of elements in S that are not in T.

Definitions

$$\emptyset[X] == \{\, x : X \mid false \,\}$$

$$
\begin{array}{l}
\underline{\quad[X]\quad} \\
\_\subseteq\_,\_\subset\_ : \mathbb{P}X \leftrightarrow \mathbb{P}X \\
\_\cup\_,\_\cap\_,\_\setminus\_ : \mathbb{P}X \times \mathbb{P}X \to X \\
\hline
\forall x : X;\ S, T : \mathbb{P}X \bullet \\
\qquad x \notin S \Leftrightarrow \neg\,(x \in X)\ \wedge \\
\qquad (S \subseteq T \Leftrightarrow (\forall x : X \bullet x \in S \Rightarrow x \in T))\ \wedge \\
\qquad (S \subset T \Leftrightarrow S \subseteq T \wedge S \neq T)\ \wedge \\
\qquad S \cup T = \{\, x : X \mid x \in S \vee x \in T \,\}\ \wedge \\
\qquad S \cap T = \{\, x : X \mid x \in S \wedge x \in T \,\}\ \wedge \\
\qquad S \setminus T = \{\, x : X \mid x \in S \wedge x \notin T \,\}
\end{array}
$$

Pairs and binary relations I

Glossary

(x, y) — The pair x,y.

$x \mapsto y$ — Maplet: x maps to y, same as (x, y).

first p — First element of pair p.

second p — Second element of pair p.

dom R — Domain: the set of first elements of all pairs in R.

ran R — Range: the set of second elements of all pairs in R.

Definitions

$$X \leftrightarrow Y == \mathbb{P}(X \times Y)$$

$$
\begin{array}{l}
[X, Y] \\
\hline
first : X \times Y \to X \\
second : X \times Y \to Y \\
\_ \mapsto \_ : X \times Y \to X \times Y \\
dom : (X \leftrightarrow Y) \to \mathbb{P}X \\
ran : (X \leftrightarrow Y) \to \mathbb{P}Y \\
\hline
\forall x : X; \; y : Y; \; R : X \leftrightarrow Y \bullet \\
\quad first(x, y) = x \wedge \\
\quad second(x, y) = y \wedge \\
\quad x \mapsto y = (x, y) \wedge \\
\quad dom\, R = \{ x : X; \; y : Y \mid x \underline{R} y \bullet x \} \wedge \\
\quad ran\, R = \{ x : X; \; y : Y \mid x \underline{R} y \bullet y \}
\end{array}
$$

Pairs and binary relations II

Glossary

$S \lhd R$ — Domain restriction: the pairs in R whose first element is in S.

$R \rhd T$ — Range restriction: the pairs in R whose second element is in T.

$S \ntriangleleft R$ — Domain antirestriction: the pairs in R whose first element is not in S.

$R \ntriangleright T$ — Range antirestriction: the pairs in R whose second element is not in T.

$R^{\sim}$ — Relational inverse: the pairs in R,

but with first and second elements exchanged.

$R(\!|S|\!)$ — Relational image: the second elements of pairs

in R whose first element is in S.

$R \oplus Q$ — Overriding: all pairs in R or Q,

except pairs in R whose first element is also in Q.

R^{+} — Transitive closure of R.

Definitions

$$
\begin{array}{l}
\underline{\quad[X, Y]\quad} \\
\hline
\_\lhd\_, \_\ntriangleleft\_ : \mathbb{P}X \times (X \leftrightarrow Y) \rightarrow X \leftrightarrow Y \\
\_\rhd\_, \_\ntriangleright\_ : (X \leftrightarrow Y) \times \mathbb{P}Y \rightarrow X \leftrightarrow Y \\
\_^{\sim} : (X \leftrightarrow Y) \rightarrow (Y \leftrightarrow X) \\
\_(\!|\_|\!) : (X \leftrightarrow Y) \times \mathbb{P}X \rightarrow \mathbb{P}Y \\
\_\oplus\_ : (X \leftrightarrow Y) \times (X \leftrightarrow Y) \rightarrow (X \leftrightarrow Y) \\
\_^{+} : (X \leftrightarrow X) \rightarrow (X \leftrightarrow X) \\
\end{array}
$$

$\forall x : X;\ y : Y;\ S : \mathbb{P}X;\ T : \mathbb{P}Y;\ Q, R : X \leftrightarrow Y\ \bullet$

$S \lhd R = \{\, x : X;\ y : Y \mid x \in S \land x\ \underline{R}\ y \bullet x \mapsto y \,\} \land$

$S \ntriangleleft R = \{\, x : X;\ y : Y \mid x \notin S \land x\ \underline{R}\ y \bullet x \mapsto y \,\} \land$

$R \rhd T = \{\, x : X;\ y : Y \mid x\ \underline{R}\ y \land y \in T \bullet x \mapsto y \,\} \land$

$R \ntriangleright T = \{\, x : X;\ y : Y \mid x\ \underline{R}\ y \land y \notin T \bullet x \mapsto y \,\} \land$

$R^{\sim} = \{\, x : X;\ y : Y \mid x\ \underline{R}\ y \bullet y \mapsto x \,\} \land$

$R(\!|S|\!) = \{\, x : X;\ y : Y \mid x \in S \land x\ \underline{R}\ y \bullet y \,\} \land$

$Q \oplus R = ((\mathrm{dom}\ R) \ntriangleleft Q) \cup R$

... predicate for $\_^{+}$ omitted ...

Pairs and binary relations III

Glossary

$Q \,\overset{\circ}{,}\, R$ — Relational composition: Q composed with R.

$R \circ Q$ — Backward relational composition, same as $Q \,\overset{\circ}{,}\, R$.

Definitions

$$
\begin{array}{l}
\underline{\qquad} [X, Y, Z] \underline{\qquad\qquad\qquad\qquad\qquad\qquad} \\
\quad \_\,\overset{\circ}{,}\,\_ : (X \leftrightarrow Y) \times (Y \leftrightarrow Z) \to (X \leftrightarrow Z) \\
\quad \_\circ\_ : (Y \leftrightarrow Z) \times (X \leftrightarrow Y) \to (X \leftrightarrow Z) \\
\underline{\qquad\qquad\qquad} \\
\quad \forall Q : X \leftrightarrow Y;\ R : Y \leftrightarrow Z \bullet \\
\qquad Q \,\overset{\circ}{,}\, R = R \circ Q = \{\, x : X;\ y : Y;\ z : Z \mid x\underline{Q}y \wedge y\,\underline{R}\,z \bullet x \mapsto z \,\}
\end{array}
$$

Numbers and arithmetic

Glossary

$\mathbb{Z}$ — The set of integers.

$\mathbb{N}$ — The set of natural numbers, starting with zero.

$\mathbb{N}_1$ — The set of strictly positive numbers, starting with one.

$+, -, *$ — Arithmetic operators: addition, subtraction, multiplication.

div, mod — Arithmetic operators: integer division and remainder (modulus).

$<, \leq$ — Comparison: less than, less than or equal.

$>, \geq$ — Comparison: greater than, greater than or equal.

$i \ldots j$ — Number range: the set of numbers starting with i up through j.

$min\ S$ — Minimum: the smallest element in S, if any.

$max\ S$ — Maximum: the largest element in S, if any.

$\#S$ — Size: the number of elements in S.

$\mathbb{P}_1$ — Nonempty sets.

$\mathbb{F}$ — Finite sets.

Definitions

$[\mathbb{Z}]$

$\mathbb{N} == \{\, n : \mathbb{Z} \mid n \geq 0 \,\}$

$\mathbb{N}_1 == \mathbb{N} \setminus \{0\}$

$\mathbb{P}_1 X == \{\, S : \mathbb{P}X \mid S \neq \emptyset \,\}$

$\mathbb{F}X == \{\, S : \mathbb{P}X \mid \ldots S \text{ is finite} \ldots \,\}$

$$
\begin{array}{|l}
\_ + \_, \_ - \_, \_ * \_ : \mathbb{Z} \times \mathbb{Z} \to \mathbb{Z} \\
\_\,div\,\_, \_\,mod\,\_ : \mathbb{Z} \times (\mathbb{Z} \setminus \{0\}) \to \mathbb{Z} \\
- : \mathbb{Z} \to \mathbb{Z} \\
\_ < \_, \_ \leq \_, \_ \geq \_, \_ > \_ : \mathbb{Z} \leftrightarrow \mathbb{Z} \\
\_ \ldots \_ : \mathbb{Z} \times \mathbb{Z} \to \mathbb{P}\mathbb{Z} \\
\# : \mathbb{F}X \to \mathbb{N} \\
min, max : \mathbb{P}_1\mathbb{Z} \twoheadrightarrow \mathbb{Z} \\
\hline
\forall a, b : \mathbb{Z} \bullet \\
\quad a \ldots b = \{\, i : \mathbb{Z} \mid a \leq i \leq b \,\} \\
\\
\quad \ldots \text{predicates for other operators omitted} \ldots
\end{array}
$$

Functions

Glossary

$X \nrightarrow Y$ — Partial function: Some members of X are paired with a member of Y.

$X \rightarrow Y$ — Total function: Every member of X is paired with a member of Y.

$X \nrightarrowtail Y$ — Partial injection: Some members of X are paired with different members of Y.

$X \rightarrowtail Y$ — Total injection: Every member of X is paired with a different member of Y.

$X \rightarrowtailtwoheadrightarrow Y$ — Bijection: Every member of X is paired with a different member of Y, covering all Ys.

Definitions

$X \nrightarrow Y == \{ \, f : X \leftrightarrow Y \mid \text{Each member of } X \text{ appears no more than once.} \, \}$

$X \rightarrow Y == \{ \, f : X \nrightarrow Y \mid \text{dom } f = X \, \}$

$X \nrightarrowtail Y == \{ \, f : X \nrightarrow Y \mid \text{Each member of } X \text{ is paired with a different member of } Y. \, \}$

$X \rightarrowtail Y == (X \nrightarrowtail Y) \cap (X \rightarrow Y)$

$X \rightarrowtailtwoheadrightarrow Y == \ldots \text{definition omitted} \ldots$

Sequences

Glossary

seq X — Sequence: the set of all sequences of Xs.

$\text{seq}_1 X$ — Nonempty sequence: the set of all sequences of Xs
with at least one element.

iseq X — Injective sequence: the set of all sequences of Xs
where each element of X appears only once.

$s \frown t$ — Concatenation: sequence s with sequence t appended.

head s — Head: the first element of sequence s.

last s — Last: the last element of sequence s.

front s — Front: all but the last element of sequence s.

tail s — Tail: all but the first element of sequence s.

$s \text{ in } t$ — Segment relation: the sequence s appears in sequence t.

Definitions

$\text{seq } X == \{\, f : \mathbb{N} \nrightarrow X \mid \text{dom } f = 1 \mathinner{\ldotp\ldotp} \#f \,\}$

$\text{seq}_1 X == \{\, f : \text{seq } X \mid \#f > 0 \,\}$

$\text{iseq } X == \text{seq } X \cap (\mathbb{N} \rightarrowtail X)$

$$
\begin{array}{l}
\hline
[X] \\
\hline
head, last : \text{seq}_1 X \rightarrow X \\
tail, front : \text{seq}_1 X \rightarrow \text{seq } X \\
\_ \frown \_ : \text{seq } X \times \text{seq } X \rightarrow \text{seq } X \\
\_ \text{ in } \_ : \text{seq } X \leftrightarrow \text{seq } X \\
\hline
\forall s : \text{seq}_1 X;\ u, v : \text{seq } X \bullet \\
\qquad head(s) = s(1) \wedge \\
\qquad last(s) = s(\#s) \wedge \\
\qquad u \frown v = u \cup \{\, i : \text{dom } v \bullet i + \#u \mapsto v(i) \,\} \\
\qquad u \text{ in } v \Leftrightarrow (\exists s, t : \text{seq } X \bullet s \frown u \frown t = v) \\
\qquad \ldots \text{predicates for other operators omitted} \ldots \\
\hline
\end{array}
$$

E Selected Laws

Logical connectives

$$true \Leftrightarrow \neg\, false \hspace{4cm} \text{[Complement]}$$

$$p \vee \neg\, p \hspace{4cm} \text{[Excluded middle]}$$

$$p \wedge p \Leftrightarrow p \hspace{4cm} \text{[Idempotence]}$$

$$p \vee p \Leftrightarrow p \hspace{4cm} \text{[Idempotence]}$$

$$p \wedge true \Leftrightarrow p \hspace{4cm} \text{[Unit of \textit{and}]}$$

$$p \wedge false \Leftrightarrow false \hspace{4cm} \text{[Zero of \textit{and}]}$$

$$p \vee false \Leftrightarrow p \hspace{4cm} \text{[Unit of \textit{or}]}$$

$$p \vee true \Leftrightarrow true \hspace{4cm} \text{[Zero of \textit{or}]}$$

$$p \wedge q \Leftrightarrow q \wedge p \hspace{4cm} \text{[Commutativity]}$$

$$p \vee q \Leftrightarrow q \vee p \hspace{4cm} \text{[Commutativity]}$$

$$(p \wedge q) \wedge r \Leftrightarrow p \wedge (q \wedge r) \hspace{4cm} \text{[Associativity]}$$

$$(p \vee q) \vee r \Leftrightarrow p \vee (q \vee r) \hspace{4cm} \text{[Associativity]}$$

$$p \wedge (q \vee r) \Leftrightarrow (p \wedge q) \vee (p \wedge r) \hspace{4cm} \text{[Distributivity]}$$

$$p \vee (q \wedge r) \Leftrightarrow (p \vee q) \wedge (p \vee r) \hspace{4cm} \text{[Distributivity]}$$

$$\neg\, (p \wedge q) \Leftrightarrow \neg\, p \vee \neg\, q \hspace{4cm} \text{[DeMorgan]}$$

$$p \Rightarrow q \Leftrightarrow \neg\, p \vee q \qquad\qquad\qquad\qquad \text{[Implication]}$$

$$p \Rightarrow q \Leftrightarrow \neg\, p \Rightarrow \neg\, q \qquad\qquad\qquad\qquad \text{[Contrapositive]}$$

$$p \Leftrightarrow q \Leftrightarrow (p \Rightarrow q) \wedge (q \Rightarrow p) \qquad\qquad \text{[Equivalence]}$$

$$p \Leftrightarrow (q \Leftrightarrow r) \Leftrightarrow (p \Leftrightarrow q) \Leftrightarrow r \qquad\qquad \text{[Associativity]}$$

$$(p \Leftrightarrow q \Leftrightarrow r) \Rightarrow (p \Leftrightarrow r) \qquad\qquad\qquad \text{[Transitivity]}$$

$$(p \wedge x' = e_1) \vee (\neg\, p \wedge x' = e_2) \Leftrightarrow x' = \textbf{if } p \textbf{ then } e_1 \textbf{ else } e_2$$
$$\text{[Z conditional expr.]}$$

Assume antecedent

$$p \Rightarrow q \qquad\qquad\qquad\qquad\qquad\qquad\qquad \text{[To prove]}$$

$$\Leftrightarrow q \qquad\qquad\qquad\qquad\qquad \text{[Assume antecedent]}$$

$$\vdots$$

$$\Leftrightarrow true \qquad\qquad\qquad\qquad \text{[Justified by antecedent } p\text{]}$$

Quantifiers

$$(\forall d \mid p \bullet q) \Leftrightarrow (\forall d \bullet p \Rightarrow q) \qquad\qquad \text{[Restricted } \forall\text{-quantifier]}$$

$$(\exists d \mid p \bullet q) \Leftrightarrow (\exists d \bullet p \wedge q) \qquad\qquad \text{[Restricted } \exists\text{-quantifier]}$$

$$(\exists x : T \bullet x = e \wedge p) \Leftrightarrow (p[e/x]) \qquad\qquad \text{[One-point rule]}$$

$$s \Leftrightarrow (\textbf{let } x == e \bullet s[x/e]) \qquad\qquad\qquad \text{[Local definition]}$$

Equality

$$x = x \qquad\qquad\qquad\qquad\qquad\qquad\qquad \text{[Reflexivity]}$$

$$x = y \Leftrightarrow y = x \qquad\qquad\qquad\qquad\qquad \text{[Symmetry]}$$

$$x = y = z \Rightarrow x = z \qquad\qquad\qquad\qquad \text{[Transitivity]}$$

$$x = y \Rightarrow e = e[x/y] \qquad\qquad\qquad\qquad \text{[Substitution]}$$

$$x = y \Rightarrow f\, x = f\, y \qquad\qquad\qquad\qquad\qquad \text{[Leibniz]}$$

Arithmetic

$$0 * n = 0 \qquad \text{[Zero]}$$

$$x < y < z \Rightarrow x < z \qquad \text{[Transitivity]}$$

$$d \neq 0 \Rightarrow n = d * (n \operatorname{div} d) + (n \operatorname{mod} d) \qquad \text{[Integer division]}$$

Sets, relations, and functions

$$p(x) \Leftrightarrow x \in (p\_) \qquad \text{[Prefix relation syntax]}$$

$$x \underline{R} y \Leftrightarrow (x, y) \in R \qquad \text{[Infix relation syntax]}$$

$$S \subseteq T \subseteq U \Rightarrow S \subseteq U \qquad \text{[Transitivity]}$$

$$\operatorname{ran} f = \{y\} \Leftrightarrow (\forall x : \operatorname{dom} f \bullet fx = y) \qquad \text{[Constant range]}$$

Sets and logic

$$\{ S \mid p \} \cup \{ S \mid q \} = \{ S \mid p \vee q \} \qquad \text{[Disjunction and union]}$$

$$\{ S \mid p \} \cap \{ S \mid q \} = \{ S \mid p \wedge q \} \qquad \text{[Conjunction and intersection]}$$

$$\{ S \mid p \} \subseteq \{ S \mid q \} \Leftrightarrow (\forall S \bullet p \Rightarrow q) \qquad \text{[Implication and subset]}$$

Set comprehensions and lambda expressions

$$x \in \{x : X \mid p(x)\} \Leftrightarrow p(x) \qquad \text{[Comprehension]}$$

$$\{ x : S \mid p \} = \{ x : X \mid x \in S \wedge p \} \qquad \text{[Set membership]}$$

$$(\lambda x : X \bullet e) = \{ x : X \bullet x \mapsto e \} \qquad \text{[Lambda expression]}$$

$$\{x : X;\ y : Y, z : Z \mid p \bullet (x, y, z)\} = \{x : X;\ y : Y;\ z : Z \mid p\}$$

$$\text{[Characteristic tuple]}$$

Sequences

$$\#\langle x \rangle = 1 \qquad \text{[Length of singleton]}$$

$$\operatorname{ran}\langle x \rangle = \{x\} \qquad \text{[Range of singleton]}$$

$$\#(s \frown t) = \#s + \#t \qquad \text{[Length and concatenation]}$$

$$\operatorname{ran}(s \frown t) = (\operatorname{ran} s) \cup (\operatorname{ran} t) \qquad \text{[Range and concatenation]}$$

Axiomatic program development

Assignment
$\{\,e$ is defined $\}\; x \;=\; e\,\{\,x' = e\,\}$

$\{\,Q[e/x']\,\}\; x \;=\; e\,\{\,Q\,\}$

Conditional branch
$\{\,U\,\}$
if $(p)\;\{\,U \wedge p\,\}\;S1;\{\,V\,\}$ else $\{\,U \wedge \neg\, p\,\}\;S2\,\{\,W\,\}$
$\{\,V \vee W\,\}$

Loop
$\{\,I\,\}$
while $(p)\;\{\,p \wedge I\,\}\;S\,\{\,I' \wedge v' < v\,\}$
$\{\,\neg\, p \wedge I\,\}$

Refinement calculus

$x \in s \;\sqsubseteq\;$ *Search for* x *in data structure* s   [Membership (data structure)]

$x \in s \;\sqsubseteq\;$ s[x]   [Membership (Boolean array)]

$u(x) \;\sqsubseteq\;$ *Find item in* u *with key* x   [Function application (data structure)]

$f(x) \;\sqsubseteq\;$ *Evaluate* f *with argument* x

[Function application (executable code)]

$u(x) \;\sqsubseteq\;$ u[x]   [Function application (array)]

$f(x) \;\sqsubseteq\;$ f(x)   [Function application (C function)]

$x' = x \;\sqsubseteq\;$ *(empty statement)*   [Skip]

$x' = e \wedge y' = y \wedge z' = z \wedge \ldots \;\sqsubseteq\;$ x $=$ e   [Assignment]

$x' = e_1(x, y) \wedge y' = e_2(x, y) \wedge z' = z \ldots \;\sqsubseteq$
    t $=$ x; x $=$ $e_1(x, y)$; y $=$ $e_2(t, y)$

[Sequential assignment]

$$x' = e_1(x) \wedge y' = e_2(y) \sqsubseteq \texttt{x = } e_1(\texttt{x})\texttt{; y = } e_2(\texttt{y})$$

[Independent assignment]

$S' = S \cup \{x\} \sqsubseteq$ *Put* x *in data structure* s   [Union]

$S' = S \cup \{x\} \sqsubseteq \texttt{s[x] = TRUE}$ [Union (Boolean array)]

$p \wedge s \sqsubseteq \texttt{if } (p) \ s$ [Guarded command]

$(p \wedge s) \vee (q \wedge t) \sqsubseteq \texttt{if } (q) \ s\texttt{; else if } (q) \ t$ [Case analysis]

$(p \wedge s) \vee (\neg p \wedge t) \sqsubseteq \texttt{if } (p) \ s\texttt{; else } t$ [Branch]

$(p \wedge x' = e_1) \vee (\neg p \wedge x' = e_2) \sqsubseteq \texttt{x = } p\texttt{?}e_1\texttt{:}e_2$

[Conditional assignment]

$(p \wedge q) \vee (\neg p \wedge r) \sqsubseteq p\texttt{?}q\texttt{:}r$ [Conditional predicate]

$(\textbf{let } x == e \bullet s(x)) \sqsubseteq \texttt{x = } e\texttt{; } s(x)$ [New variable]

$\forall x : S \bullet p(x) \sqsubseteq \texttt{b = 1; for } (x \textit{ in } S) \texttt{ if } (!p(x)) \texttt{ b = 0}$

[Universal test]

$\exists x : S \bullet p(x) \sqsubseteq \texttt{b = 0; for } (x \textit{ in } S) \texttt{ if } (p(x)) \texttt{ b = 1}$

[Existential test]

$\forall x : S \bullet p(x) \sqsubseteq \texttt{b = 1; for (i = 0; i < n; i++)}$
$$\texttt{if } (!p(\texttt{s[i]})) \texttt{ b = 0}$$

[Universal test (array of length n)]

$\forall x : S \bullet s(x) \sqsubseteq \texttt{for } (x \textit{ in } S) \ s(x)$ [Universal assignment]

$\exists x : S \bullet s(x) \sqsubseteq$ *Choose any or all x in S;* $s(x)$ [Existential assignment]

C source language transformations

$$x \mathrel{!=} 0 \equiv x \qquad\qquad\qquad\qquad \text{[C true]}$$

$$(*x).z \equiv x\text{->}z \qquad\qquad\qquad\qquad \text{[C pointer]}$$

$$x = x + 1 \equiv x\text{++} \qquad\qquad\qquad \text{[C increment]}$$

$$x[y] \equiv *(x+y) \qquad\qquad\qquad\qquad \text{[C array]}$$

$$\texttt{if (p) x = y; else x = z} \equiv \texttt{x = p ? x : z}$$
$$\text{[C conditional expression]}$$

$$\texttt{s; while (p) \{ t; u; \}} \equiv \texttt{for (s; p; u) t;} \qquad \text{[C for]}$$

F Solutions to selected exercises

From Chapter 6

6.5.1   The state machine model did not specify the initial state. The only reasonable choice is the PATIENTS state.

From Chapter 10

10.4.5.1   *beam = on* $\Leftrightarrow$ *door = closed* means the beam is on when the door is closed and the beam is off when the door is open. This is a bad requirement because the beam will turn on the moment the door is closed.

 beam = on $\wedge$ *door = closed* means the beam is always on and the door is always closed. Obviously useless.

 beam = on $\vee$ *door = open* means the beam is on or the door is open, or both. This is a bad requirement because it allows the beam to be on when the door is open.

 beam = off $\vee$ *door = closed* means the beam is off or the door is closed, or both. This is a good requirement, and means exactly the same thing as *beam = on* $\Rightarrow$ *door = closed*, according to the law $p \Rightarrow q \Leftrightarrow \neg\, p \vee q$.

10.8.1 $x \in \mathrm{dom}\ f \Rightarrow f\ x = y$ is *true* when $x \in \mathrm{dom}\ f$ is *false*, otherwise it has the same truth value as $f\ x = y$.

From Chapter 11

11.1.1   Represent each triangle as a tuple whose components are the lengths of its three sides. These tuples are called *Pythagorean triples* because their components are related by the Pythagorean theorem; $(3, 4, 5)$ is a Pythagorean triple because $3^2 + 4^2 = 5^2$.

$$right\_triangles == \{\, a, b, c : \mathbb{N} \mid a < b \wedge a * a + b * b = c * c \,\}$$

Here c must be the longest side, which prohibits rotations such as $(5, 3, 4)$ or $(4, 5, 3)$, and $a < b$ ensures that the sides appear in order of increasing length, which prohibits reflections such as $(4, 3, 5)$.

11.1.2   Define *window*, then *segment = line $\cap$ window*.

11.3.1   *PRIME* is not constructive because $\mathbb{N}_2$ and $\{\, n, m : \mathbb{N}_2 \bullet n * m \,\}$ are both infinitely large. It is not possible to construct both sets and then take the difference.

11.5.1   This solution uses pattern matiching:

> *month* : *DATE* $\rightarrow$ *MONTH*
> ―――――――――――――――
> $\forall d : DAY;\ m : MONTH;\ y : YEAR \bullet month\,(d, m, y) = m$

This equivalent shorter definition uses the characteristic tuple:

$$month == (\lambda\, d : DAY;\ m : MONTH;\ y : YEAR \bullet m)$$

From Chapter 12

12.4.1.1   The precondition of *ForwardTwo* is #*right* ≥ 2.

From Chapter 13

13.2.1   Hint: Define *Next* using schema disjunction to handle leap years.

From Chapter 15

15.1.1   Inequality is not transitive. Consider $x \neq y \neq x$.

15.2.1   "Divide both sides by three" is an application of Leibniz' law where $f = (\lambda\, e : \mathbb{Z} \bullet e$ div 3) and so on.

15.3.1   We have $x = y \Leftrightarrow f\, x = f\, y$ when the inverse of f is also a function, that is when f is an injection.

From Chapter 17

17.3.1   *Format* requires that no word in the text is larger than *width*.

From Chapter 18

18.1, 18.2   Model the queen's and knight's moves as relations on *SQUARE*

```
queen, knight : SQUARE ↔ SQUARE
────────────────────────────────
. . .
```

18.2   A knight's tour is a sequence of squares, where each square appears once and each successive pair of squares is a knight's move:

```
┌─ Tour ──────────────────────────
│ tour : iseq SQUARE
├──────────────────────────────────
│ ran tour = SQUARE
│ ∀ s1, s2 : SQUARE | ⟨s1, s2⟩ in tour • (s1, s2) ∈ knight
```

From Chapter 26

26.6.1

x	x'	$x' = x + 1$	$x' > x$	$x' = x + 1 \Rightarrow x' > x$
1	1	*false*	*false*	*true*
1	3	*false*	*true*	*true*
−	−	*true*	*false*	*false*
1	2	*true*	*true*	*true*

There is no way to choose x and x', so $x' = x + 1$ is *true* but $x' > x$ is *false*, so the entries in the third row are left empty.

26.3.1   Use function overriding to model assignment to an array element. The concrete state must include the index of the last array element in use.

```
┌─ Concrete1 ─────────────────────
│ nmax : ℕ
│ ss : seq X
```

```
┌─ CStore1 ───────────────────────
│ ΔConcrete1
│ x? : X
├──────────────────────────────────
│ nmax' = nmax + 1
│ ss' = ss ⊕ {nmax ↦ x?}
```

26.3.2 The domain of the hash function must be X, the type of the elements to be stored, and its range must be $\mathbb{N}_1$, the domain of a sequence. The hash function must map each member of X to a different member of $\mathbb{N}_1$. In other words, it must be a total injection.

$$hash : X \rightarrowtail \mathbb{N}_1$$

$\begin{array}{l} \underline{\quad CStore2 \underline{}} \\ \Delta Concrete \\ x? : X \\ \hline ss' = ss \oplus \{hash\ x? \mapsto x?\} \\ \hline \end{array}$

From Chapter 27

27.1.2.1 The verification conditions are implications, so assume the antecedent:

$$p \Rightarrow (q \Leftrightarrow p \wedge q) \qquad\qquad\qquad\qquad \text{[Given]}$$

$$\Leftrightarrow (q \Leftrightarrow true \wedge q) \qquad\qquad \text{[Assume antecedent]}$$

$$\Leftrightarrow (q \Leftrightarrow q) \qquad\qquad\qquad\qquad \text{[Unit of } and\text{]}$$

$$\Leftrightarrow true \qquad\qquad\qquad\qquad \text{[Reflexivity of } \Leftrightarrow\text{]}$$

27.1.3.1 When the variant falls below bound k, the guard becomes *false*. It is easiest to solve for k formally. The bound k is defined by item 4 in the checklist: $I \wedge v < k \Rightarrow \neg p$. Filling in the definitions of I, v, and p from our example, we get

$$(0 \leq r * r \leq a) \wedge (a - (r+1) * (r+1) < k) \Rightarrow \neg a \geq (r+1) * (r+1)$$

$$\text{[Defn]}$$

$$\Leftrightarrow a - e < k \Rightarrow \neg a \geq e \qquad \text{[where } e \text{ is } (r+1) * (r+1)]$$

$$\Leftrightarrow a - e < k \Rightarrow a < e \qquad\qquad \text{[Def'ns } \neg, \geq, <]$$

$$\Leftrightarrow a < k + e \Rightarrow a < e \qquad\qquad \text{[Arithmetic, } e \geq 0]$$

$$\Leftrightarrow k \leq 0 \qquad\qquad\qquad\qquad \text{[Arithmetic]}$$

The bound k is the largest value that makes the final inequality true, so k is zero.

G Other formal notations

Here is a sample of notations that might be useful to people who are considering Z. All are based on the discrete mathematics taught in Chapters 8 to 11.

In addition to Z itself, the Z family includes several object-oriented dialects including Object-Z, MooZ, OOZE, and Z++ [Stepney, Barden, and Cooper , 1992a; Stepney *et al.*, 1992b; Lano and Haughton, 1993]. Some early contributors to Z went on to create a development method called B that includes a specification language and a tool for automating calculations and proofs [Lano and Haughton, 1995].

Of the other formal notations, VDM [Jones, 1990] is most similar to Z. Like Z, VDM is a *model-based notation*. You model a system by representing its state and a collection of operations that can change its state. VDM lacks the boxed paragraphs of Z and has nothing quite like the Z schema calculus. VDM stands for the *Vienna Development Method*. The VDM community emphasizes refinement, not just modelling. Z and VDM are compared in Hayes [1992b].

Combinations of conditions that define complex predicates can sometimes be made easier to grasp by presenting them in a two-dimensional tabular format. A particularly rigorous and comprehensive tabular notation was invented by Parnas and others [Parnas, 1994] and has been applied to nuclear reactor shutdown software. Leveson and colleagues invented a tabular notation called *AND/OR* tables and applied it to an aircraft collision avoidance system [Leveson *et al.*, 1994].

Z provides no built-in way to represent concurrent processes, although it is possible to express them in Z using the methods of Chapter 25. Other formal notations provide built-in constructs to represent concurrency. Some retain the concept of state and a model-oriented world view: These include Unity [Chandy and Misra, 1988] and the Temporal Logic of Actions (TLA) [Lamport, 1994]. The *process algebras* hide the state, focusing instead on the processes and their interactions. Examples are CCS [Milner, 1989], CSP [Hoare, 1985], and the Pi calculus [Milner, 1993].

Some systems can be modelled by a feasibly small number of discrete states. Such *state transition systems* lend themselves to pictorial notations and exhaustive analyses. Statecharts [Harel, 1987] and Petri nets [Jensen and Rozenberg, 1991] use pictures to represent state transitions, concurrency, and synchronization. They are far more substantive and rigorous than most of the other bubble-and-arrow notations that they superficially resemble. Models expressed in some discrete state notations can be executed; they can serve as *executable specifications* or *prototypes* [Harel *et al.*, 1990].

Models that include numbers or indefinitely large sets usually cannot be subjected to exhaustive analyses, but if a model has a limited number of states it can be feasible to search the entire state space. Exhaustive search is used in reachability analysis [Leveson and Stolzy, 1987] and model checking [Clarke, Emerson, and Sistla, 1986], which can automatically detect certain kinds of errors or confirm desired properties. In some cases model checking can provide a completely automatic alternative to the kind of proof taught in Chapter 15.

Integrated systems such as EVES [Craigen, 1995] combine a specification language, a theorem prover, and a programming language. Larch [Guttag and Horning, 1993] splits the specification language into a core *shared language* and a number of *interface languages*, each matched to a target programming language such as C, Ada, or Modula-3.

More information about most of these notations can be found on the Formal Methods home page maintained by Jonathan Bowen on the World Wide Web at http://www.comlab.ox.ac.uk/archive/formal-methods/.

Bibliography

Abelson Harold, and Sussman, Gerald Jay. *Structure and Interpretation of Computer Programs*. MIT Press, Cambridge, MA, 1984.

Ackerman, A. Frank, Buchwald, Lynne S., and Lewski, Frank H. Software inspections: An effective verification process. *IEEE Software*, **6**(3) (May 1989), 31–36.

Adams, James L. *Flying Buttresses, Entropy, and O-Rings: The World of an Engineer*. Harvard University Press, Cambridge, MA, 1991.

Agre, Philip E. Risks of ATM manufacturers. *RISKS-FORUM Digest*, **7**(9) (June 22, 1988).

Alagić, Suad and Arbib, Michael A. *The Design of Well-Structured and Correct Programs*. Springer-Verlag, New York, 1978.

Austin-Seymour, Mary, Kalet, Ira, McDonald, John, Kromhout-Schiro, Sharon, Jacky, Jon, Hummell, Sharon, and Unger, Jonathan. Three-dimensional planning target volumes: A model and a software tool. *International Journal of Radiation Oncology Biology Physics*, **33**(5) (1995), 1073–1080.

Barden, Rosalind, Stepney, Susan, and Cooper, David. *Z in Practice*. Prentice Hall, 1994.

Barrett, G. Formal methods applied to a floating-point number system. *IEEE Transactions on Software Engineering*, **15**(5) (May 1989), 611–621.

Bird, R. S. Transformational programming and the paragraph problem. *Science of Computer Programming*, **6** (1986), 159–189.

Bird, Richard and Wadler, Philip. *An Introduction to Functional Programming*. Prentice Hall International Ltd., Hertfordshire, UK, 1988.

Bjerknes, Gro, Ehn, Pelle, and Kyng, Morten. *Computers and Democracy : A Scandinavian Challenge*. Avebury, Brookfield, VT, 1987.

Bloomfield, R. E. and Froome, P. K. D. The application of formal methods to high integrity software. *IEEE Transactions on Software Engineering*, SE-**12**(9) (1986), 988–993.

Bohm, C. and Jacopini, G. Flow diagrams, Turing machines, and languages with only two formation rules. *Communications of the ACM*, **9**(5), (May 1966).

Bowen, J. P., ed. *Proc. Z Users Meeting*, Oxford University Computing Laboratory, Oxford, UK, 1987a.

Bowen, J. P. Formal specification and documentation of microprocessor instruction sets. *Microprocessing and Microprogramming*, **21** (August 1987b), 223–230. (Proc. EUROMICRO'87, Microcomputers: Usage, Methods and Structures.)

Bowen, J. P., ed. *Proc. Third Annual Z Users Meeting*, Oxford University Computing Laboratory, Oxford, UK, 1988.

Bowen, J. P. Formal specification of the ProCoS/safemos instruction set. *Microprocessors and Microsystems*, **14**(10) (December 1990), 631–643.

Bowen, Jonathan P. X: Why Z? *Computer Graphics Forum*, **11**(4) (October 1992), 221–234.

Bowen, Jonathan P. and Gordon, Mike. A shallow embedding of Z in HOL. *[Bowen and Hinchey, 1995b]*, (1995) 269–276.

Bowen, J. P. and Hall, J. A., eds. *Z User Workshop, Cambridge 1994*, Workshops in Computing. Proceedings of the Eighth Annual Z User Meeting, Springer-Verlag, 1994.

Bowen, J. P. and Hinchey, M. G., eds. *ZUM '95: The Z Formal Specification Notation*. Lecture Notes in Computer Science 967. Ninth International Conference of Z Users, Springer-Verlag, 1995a.

Bowen, Jonathan and Hinchey, Mike. Z Special Issue. *Information and Software Technology*, **37** (May–June 1995b), 5–6.

Bowen, J. P. and Nicholls, J. E., eds. *Z User Workshop, London 1992*, Workshops in Computing. Proceedings of the Seventh Annual Z User Meeting, Springer-Verlag, 1993.

Bowen, J. P. and Stavridou, V. Safety-critical systems, formal methods and standards. *Software Engineering Journal*, **8**(4) (July 1993), 189–209.

Bowen, Jonathan, Stepney, Susan, and Barden, Rosalind. Annotated Z bibliography. *[Bowen and Hinchey, 1995b]*, (1995), 317–332.

Boyer, R. S. and Moore, J. S. *A Computational Logic Handbook*. Academic Press, 1988.

Burton, David M. *Elementary Number Theory*. Allyn and Bacon Inc., 1980.

Carrol, Paul B. Getting IBM back on track. *Seattle Times – Post-Intelligencer*, Sunday, December 8, 1991, p. E1. (Reprinted from *Wall Street Journal*.)

Chandy, K. Mani and Misra, Jayadev. *Parallel Program Design: A Foundation*. Addison-Wesley, 1988.

Clarke, E. M., Emerson, E. A., and Sistla, A. P. Automatic verification of finite-state concurrent systems using temporal logic specifications. *ACM Transactions on Programming Languages and Systems*, **8**(2) (April 1986), 244 – 263.

Clutterbuck, D. L. and Carré, B. A. The verification of low-level code. *Software Engineering Journal*, **3** (May 1988), 97–111.

Cohen, Edward. *Programming in the 90s: An Introduction to the Calculation of Programs*. Springer-Verlag, New York, 1990.

Craig, Iain D. *Formal Specification of Advanced AI Architectures*. Ellis Horwood, 1991.

Craigen, Dan. Reference manual for the language Verdi. Technical Report TR-91-5429-09c, ORA Canada, Ottawa, ON, October 1995.

Craigen, Dan, Gerhart, S., and Ralston, T. J. An international survey of industrial applications of formal methods (Vol. 1: Purpose, approach, analysis and conclusions; Vol. 2: Case studies). Technical Report NIST GCR 93/626-V1 & NIST GCR 93-626-V2 (Order numbers: PB93-178556/AS & PB93-178564/AS), Atomic Energy Control Board of Canada, U.S. National Institute of Standards and Technology, and U.S. Naval Research Laboratories, National Technical Information Service, Springfield, VA, 1993.

Craigen, Dan, Gerhart, Susan, and Ralston, Ted. Formal methods reality check: Industrial usage. *IEEE Transactions on Software Engineering*, **21**(2) (February 1995), 90–98. (Also in [Woodcock and Larsen, 1993].)

Cullyer, W. J., Goodenough, S. J., and Wichmann, B. A. The choice of computer languages for use in safety-critical systems. *Software Engineering Journal*, (March 1991), 51–58.

Davis, Bob. As complexity rises, tiny flaws in software pose a growing threat. *Wall Street Journal*, January 28, 1987, p. 1.

Delisle, Norman and Garlan, David. Formally specifying electronic instruments. in *Proceedings of the Fifth International Workshop on Software Specification and Design*, IEEE Computer Society Press, Washington, DC, 1989. (Also ACM Software Engineering Notes **14**(3) May 1989.)

Delisle, Norman and Garlan, David. A formal specification of an oscilloscope. *IEEE Software*, **7**(5) (September 1990), 29–36.

DeMillo, Richard A., Lipton, Richard J., and Perlis, Alan J. Social processes and proofs of theorems and programs. *Communications of the ACM*, **22**(5) (May 1979), 271–280.

Denninger, Karl. Risks of bank ATM cards. *RISKS-FORUM Digest*, **7**(5), (June 7, 1988).

DeRemer, F. and Kron, H. H. Programming-in-the-large versus programming-in-the-small. *IEEE Transactions on Software Engineering*, SE-2 (1976), 80–86.

Diller, Antoni. *Z: An Introduction to Formal Methods*. John Wiley and Sons, UK, 1990.

Diller, Antoni. *Z: An Introduction to Formal Methods*. John Wiley and Sons, UK, 2nd ed., 1994.

Dunham, William. *Journey Through Genius: The Great Theorems of Mathematics*. John Wiley and Sons, New York, 1990.

Evans, Andy S. Specifying and verifying concurrent systems using Z. in *FME '94:*

Industrial Benefit of Formal Methods, Maurice Naftalin, Tim Denvir, and Miquel Bertran, eds. Springer-Verlag, 1994a, 366–380. (Lecture Notes in Computer Science number 873.)

Evans, Andy S. Visualizing concurrent Z specifications. in *Z User Workshop,Cambridge 1994*, Bowen, J. P. and Hall, J. A., eds. Springer-Verlag, 1994b. 269–281. (Workshops in Computer Science.)

Fagan, M. E. Advances in software inspections. *IEEE Transactions on Software Engineering*, SE-**12**(7) (1986), 744–751.

Fasel, Joseph H. Hudak, Paul, Peyton-Jones, Simon, and Wadler, Philip. Special issue on the functional programming language Haskell. *ACM SIGPLAN Notices*, **27**(5), (May 1992).

Fields, Bob and Elvang-Gøransson, Morten. A VDM case study in Mural. *IEEE Transactions on Software Engineering*, **18**(4) (April 1992), 279–295.

Fitzgerald, John S. Unification: Specification and development. in *Case Studies in Systematic Software Development*, Jones, Cliff B. and Shaw, R. C., eds. Prentice-Hall International, 1990, 127–162.

Garlan, David and Delisle, Norman. Formal specifications as reusable frameworks. in *VDM '90: VDM and Z — Formal Methods in Software Development*, Bjorner, D., Hoare, C. A. R., and Langmaack, H., eds. Kiel, FRG, April 1990, 150–163. Third International Symposium of VDM Europe, Springer-Verlag. Lecture Notes in Computer Science Number 428.

Gehani, N. and McGettrick, A. D., eds. *Software Specification Techniques*. International Computer Science Series. Addison-Wesley Publishing Co., 1986.

Gerhart, Susan and Yelowitz, Lawrence. Observations of fallibility in applications of modern programming methodologies. *IEEE Transactions on Software Engineering*, SE-**2**(3) (September 1976), 195–207.

Gerhart, Susan, Craigen, Dan, and Ralston, Ted. Experience with formal methods in critical systems. *IEEE Software*, **11**(1) (Jan. 1994a), 21–28.

Gerhart, Susan, Craigen, Dan and Ralston, Ted. Regulatory case studies. *IEEE Software*, **11**(1) (Jan. 1994b), 30–39.

Gleick, James. Chasing bugs in the electronic village. *New York Times Magazine*, Sunday, June 14, 1992, 38 ff.

Goguen, Joseph A. and Luqi, Formal methods and social context in software development. *[Mosses* et al.*, 1995]*, (1995), 62–81.

Gordon, M. J. C. and Melham, T. F. *Introduction to HOL*. Cambridge University Press, 1993.

Gravell, A. M. What is a good formal specification? in *Z User Workshop, Oxford 1990*, Nicholls, J.E., ed. Workshops in Computing, Springer-Verlag, 1991, 137–150.

Greenbaum, Joan and Kyng, Morten, eds. *Design at Work: Cooperative Design of Computer Systems*. L. Erlbaum Associates, Hillsdale, NJ, 1991.

Gries, David. *The Science of Programming*. Springer-Verlag, New York, 1981.

Gries, David and Schneider, Fred B. *A Logical Approach to Discrete Mathematics*. Springer-Verlag, New York, 1993.

Guttag, John V. and Horning, James J., eds. *Larch: Languages and Tools for Formal Specification*. Springer-Verlag, 1993.

Harel, David, Lachover, Hagi, Naamad, Amnon, Pnueli, Amir, Politi, Michal, Sherman, Rivi, Shtull-Trauring, Aharon, and Trakhtenbrot, Mark. STATEMATE: A working environment for the development of complex reactive systems. *IEEE Transactions on Software Engineering*, **16**(4) (April 1990), 403–414.

Harel, David. Statecharts: A visual formalism for complex systems. *Science of Computer Programming*, **8** (1987), 231–274.

Hart, Johnson M. Experience with logical code analysis in software maintenance. *Software Practice and Experience*, **25**(11) (November 1995), 1243–1262.

Hartmann, David C. Software safety in medical devices. The MITRE Corporation, 1993.

Hatton, Les. *Safer C: Developing Software for High-Integrity and Safety-Critical Systems*. McGraw-Hill, 1995.

Hayes, I. J. Applying formal specification to software development in industry. *IEEE Transactions on Software Engineering*, **11**(2) (February 1985), 169–178.

Hayes, Ian, ed. *Specification Case Studies*. Prentice Hall International, Englewood Ciffs, NJ, 1987.

Hayes, Ian, ed. *Specification Case Studies*. Prentice Hall International, Englewood Ciffs, NJ, 2nd ed. 1992a.

Hayes, I. J. VDM and Z: A comparative case study. *Formal Aspects of Computing*, **4**(1) (1992b), 76–99.

Hehner, Eric C. R. What's wrong with formal programming methods? in *Advances Computing and Information — ICCI '91*, Dehne, F., Fiala, F., and Koczkodaj, W. W., eds. Lecture Notes in Computer Science 497. Springer-Verlag, 1991, 2–23.

Hehner, Eric. *A Practical Theory of Programming*. Springer, 1993.

Heninger, K. L. Specifying software requirements for complex systems: New techniques and their application. *IEEE Transactions on Software Engineering*, SE-**6**(1) (1980), 2–13.

Hinchey, M. G. and Bowen, J. P., eds. *Applications of Formal Methods*. International Series in Computer Science. Prentice-Hall, 1995.

Hoare, C. A. R. *Communicating Sequential Processes*. Prentice-Hall, 1985.

Hoare, C. A. R. An overview of some formal methods for program design. *Computer*, **20**(9) (September 1987), 85–91.

Hoare, C. A. R. and Wirth, N. An axiomatic definition of Pascal. *Acta Informatica*, **3** (1973), 335–355.

IEEE. ANSI/IEEE Std 729-1983. Glossary of software terminology, 1987. In *[Institute of Electrical and Electronics Engineers, 1987]*.

Institute of Electrical and Electronics Engineers. *Software Engineering Standards.* IEEE and Wiley-Interscience, New York, 1987.

Jackson, Daniel. Abstract model checking of infinite specifications. In *[Naftalin et al., 1994]*, 1994.

Jackson, Daniel and Damon, Craig A. Elements of style: Analyzing a software design feature with a counterexample detector. In Steven J. Zeil, editor, *Proceedings of the 1996 International Symposium on Software Testing and Analysis (ISSTA)*, 1996, 239–249. (*ACM Software Engineering Notes* **21**(3), May 1996).

Jacky, Jonathan. Programmed for disaster: Software errors that imperil lives. *The Sciences*, **29**(5) (September/October 1989), 22–27.

Jacky, Jonathan. Formal specifications for a clinical cyclotron control system. in *Proceedings of the ACM SIGSOFT International Workshop on Formal Methods in Software Development*, Moriconi, Mark, ed. Napa, CA, May 9–11, 1990, 45–54. (Also in *ACM Software Engineering Notes*, **15**(4), Sept. 1990.)

Jacky, Jonathan. Safety-critical computing: Hazards, practices, standards, and regulation. in *Computerization and Controversy: Value Conflicts and Social Choices.* Dunlop, Charles and Kling, Rob, eds. Academic Press, 1991.

Jacky, Jonathan. Formal specification and development of control system input/output. in *Z User Workshop, London 1992*, Bowen, J. P. and Nicholls, J. E., eds. Workshops in Computing Series. Proceedings of the Seventh Annual Z User Meeting, Verlag, 1993a.

Jacky, Jonathan. Specifying a safety-critical control system in Z. in *FME '93: Industrial-Strength Formal Methods*, Woodcock, J. C. P. and Larsen, P. G., eds. Lecture Notes in Computer Science 670. First International Symposium of Formal Methods Europe, Springer-Verlag, Odense, Denmark, 388–402, 1993b.

Jacky, Jonathan. Specifying a safety-critical control system in Z. *IEEE Transactions on Software Engineering*, **21**(2) (1995), 99–106. (Also in [Woodcock and Larsen, 1993], 388–402).

Jacky, Jonathan. Safety-critical computing: Hazards, practices, standards, and regulation (revised). in *Computerization and Controversy: Value Conflicts and Social Choices.* Rob Kling, ed. Academic Press, 2nd ed., 1996.

Jacky, Jonathan and Unger, Jonathan. From Z to code: A graphical user interface for a radiation therapy machine. In *[Bowen and Hinchey, 1995a]*, (1995), 315–333.

Jacky, Jonathan, Risler, Ruedi, Kalet, Ira, and Wootton, Peter. Clinical neutron therapy system, control system specification, part I: System overview and hardware organization. Technical Report 90-12-01, Radiation Oncology Department, University of Washington, Seattle, WA, December 1990.

Jacky, Jonathan, Risler, Ruedi, Kalet, Ira, Wootton, Peter, and Brossard, Stan. Clinical neutron therapy system, control system specification, part II: User operations. Technical Report 92-05-01, Radiation Oncology Department, University of Washington, Seattle, WA, May 1992.

Jacky, Jonathan, Kalet, Ira, Chen, Jun, Coggins, James, Cousins, Steve, Drzymala, Robert, Harms, William, Kahn, Michael, Kromhout-Schiro, Sharon, Sherouse, George, Tracton, Gregg, Unger, Jonathan, Weinhous, Martin, and Yan, Di. Portable software tools for 3-D radiation therapy planning. *International Journal of Radiation Oncology, Biology and Physics*, **30**(4) (November 1994), 921–928.

Jaffe, Matthew S., Leveson, Nancy G., Heimdahl, Mats P. E., and Melhart, Bonnie E. Software requirements analysis for real-time process control systems. *IEEE Transactions on Software Engineering*, **17**(3) (March 1991), 241–258.

Jensen, K. and Rozenberg, G., eds. *High-level Petri Nets: Theory and Application*. Springer-Verlag, 1991.

Jensen, Kathleen and Wirth, Nicklaus. *PASCAL User Manual and Report*. Springer-Verlag, Berlin, 2nd ed., 1974.

Johns, Harold E. and Cunningham, John R. *The Physics of Radiology*. Charles C. Thomas, 4th ed., 1983.

Jones, Cliff B. *Systematic Software Development Using VDM*. Prentice-Hall, Englewood Cliffs, NJ, 2nd ed., 1990.

Jones, C. B. The search for tractable ways of reasoning about programs. Technical Report UMCS-92-4-4, Department of Computer Science, University of Manchester, Manchester, UK, 1992.

Kaldewaij, Anne. *Programming: The Derivation of Algorithms*. Prentice-Hall, 1990.

Kalet, Ira J., Jacky, Jonathan, Cho, Paul, and Martin, Mark. Prism dose computation methods. Technical Report 93-09-01, Radiation Oncology Department, University of Washington, Seattle, WA, 1993.

Kalet, Ira J., Jonathan P. Jacky, Mary M. Austin-Seymour, Sharon M. Hummel, Kevin J. Sullivan, and Jonathan M. Unger. Prism: A new approach to radiotherapy planning software. *International Journal of Radiation Oncology, Biology and Physics*, 1996. in press.

Keefe, Patricia. Tomorrow is D Day for Dbase, *Computerworld* July 30, 1990.

Kernighan, Brian W. and Plauger, P. J. *The Elements of Programming Style*. McGraw Hill, New York, 1978.

Khan, Faiz M. *The Physics of Radiation Therapy*. Williams and Wilkins, Baltimore, 1984.

Knight, John C. and Myers, E. Ann. An improved inspection technique. *Communications of the ACM*, **36**(11) (November 1993), 51–61.

Knuth, Donald E. *Literate Programming*. Center for the Study of Language and Information, Stanford, CA, 1992.

Koenig, Andrew. *C Traps and Pitfalls*. Addison-Wesley, 1988.

Lamb, David Alex. *Software Engineering: Planning for Change.* Prentice Hall, Englewood Cliffs, NJ, 1988.

Lamport, Leslie. The temporal logic of actions. *ACM Transactions on Programming Languages and Systems*, May 1994, 872–923.

Landauer, Thomas K. *The Trouble With Computers: Usefulness, Usability, and Productivity.* MIT Press, 1995.

Landwehr, Carl E. Formal models of computer security. *ACM Computing Surveys*, **13**(3) (September 1981), 247–278.

Lano, Kevin and Haughton, Howard, eds. *Object-oriented Specification Case Studies.* Object-Oriented Series. Prentice Hall International, 1993.

Lano, Kevin and Haughton, Howard. Formal development in B Abstract Machine Notation. *[Bowen and Hinchey, 1995b]*, 1995, 303–316.

Lee, Leonard. *The Day the Phones Stopped: How People Get Hurt When Computers Go Wrong.* Primus, New York, 1992.

Leveson, Nancy G. *Safeware: System Safety and Computers.* Addison-Wesley, 1995.

Leveson, Nancy G. and Stolzy, Janice L. Safety analysis using Petri nets. *IEEE Transactions on Software Engineering*, SE-**13**(3) (1987), 386–397.

Leveson, Nancy G. and Clark S. Turner. An investigation of the Therac-25 accidents. *IEEE Computer*, **26**(7) (July 1993), 18–41.

Leveson, Nancy G. Heimdahl, Mats Per Erik, Hildreth, Holly, and Reese, Jon Damon. Requirements specification for process control systems. *IEEE Transactions on Software Engineering*, **20**(9) (Sept. 1994), 684–707.

Lewis, Peter. Can the new dBASE solve Ashton-Tate's problems? *New York Times*, Sunday, August 19, 1990, p. F9.

Linger Richard C. Cleanroom software engineering for zero-defect software. In *Proceedings 15th International Conference on Software Engineering*, 2–13. IEEE Computer Society Press, 1993.

Macdonald, Ruaridh. Z usage and abusage. Technical Report 91003, Royal Signals and Radar Establishment, Malvern, Worcestershire, UK, February 1991.

Mackenzie, Donald. The automation of proof: A historical and sociological exploration. *IEEE Annals of the History of Computing*, **17**(3) (Fall 1995), 7–29.

Markoff, John. Marketer's dream, engineer's nightmare. *New York Times* (Business Section), Sunday, December 12, 1993, p. 1.

Marshall, Lynn S. Line representations on graphics devices. in *Case Studies in Systematic Software Development*, Jones, Cliff B. and Shaw, R. C., eds. Prentice-Hall International, 1990, 337–364.

McDermid, J. Special section on Z. *Software Engineering Journal*, **4**(1) (1989), 25–70.

Meisels, Irwin and Saaltink, Mark. The Z/EVES reference manual. Technical Report TR-95-5493-03, ORA Canada, Ottawa, ON, December 1995.

Meyer, Bertrand. On formalism in specifications. *IEEE Software*, **2**(1) (1985), 6–26.

Milner, Robin. *Communication and Concurrency*. Prentice Hall International, 1989.

Milner, Robin. Elements of interaction. *Communications of the ACM*, **36**(1) (January 1993), 78–89.

Mitchell, Chris and Stavridou, Victoria, eds. *Mathematics of Dependable Systems*, Clarendon Press, Oxford, 1995.

Morgan, Carroll. *Programming from Specifications*. Prentice-Hall International, Hemel Hempstead, Hertfordshire, UK, 1994 (Second edition).

Morgan, Carroll and Sufrin, Bernard. Specification of the UNIX file system. *IEEE Transactions on Software Engineering*, SE-**10**(2) (March 1984), 128–142. (Also appears in [Hayes, 1987].)

Mosses, Peter D., Nielson, Mogens, and Schwartzbach, Michael I., eds. *TAPSOFT 95: Theory and Practice of Software Development*. Lecture Notes in Computer Science, **915**, Springer, 1995.

Naftalin, Maurice, Denvir, Tim, and Bertran, Miquel, eds. *FME '94: Industrial Benefit of Formal Methods*. Springer-Verlag, 1994. (Lecture Notes in Computer Science Number 873.)

Naftalin, Maurice Correctness for beginners. in *VDM '88: VDM — The Way Ahead (Lecture Notes in Computer Science No. 328)*, Bloomfield, R., Marshall, L., and Jones, R., eds. Springer-Verlag, Berlin, 1988. Proceedings of the 2nd VDM-Europe Symposium, Dublin, Ireland.

Neumann, Peter G. *Computer-Related Risks*. Addison-Wesley, Reading, MA, 1994.

Neumann, Peter G. Illustrative risks to the public in the use of computer systems and related technology. *ACM Software Engineering Notes*, **21**(1) (January 1996), 16–30.

Neuport, John R. *Avionics Systems Design*. CRC Press, 1994.

Newton-Smith, W. H. *Logic: An Introductory Course*. Routledge and Kegan Paul, 1985.

Nicholls, J. E., ed. *Z User Workshop, Oxford 1989*, Workshops in Computing. Proceedings of the Fourth Annual Z User Meeting. Springer-Verlag, 1990.

Nicholls, J. E., ed. *Z User Workshop, Oxford 1990*, Workshops in Computing. Proceedings of the Fifth Annual Z User Meeting. Springer-Verlag, 1991.

Nicholls, J. E., ed. *Z User Workshop, York 1991*, Workshops in Computing. Proceedings of the Sixth Annual Z User Meeting. Springer-Verlag, 1992.

Nicholls, J. E., ed. *Z Notation*. Z Standards Panel: BSI Panel IST/5/19/2, ISO Panel JTC1/SC22/WG19, Version 1.2, September 14, 1995.

Nye, Adrian. *Xlib Programming Manual*. O'Reilly and Associates, Inc., Sebastopol, CA, 1988.

Ohlbach, Hans Jurgen. Predicate logic hacker tricks. *Journal of Automated Reasoning*, **1** (1985), 435–440.

O'Rourke, Joseph. *Computational Geometry in C*. Cambridge University Press, 1994.

Owre, Sam, Rushby, John, Shankar, Natarajan, and von Henke., Friedrich. Formal verification for fault-tolerant architectures: Prolegomena to the design of PVS. *IEEE Transactions on Software Engineering*, **21**(2) (February 1995), 107–125. (Also in [Woodcock and Larsen, 1993].)

Palfreman, Jon and Swade, Doran. *The Dream Machine*. BBC Books, 1991.

Parnas, David Lorge and Clements, Paul C. A rational design process: How and why to fake it. *IEEE Transactions on Software Engineering*, SE-**12**(2) (February 1986), 251–257.

Parnas, David Lorge, Jan Madey, and Michael Iglewski. Precise documentation of well-structured programs. *IEEE Transactions on Software Engineering*, 20(12): 948–976, December 1994.

Parnas, David Lorge. Using mathematical models in the inspection of critical software. *[Hinchey and Bowen, 1995]* 1995.

Paulson, Laurence C. *ML for the Working Programmer*. Cambridge University Press, New York, 1991.

Pfleeger, C. P. Uses and misuses of formal methods in computer security. *[Mitchell and Stavridou, 1995]*, 1995, 249–256.

Poltrock, Steven E. and Grudin, Jonathan. Organizational obstacles to interface design and development: Two participant-observer studies. *ACM Transactions on Computer-Human Interaction*, **1**(1) (1994), 52–80.

Potter, Ben, Sinclair, Jane, and Till, David. *An Introduction to Formal Specification and Z*. Prentice Hall International Ltd., Hemel Hempstead, Hertfordshire, UK, 1991.

Risler, Ruedi, Eenmaa, Jüri, Jacky, Jonathan P., Kalet, Ira J., Wootton, Peter, and Lindbaeck, S. Installation of the cyclotron based clinical neutron therapy system in Seattle. in *Proceedings of the Tenth International Conference on Cyclotrons and their Applications*, IEEE, East Lansing, MI, May 1984, 428–430.

Rosen, Kenneth. *Elementary Number Theory and its Applications*. Addison Wesley, 1993.

Rushby, John and von Henke, Fredrich. Formal verification of algorithms for critical systems. in *Proceedings of the ACM SIGSOFT '91 Conference on Software for Critical Systems*, (1991), 1–15. (Published as *ACM Software Engineering Notes* **16**(5), December 1991.)

Rushby, John. Formal methods and the certification of critical systems. Technical Report SRI-CSL-93-07, SRI International, Menlo Park, CA, November 1993.

Russell, Glen W. Experience with inspection in ultralarge-scale developments. *IEEE Software*, (January 1991), 25–31.

Saaltink, M. Z and EVES. Technical Report TR-91-5449-02, Odyssey Research Associates, Ottawa, ON, October 1991.

Saaltink, M. Z and EVES. In *[Nicholls, 1992]*, (1992), 223–242.

Sabbagh, Karl. *Skyscraper*. Viking, New York, 1990.

Scheifler, R. W. and Gettys, J. The X window system. *ACM Transactions on Graphics*, **5**(2) (1986), 79–109.

Schneier, Bruce. *Applied Cryptography: Protocols, Algorithms and Source Code in C*. John Wiley and Sons, New York, 1994.

Schuler, Douglas and Namioka, Aki. *Participatory Design: Principles and Practices*. L. Erlbaum Associates, Hillsdale, NJ, 1993.

Shepherd, David and Wilson, Greg. Making chips that work. *New Scientist*, May 13, 1989, 61–64.

Shepherd, David. Verified microcode design. *Microprocessors and Microsystems*, **14**(10) (December 1990), 623–630.

Smith, D. R. Kids: A semiautomatic program development system. *IEEE Transactions on Software Engineering*, **16**(9) (September 1990).

Spivey, J. M. *Understanding Z: A Specification Language and its Formal Semantics*, Vol. 3 of *Cambridge Tracts in Theoretical Computer Science*. Cambridge University Press, Cambridge, UK, January 1988.

Spivey, J. Michael. Specifying a real-time kernel. *IEEE Software*, **7**(5) (September 1990), 21–28.

Spivey, J. M. *The fuzz Manual*. J. M. Spivey Computing Science Consultancy, Oxford, 2nd ed., July 1992a.

Spivey, J. M. *The Z Notation: A Reference Manual*. Prentice-Hall, New York, 2nd ed., 1992b.

Stepney, Susan. *High Integrity Compilation: A Case Study*. Prentice Hall, 1993.

Stepney, Susan, Barden, Rosalind, and Cooper, David, eds. *Object Orientation in Z*. Workshops in Computing. Springer-Verlag, 1992a.

Stepney, Susan, Barden, Rosalind, and Cooper, David. A survey of object orientation in Z. *Software Engineering Journal*, **7**(2) (March 1992b), 150–160.

Sufrin, Bernard. Formal specification of a display-oriented editor. *Science of Computer Programming*, **1** (1982), 157–202. (Also in [Gehani and McGettrick, 1986], 223–267.)

Sufrin, Bernard. Effective industrial application of formal methods. in *Information Processing 89*, Ritter, G. X., ed. Elsevier Science Publishers B. V., North-Holland, 1989, 61–69.

Tichy, W. Design, implementation and evaluation of a Revision Control System. in *Proceedings of the Sixth International Conference on Software Engineering*, 1982.

Tierney, M. The evolution of def stan 00-55. in *Social Dimensions of System Engineering*. Quintas, Paul ed. Ellis Horwood, 1993.

Toeplitz, Otto. *The Calculus: A Genetic Approach*. University of Chicago Press, Chicago, 1963.

Turner, David. An overview of Miranda. *ACM SIGPLAN Notices*, **21**(12) (December 1986).

Vadera, Sunil. Building a theory of unification. in *Case Studies in Systematic Software Development*, Jones, Cliff B. and Shaw, R. C., eds. Prentice-Hall International, 1990, 163–194.

Valentine, Samuel H. The programming language $Z - -$. *[Bowen and Hinchey, 1995b]*, 1995, 293–301.

van Gasteren, A. J. M. *On the Shape of Mathematical Arguments*, Vol. 445 of *Lecture Notes in Computer Science*. Springer-Verlag, 1990.

Weinhous, Martin S., Purdy, James A., and Granda, Conrad O. Testing of a medical linear accelerator's computer-control system. *Medical Physics*, **17**(1) (Jan/Feb 1990), 95–102.

Weizenbaum, Joseph. *Computer Power and Human Reason: From Judgment to Calculation*. W. H. Freeman, San Francisco, 1976.

Welsh, J., Sneeringer, W. J., and Hoare, C. A. R. Ambiguities and insecurities in Pascal. *Software: Practice and Experience*, **7** (1977), 685–696.

WGBH. The paperback computer. Episode of *The Machine That Changed the World*, public television series, 1992a. (First broadcast April 20, 1992.)

WGBH. The world at your fingertips. Episode of *The Machine That Changed the World*, public television series, 1992b. (First broadcast May 4, 1992.)

Wiener, Lauren. *Digital Woes: Why We Should Not Depend on Software*. Addison-Wesley, Reading, MA, 1993.

Wing, Jeannette M. and Vaziri-Farahani, Mandana. Model checking software systems: A case study. in *Proceedings of the Third ACM SIGSOFT Symposium on the Foundations of Software Engineering*, 1995, 128–139. (Published as *ACM Software Engineering Notes* **20**(4), October 1995.)

Winston, Patrick Henry. *Artificial Intelligence*. Addison-Wesley, 1977.

Wirth, Nicklaus. *Algorithms + Data Structures = Programs*. Prentice Hall, 1976.

Woodcock, J. C. P. Calculating the properties of Z specifications. *ACM Software Engineering Notes*, **14**(5) (July 1989a), 43–54.

Woodcock, J. C. P. Structuring specifications in Z. *Software Engineering Journal*, **4**(1) (January 1989b), 51–66.

Woodcock, J. C. P. and Larsen, P. G., eds. *FME '93: Industrial-Strength Formal Methods*, Lecture Notes in Computer Science 670. First International Symposium of Formal Methods Europe, Springer-Verlag, Odense, Denmark, April 1993.

Woodcock, J. C. P. and Loomes, Martin. *Software Engineering Mathematics*. Addison Wesley, Reading, MA, 1990.

Wordsworth, J. B. *Software Development With Z: A Practical Approach to Formal Methods in Software Engineering*. Addison-Wesley Publishers, Ltd., 1992.

Zachary, G. Pascal. *Showstopper: The Breakneck Race to Create Windows NT and the Next Generation at Microsoft*. Free Press, 1994.

Index